Praise for *Necropolis: London and Its Dead*

'There has always been a certain relish in recounting the decay of flesh ... That is why *Necropolis* is deeply pleasing: it satisfies the desire for wayward knowledge, being a compendium of death in all its forms while at the same time providing entertainment of the most garish and exquisite kind ... if you wish to go on a pilgrimage down these gravel paths and among these white sepulchres, this book should be your guide. It is a Baedeker of the dead'
Peter Ackroyd, *The Times*

'Enthusiastic, good-humoured and constantly engaging'
Sinclair McKay, *Daily Telegraph*

'Grimly entertaining ... Arnold's book abounds in deliciously uncanny detail ... Poignant or dramatic figures crowd these pages, from swindling Victorian speculators to expiring infants, from the grandest of royals to the most pathetic of executed criminals'
Suzi Feay, *Independent on Sunday*

'Catharine Arnold romps across the cemeteries, plague pits and tumuli of the capital in her survey of London's stiffs ... Luminous and often touching details crowd these pages ... Well-researched and elegantly written'
Melanie McGrath, *Sunday Telegraph*

'An elegant saunter through the land of the dead'
Jad Adams, *Guardian*

'This book allows a fascinating ramble through the cadavers of London's history, with the irresistible draw of finding out more about what lies under our pavements'
Anna Metcalfe, *Financial Times*

BEDLAM

London and Its Mad

CATHARINE ARNOLD

**SIMON &
SCHUSTER**

London · New York · Sydney · Toronto

A CBS COMPANY

First published in Great Britain in 2008 by Simon & Schuster UK Ltd
A CBS COMPANY

1 3 5 7 9 10 8 6 4 2

Simon & Schuster UK Ltd
Africa House
64–78 Kingsway
London WC2B 6AH

www.simonsays.co.uk

Simon & Schuster Australia
Sydney

Picture credits
Rex: p. 7
Mary Evans: p. 69, p. 161
From *The Story of Bethlehem Hospital From Its Foundation In 1247* by
E. G. O'Donoghue: p. 90, p. 93, p. 94, p. 131, p. 176, p. 188, p. 210
TopFoto: p. 204
Corbis: p. 252
Getty: p. 272
Lebrecht: p. 272

A CIP catalogue for this book is available
from the British Library.

ISBN: 978-1-84737-000-6

Typeset in Granjon by M Rules
Printed in the UK by CPI Mackays, Chatham ME5 8TD

For my husband

Contents

BEDLAM

A PLAN of the CITY and LIBERTIES of LON

The Blank Part whereof represents the Ruins and

THE RIVER

Acknowledgements

Bedlam: London and Its Mad is by no means an exhaustive history of madness. For further reading I recommend Jonathan Andrews's monumental *History of Bethlem* (1997), David Russell's *Scenes from Bedlam* (1997) and Andrew Scull's extensive chronicles of English madness including *Madhouses, Mad-Doctors, and Madmen: The Social History of Psychiatry in the Victorian Era* (1981), *Museums of Madness: The Social Organization of Insanity in Nineteenth-Century England* (1979) and his *Undertaker of the Mind* (2001), a portrait of the life and times of Dr John Monro. I also recommend Andrew Roberts's Mental Health Timeline (http://www.mdx.ac.uk/www/study/mhhtim.html), which is an excellent resource.

I would like to thank the following for their help and support with this project: The Hallward Library and the Medical School Library, University of Nottingham; Cambridge University Library; Colin Gale and Royal Bethlem Hospital Museum; my editors, Andrew Gordon and Kerri Sharp; my agent, Charlie Viney; Dr Vanessa Dale; and last but not least, my family for their enduring patience during the research and writing of this book.

Introduction

The mad, like the poor, have always been with us. Madness runs like a watermark through the history of London, from the earliest times, when the city was little more than a ramshackle collection of huts along the banks of the tidal river. In those days, lost souls tormented by invisible voices or stricken with the falling sickness were tended by their uncomprehending families, medicated with tinctures distilled from bark and berries or blessed in some mysterious ritual by a tribal elder. When the Romans arrived in the first century AD, they treated their mad with remedies from the classical world, cold baths and purges, sleeping draughts infused from the poppy, even a primitive form of electric shock treatment using live eels (or powdered eel mixed with olive oil, where fresh eels were not available). The Romans also favoured trepanning, a primitive form of neurosurgery involving drilling a hole in the patient's skull to let out the bad spirits. Many of these trepanned skulls have been recovered from the Thames, with bone tissue indicating that patients survived the operation, although we have no idea whether they recovered their wits after this dangerous procedure.

In Saxon times, the mad fared little better. Beating had become established as the standard treatment. It was believed this barbaric technique would exorcise the devils which caused mental illness. One account tells of a poor, 'moon-sick' individual found wandering the Roman Ridgeway, half naked, a clovewort tied round his neck by a red thread (the plant was believed to cure madness). As if he had not suffered enough, he was seized and given a good thrashing with a whip of porpoise hide.

Life for London's mad should have improved during the mediaeval period, with hospitals developing as extensions of religious orders, but provision for sane and insane alike was erratic, and there was no overall responsibility for the mad. Those troubled in mind had to compete for beds with the lepers, the blind, the crippled, the toothless hags and the abandoned children, scrabbling for scraps of bread and cheese, a jug of ale and a bed of straw. But one of these sanctuaries went on to become synonymous with London and the mad. Bethlehem Hospital, or 'Bethlem' as it soon became in the Cockney argot, was founded in Bishopsgate in 1247, by Simon FitzMary, a shrewd politician with a passion for social justice, who rose from modest origins to become sheriff of London – twice. Simon had a particular veneration for the Blessed Virgin Mary and the Star of Bethlehem, believing that on one occasion the star had saved his life. Lost behind enemy lines during the Crusades, Simon had almost despaired when he saw the Star of Bethlehem shining in the night sky, enabling him to navigate safely back to his own camp.

Despite Simon's intention to found a religious order devoted to his ideals, Bethlem fell into disrepute over the following centuries. The monks sold off land and the chapel roof fell in; Bethlem developed an appalling reputation and only the most desperate made their way to its battered wooden door. Bethlem became a byword for thieving, degeneracy and institutionalised corruption. One of the most notorious employees was Peter the Porter, who left his miserable charges to starve and shiver while he traded in their food and bedding. Peter's wife, meantime, a terrifying old harpy, ran a pub on the premises patronised by the local low life: tramps, sluts and drunkards, disgraced ex-soldiers and beggars who crippled their own children.

The mad first came to Bethlem in the 1370s, after Richard II closed down the Stone House, a small hospital in Charing Cross, on the grounds that the residents were so noisy they disturbed his falcons. Conditions at Bethlem would have been primitive, little better than a ramshackle hovel built over two drains blocked with human excrement, but at least they offered a modicum of protection for those ill-equipped to deal with the hostile outside world.

By the mid-sixteenth century, Bethlem had become 'Bedlam', a byword for pandemonium. Bedlam was familiar to Shakespeare's groundlings who knew all about madness: shoehorned into the Globe, they gawped at insane King Henry VI, clinically depressed Hamlet, besotted Ophelia and demented Lear, howling against the storm with a fool and Tom of Bedlam for company. Even the dancing bears on the South Bank referenced the madhouse: reminiscent of the inmates, with their lumbering gait and incoherent bellowing, the bears were christened 'Bess' and 'Rose' of Bedlam. Elizabethan dramatists toured the hospital, in search of inspiration. Madness became the English Disease (Hamlet, Prince of Denmark was to be sent to England because his own insanity would pass without comment there) and bizarre remedies for the condition abounded: herbal cures of borage and hellebore; leeching and vomiting; and even the suggestion that 'a roasted mouse, eaten whole' was a sterling cure for madness.

By the seventeenth century, Bethlem took on a more sinister role: it became a dumping ground for political prisoners, such as the Colchester weaver Richard Farnham, who claimed to be Jesus Christ and had gathered considerable support when he tried to overthrow Charles I and seize power. Too popular to execute, incarceration in Bethlem kept him out of harm's way without making him a martyr. In 1607, Bartholomew Helston went around London claiming to be the son of Mary, Queen of Scots. He ended up in Bethlem on the grounds that he was violently disturbed – or because he represented a real hazard to the monarchy.

Against all odds, Bethlem survived. The Bishopsgate building endured the Civil War, the Great Plague of 1665 and the Fire of London a year later, after which the hospital's governors realised that it needed a new home. In 1676 'New Bedlam' opened in Moorfields, with patients transferred to a 'palace beautiful' designed by the genius polymath Robert Hooke. Soon this magnificent building, reminiscent of Versailles, became a freak show and a pickup joint, with visitors crowding in to view the lunatics every holiday. Bethlem became, for the nation's satirists, a 'mirror of madness' reflecting the city's disordered psyche, designed by the city fathers as an asylum for their own impending insanity. And, by the eighteenth century, it did seem as if London was going mad. The witty Jonathan Swift suggested that politicians and generals be recruited from Bethlem as they could not be any more insane than the ones currently in charge. The establishment itself was riddled with insanity. Cartoonists of the day depicted leading politicians such as Charles James Fox raving in a straitjacket. Pitt the Elder suffered such a severe breakdown that he became a recluse in his Hampstead mansion. He could bear to see nobody: the sound of a child's voice would drive him to fury and meals had to be delivered on a tray through a hatch in the bedroom door. The king himself, George III, went spectacularly mad, and his insanity became public knowledge despite the best efforts of his advisers. The world of culture was not immune: Jonathan Swift succumbed to madness, the curmudgeonly Samuel Johnson battled with depression, and the dreamer William Blake witnessed angels in Peckham Rye and concluded that London itself was driving its citizens crazy. The prospect of total anarchy threatened as attempts were made on the life of the king. Unemployed seamstress Margaret Nicholson, reduced to penury and crossed in love, attacked George III with a dessert knife. The king was shrewd enough to recognise this as a cry for help and Margaret escaped capital punishment, although she spent the rest of her life in Bethlem, a model patient with a passion for snuff. Margaret presented less of a challenge to the status quo than Lord George Gordon, whose rioters, 50,000 strong, marched on Parliament and burst into the House of Commons. Under the leadership of the erratic anti-Papist, the rioters laid waste to London and reduced it to anarchy for a week, torching Newgate gaol and threatening to liberate Bethlem. In a final, appalling act before they surrendered to the militia, the rioters set fire to a distillery and men, women and even children died in agony after drinking from rivers of flaming alcohol as it ran down the gutters.

It was against this background that the first proper asylums were introduced into Britain. Asylums had originated in France in the seventeenth century, under the influence of Louis XIV, who, during the 1660s, locked up anyone likely to oppose him in a giant police operation described by Foucault as 'the Great Confinement', when over 6,000 people were incarcerated in the Hôpital Général. The practice of building asylums soon spread across Europe (and later to the United States). On one level, these institutions symbolised progress, and the 'therapeutic optimism' with which eighteenth-century scientists believed they could 'cure' the mad; on another, asylums were instruments of social control, prisons disguised as hospitals, where the poor and incurable could be swept out of sight. This led to the establishment of asylums such as St Luke's in London and Hanwell in Middlesex which were founded under the County Asylums Act, 1808, an early form of social welfare. The foundation of these hospitals marked the start of psychiatric medi-cine, as we know it, with pioneering visionaries such as William Battie (who gave his name to a slang term for the mad). Battie believed that madness could, and would, respond to treatment, unlike his rival, Dr John Monro, the suave, silk-hatted society doctor and trader in lunacy whose descendants were to dominate Bethlem Hospital for four generations. Under the Monro dynasty, Bethlem was to become notorious. During the nineteenth century, the hospital's reputation was rocked by scandals: William Norris, an American marine, was kept chained up for twelve years in such confined conditions that he died when his intestines burst as a result of constipated bowels; young Hannah Hyson died within days of being rescued by her father from Bethlem, her body covered in scabs and her knuckles red raw where she had crawled about her cell on her hands and knees. Ann Morley, a former patient at Bethlem, was admitted to Northampton Asylum in a skeletally weak condition, incontinent, prolapsed and close to death. Upon recovery, she testified to being punched in the face by a bad-tempered nurse called Black Sall (the name referred to Sall's moods), hosed down with freezing water and being made to sleep naked on straw in a cellar. It was only with the arrival of William Charles Hood, in 1853, that Bethlem began its long process of reform, and even after this date episodes of cruelty and neglect surfaced, with a high suicide rate attracting press coverage in the 1880s. By the turn of the century, Bethlem had undergone a transformation: pauper lunatics had been banished to the great asylums on the fringes of London; the worried well and the shabby genteel, driven to madness by the pressures of middle-class life, inhabited a comfortable asylum that appeared, at first glance, more like a Pall Mall club than a psychiatric institution. In 1930, the hospital was relocated to Kent, while the imposing Victorian building in Southwark, with its distinctive pumpkin-shaped dome, took on a new role as the Imperial War Museum.

*

For all its trials and tribulations, its reputation as a byword for horror and chaos, Bethlem has still benefited generations of Londoners. This is the story of Bethlem, in fact and fiction, from 1247 to the present day, from Bishopsgate hovel to the 'palace beautiful' in Moorfields, to the imposing Victorian building in Lambeth. I am by no means the first to chronicle Bethlem's vivid history. In 1914, the Reverend Geoffrey O'Donoghue, the hospital chaplain, published his *History of Bethlehem Hospital*, an eccentric and some would say fantastic rendering of the institution's story which started as a series of articles for *Under the Dome*, the hospital's magazine. Never afraid to let the facts get in the way of a good story, O'Donoghue serves as a flamboyant guide to Bethlem; he is genial and colourful, an inspiration but sometimes an irritation, steeped in the prejudices of his age.

*'Bedlam' goes Hollywood: a poster for the 1940s shocker starring
Boris Karloff as a sinister medical superintendent.*

In donning the Reverend's mantle, I have retained the use of the
term 'mad' for Bethlem's residents. The term 'mad' is not intended
to cause offence, but to reflect the generic use of the word, reserving
explicit clinical terms for the appropriate context. By the same
token, the specific institution of Bethlehem Hospital is referred to as
'Bethlem', to distinguish between the actual hospital and the social
construct of 'Bedlam', a place of madness.

My own interest in Bethlem and madness came from a number
of sources; the onomatopoeic clangour of the word 'Bedlam' itself,
suggesting an infernal din, like a bedstead falling downstairs, some-
how echoed in the vast Victorian asylum near my childhood home,
and its noisy but harmless residents, who occasionally spilled out

into the streets, weeping and shouting. A preoccupation with literary madness, from the terrifying first Mrs Rochester in *Jane Eyre* to the mad poets John Clare and Kit Smart; a lurid movie from the 1940s, starring Boris Karloff as the sinister medical director of 'Bedlam', whose destiny is to be walled up alive by his long-suffering patients; leafing through Sigmund Freud, R. D. Laing, and Anthony Storr, in early attempts to make sense of my parents' friends, so many of whom seemed vulnerable to mental health problems; a doomed relationship with a young man whose life was blighted by severe mental illness, despite all the efforts of his family and his doctors; and, finally, from my own experiences of bereavement and depression. Mental illness is no respecter of persons: we are all vulnerable, ourselves and those close to us. This is why this book is for all whose lives are touched by madness.

FOUNDATION

Bishopsgate, London, circa 1377: outside St Botolph's Church a herbalist plied his trade in natural remedies, wrapped in scraps of parchment. Suddenly, the sound of shouting reached the gate, and his customers deserted him as they rushed off to discover the source of the uproar. They were confronted with the clank of chains and the swish of whips as the latest residents arrived. For the first time, those diseased in brain or nerve were coming to Bethlem. Pitiless, the crowd watched the poor, miserable wretches; they threw mud and jeered, letting rip with volleys of abuse and profanity.

But how did this come to pass? Why were London's mad being herded to one small priory, to seek asylum in the straw? To answer this question, we must travel back in time, long ago and far away, to Palestine, to be precise. The name 'Bethlem' is a contraction of 'Bethlehem'. From the Hebrew, it means 'House of Bread' or refuge. The original 'Bethlem' was the Church of the Nativity in Bethlehem, which still stands on Manger Square, five miles from Jerusalem. Built over a grotto where Mary was said to have given birth to Jesus, the area became associated with the fourth-century saints Jerome (c. 342–420) and Paula (347–404). St Paula built a hostelry for pilgrims close to the basilica, thus beginning Bethlehem's long association with the care of the sick and the poor.

For 600 years, Jews, Muslims and Christians lived peacefully together, until the Crusades, inspired by the Pope's orders to seize Jerusalem from its Arab rulers. As European forces slaughtered Jews and Muslims alike, Saladin, Sultan of Egypt and Syria, began his assault on Jerusalem in 1187. When the crusaders were beaten at the battle of Tiberias, the bishops, canons and priests were driven away from Bethlehem. By 1217, not a single priest dared stay there. In 1224, Regnier, its bishop, sought sanctuary in France, at Clamecy. Seized and fought over by Christian and Muslim forces alike, it was miraculous that the structure of the Church of the Nativity withstood the onslaught. But, in 1229, some of the clerics had the temerity to steal back to Bethlehem and take up residence once more. Their presence was tolerated by Muslim rulers who recognised that the church was a shrine, a golden goose that brought tourist revenue from the pilgrims who flocked to Christ's birthplace.

One of the first clerics to return to the Church of the Nativity was a bishop, 'John the Roman'. Unfortunately, John proved to be a bad influence, the first in a long line of Bethlem's corrupt officials. In complicity with the canons, John sold off all the property of his see, the houses, castles, indulgences (documents permitting 'remission from sin') and a number of precious holy relics, spoils from the sacking of Constantinople in 1204, including the hammer and a nail allegedly used in the crucifixion of Jesus, and a hand from the body of St Thomas the Apostle. The haul also included some relics from the Church of the Nativity. Centuries later, in 1869, during the excavation of an ancient cloister which formed part of the Franciscan church of Bethlehem, archaeologists disinterred a pair of chandeliers and two copper basins dating from the twelfth century. The base of each chandelier was inscribed: 'Cursed be he who removes me from the place of the Holy Nativity, Bethlehem.' History does not tell us whether John the Roman was the recipient of that curse, but it is tempting to speculate that Bethlem's troubled past might have originated with that imprecation. The items themselves may have been returned by Goffredo di Prefetti, bishop elect of Bethlehem, in his capacity as the Pope's roving eye. In 1245, Goffredo had taken it upon himself to redeem as much of the treasure and property of the basilica as was still for sale. John the Roman was condemned by the Pope, who declared all his property dealings to be invalid, but it was too late. All the money had been dissipated, and the Church of the Nativity lay on the roadside, stripped of its dignity, as if it had fallen among thieves. Meanwhile, the 'Bethlemites' dispersed, to Italy, to France and subsequently to England, founding hospitals and churches.[1]

The remaining chapter appealed to Pope Innocent IV for help. The Pope responded by composing an encyclical to be circulated throughout Italy, England and Scotland. Designed to be read aloud at Mass, it commanded his flock, from archbishops and bishops to abbots and priors, and all the faithful to welcome the Bethlemites, who were dedicated to offering shelter to the poor, the sick and the homeless. The Pope decreed that Bethlemite brothers should be allowed to address the congregations and ask for alms. In addition, any citizen who donated large sums of money to the Bethlemite order was guaranteed forty days reduction of his penances.[2]

*

Two years later, this encyclical reached London. Among those who listened reverently, at St John's, Walbrook, was a wealthy alderman and former sheriff of London. His name was Simon FitzMary and he was to become the founder of Bethlehem Hospital.

Twice sheriff of London, Simon FitzMary was rich and influential both on the streets of London and at the court of King Henry III. He appears in the cartulary of the Holy Trinity, Aldgate, as an alderman in 1249 and 1250, was associated with the parish of St John, Walbrook and had an estate in Bishopsgate.[3] But little is known of his origins; indeed, his mysterious background evokes Bede's comparison of the passage of a man's life with the flight of a single sparrow through a chieftain's banqueting hall. As the king and his men sit by the blazing fire, and the wind howls without, a sparrow flies swiftly through the house, entering at one door and passing out through the other. In the same way, the life of a man is visible for a time, but as to what follows or what went before, we know nothing. This could well be a description of Simon FitzMary. Emerging briefly from the shadows into the light and warmth of history, he glimmers and is gone, disappearing once more into darkness. But he was clearly a man of wealth and influence, able to donate one estate and purchase another within a year. A conveyance in the Public Record Office shows him buying thirty-five acres of land for £20 in the village of Shoreditch. One explanation for Simon's mysterious background lies in his actual name: 'fitz' means 'son of' but FitzMary is in fact a matronymic (i.e. derived from his mother's Christian name) which commonly denoted illegitimate birth (as in Martin FitzAlice, alderman of St Michael's, Paternoster Royal, in 1281). Earlier historians assumed that Simon's father was unknown,[4] but recent research suggests that he was one Walter of Fulham, with whom Simon held some property in Bread Street, and he was related either by blood or marriage to a wealthy London family called the Baluns. The picture suggests a family of moderate status, with aspirations to greater things.[5] Simon appears to have been married twice, to a woman called Avice in 1241 and subsequently to an Edith, in Leicestershire. There are no immediate references to children – for instance, in the deed poll of the foundation of Bethlehem, he requests that masses be sung for the souls of his departed ancestors and descendants, and for his friends Guy of Marlow, John Durant, Ralph Anway, of Matilda, Margery and for Dionysia their wives, but no mention is made of children.

Whoever his father may have been, Simon appeared devoted both to the memory of his own mother, and to the Church of Bethlehem, 'where the same Virgin brought forth her first born son, our Incarnate Saviour, Jesus Christ, and fed him as he lay in the manger with her own milk, where too, the author of our salvation and the King of kings was pleased to be worshipped by kings [the wise men], before whom went a new star.'[6]

Simon may have owed his life to that star, following an incident during the Crusades. Legend has it that, one pitch-black night, he was lost, and panicked as he realised he could easily stumble into Saladin's clutches. Then, a bright star appeared over Bethlehem, just like the one which led the three wise men to the birthplace of the infant Jesus, and guided him safely back to his own camp. This star was the inspiration for the motif that appears on the hospital's crest to this very day.

Although little is known of Simon's private life, there are plenty of references to his public one as a man of the people, for the people, whose illegitimate birth gave him a motive for espousing the cause of the craftsmen against the mercantile oligarchy. One contemporary account tells of Simon setting off from his mansion to ride to Westminster, to lobby Henry III on behalf of the craftsmen, who felt they were paying unfairly high taxes. After riding through filthy streets, past the overflowing gutters and the rubbish thrown from unglazed windows to the swine which roamed free below, Simon was mobbed by admirers. 'You have been harshly oppressed by the mighty,' he told them, 'and felt the hard hand of those who spare themselves and spoil the poor. I go to see your lord, the king, who will be the saviour of poor men. Rejoice in him, for your time of redemption draws near.'[7]

By now riotous, the procession made its way between the market stalls of Cheapside to the New Gate, accompanied by tumult and shouting. But according to Arnold FitzThedmar, the aristocratic diarist who recorded these events for posterity, Simon was playing a dangerous game, manipulating voters to elect him as sheriff whilst bribing King Henry.

At this point in London's history, there were two factions: the patrician burghers, men of wealth and family, and the traders and artisans, who believed they paid more than their fair share of taxes. The power rested in the hands of the ruling class; they were supposed to govern with the consent of the people, but craftsmen frequently complained that they had no voice. Simultaneously, King Henry III made insatiable demands to fund his programme of construction projects, including the rebuilding of Westminster Abbey, which began in 1245. The ruling families were beginning to protest at the king's financial demands; even Simon FitzMary appears to have sided with them, refusing to pay the king some of the money he demanded. According to records at the Guildhall, during both his periods of office as sheriff (1235–6 and 1246–7) he failed to pay the whole of his tax into the Exchequer, and was fined £20 on the first occasion. On the second, he was arrested.

Henry III wanted to humiliate the aristocracy, who were refusing to pay the additional taxes he demanded, and to extort every penny he could from Londoners. To this end, he triangulated the situation by playing one party off against the other, while waiting for the opportunity to overthrow the city's liberties altogether. Henry appears to have been assisted in this by Simon, who may have gained a reputation as the people's champion, but was regarded by his fellow aldermen as a tool of the king. FitzThedmar described him as a traitor to the city: 'He has bribed the king; he has fomented an artificial law-suit, so that the King might intervene as a Court of Appeal against the jurisdiction and privileges of London. He has oppressed the re-election of a member of one of the ruling families as sheriff, shouting that he was a "perjurer". And there were also many evil and detestable actions, of which he had been secretly guilty against the franchises of the city.'[8] As a result, in 1248, the mayor, who was willing to side with the king in order to get rid of a popular agitator, deprived Simon of his aldermanry; the men of his ward selected Alexander the ironmonger, from Shoreditch, in his place.

*

After this brief appearance in the records, Simon vanishes from history again, passing swiftly out by the other door, leaving conflicting images of a benevolent populist, a pious founder of Bethlehem hospital and a shifty London politician. One source suggests he may have retired to Leicestershire and married a second wife, Edith.[10] However, one other reference to Simon throws light on his mysterious personality. This is an incidental allusion to him on the cartulary of Holy Trinity Priory, Aldgate, which shows him in a more favourable light. According to this record, one Osbert, rector of St Mary Bothaw, near St Paul's Churchyard, donated land to Bermondsey Abbey, an act witnessed by Simon with his signature in 1248. Osbert was descended from an aristocratic family noted for good works: an ancestor, William FitzOsbert, notorious for sporting a long beard in defiance of Norman convention, died as a martyr in 1196, for a cause that we would now term civil rights. Deserting his own class, FitzOsbert gathered the workers to his standard, maintaining that he would go to King Richard I and expose the selfishness and corruption of the aldermen. Instead, he was dragged out of the church where he had taken sanctuary and hanged under the elms at Smithfield for his trouble, in full view of his wife. But the people believed him to be a saint, and women spent nights praying at the scene of his execution. Despite the archbishop's attempts to suppress them, reports soon broke out of miracles, of the sick being cured by contact with his chains and clothes. Memories of his martyrdom and teaching survived: it is possible they inspired Simon FitzMary to follow the example of a man whose career and convictions in so many ways resembled his own; and they may have been a link between him and the Osbert of the document.[9]

Whatever the original source of his inspiration, Simon FitzMary was sufficiently motivated to hand over his estate to the bishop of Bethlehem, to establish a priory, with canons, brothers and sisters.[10] The ceremony took place on Wednesday, 23 October 1247. Just outside Bishopsgate (so called because Bishop Erkenwald built a gate there in 685), craftsmen in leather jackets were listening to a chantry priest, who was urging them to rally round Simon FitzMary. O'Donoghue, Bethlem's Edwardian historian, draws a vivid picture of the scene: from the kennels across the marshes of Moorfields drifted the yelping of hounds, which were to draw a fox in Marylebone that afternoon. The procession of clerics set off with Goffredo de Prefetti, bishop elect of Bethlehem and papal troubleshooter, at its centre, carrying a phial of blood, believed to be that of Christ, and sent by the Templars. Incense wafted through the air and holy water sparkled as the priests consecrated the boundaries of the ground that Simon had donated. It was a land of orchards and gardens, of ditches and marshes. To the east was the highway into Essex; to the south, St Botolph's Church; to the west, reeds grew beside the sluggish stream of Depeditch, which broadened out to meet the waters of the Walbrook; to the north lay the estate of Ralph Dunning, a local worthy. Beneath the land lay the remains of a Roman cemetery. A makeshift altar had been set up until the priory church itself could be built. The phial of blood was placed upon the altar; it was anointed with holy oils, and the sign of the cross executed in the smoke from the censer. On his knees, Simon FitzMary offered the land to the worship of the glorious Virgin Mary of Bethlehem, for the foundation of a religious institution there, free from all secular control, governed by canons and priors and sisters and brothers, who were to wear upon their mantles the badge of a star. This institution, like many others, would become a prototype hospital, dedicated to Christian charity, including the care of the homeless, the sick and the aged. Simon may have been operating for a variety of motives: he was eager to placate Henry, and improve his standing; on a spiritual level, he knew that if he gave land for a priory the gesture would curtail his time in Purgatory and lead to the salvation of his eternal soul.

Simon's decision was immortalised in 'The Ballad of John the Roman': the title refers, of course, to the infamous bishop who sold off so much of the see of Bethlehem in the first place:

> Good people all, come hear me now,
> Till John the Roman's guilt be told,
> And how he broke his priestly vow,

And Judas-like his Master sold.
Castles and lands and relics bless'd
He seized, he stole. He scattered them,
And sore despoiled, and sore oppress'd,
The holy Church of Bethlehem.
Yet out of evil good shall come –
Adoremus Dominum.

For, as FitzMary knelt to pray,
An angel whispered in his ear
'The Holy Land is far away,
Prepare another Manger here.
Build you a second House of Bread
In this fair city of renown,
And God His Son,' the angel said,
'Shall come to dwell in London Town.'
So spake the angel, bending low
Reddens laudes Domino.

From earth to heaven the righteous win,
And from base clay sweet flowers arise,
As Eve's offence and Adam's sin
Brought God His Son from out the skies.
So John the Roman's evil deed
Touched good FitzMary's heart to grace,
And, where the sick find care at need,
The Lord shall make His dwelling-place.
Wherefore let it merry be:
Gloria Tibi, Domine![11]

It is centuries now since masses were sung for Bethlem's founder.
Simon FitzMary's tomb by the high altar did not survive its removal
to St Thomas's, Southwark, in 1800. While Simon's original dona-
tion of land went on to bear dividends centuries after his death, he

was long forgotten. For, although Rahere, the court jester and founder of St Bartholomew's Hospital, was commemorated in Rahere ward and Rahere Street, there was neither a ward in Bethlem nor a tablet in Bishopsgate to perpetuate the memory of Simon FitzMary, twice sheriff of London and champion of the craftsmen. Perhaps this brief account of Simon's life will serve to bring out of darkness and oblivion into the light of day the true founder of Bethlem.

*

For the next 100 years, between 1247 and 1346, there is little mention of the priory. It is a dark period, referred to by O'Donoghue, with good reason, as a century of silence and disaster, during which, on three separate occasions, the death crier, in his gruesome livery, rang his bell outside Bethlem and exhorted Londoners to pray for the departed souls of Henry III, Edward I and Edward II. Despite the fact that Bethlem occupied a valuable piece of real estate, the brothers were desperately short of funds. The revenues of the order were insufficient to maintain the work of a hospital, however modest the demands – patients were offered little more than bread, cheese, ale and fresh straw – and they were forced to travel the country begging, a practice that was acceptable at the time. Half a dozen licences were issued to the brothers by Edward III, one of which, dating from 1329, is the first document in which the word 'hospital' is applied to Bethlem. The licence recommends that the clergy extend a kindly welcome to anyone from Bethlem who appears before them to gather alms.[12]

There are few references to Bethlem during the fourteenth century, a fact which O'Donoghue interpreted as an 'ominous silence', portending a tragedy which lay buried in the innocent phrases of the official calendar. 'As I translated the whole of the original, I felt as if I was reading the diary of those who sat through the long vigil of the night by the bedside of a sufferer, stripped of everything, abandoned by nearly everybody, and, as it seemed, at the point of death.'[13]

This document is a petition, presented to the mayor and aldermen in 1346 by the master, Brother John Matthew de Norton, and brethren of the order of knighthood of the Blessed Mary of Bethlehem, pleading to be taken under the protection of the City of London. It reveals a century of poverty and neglect, hardship and failure, during which the hospital was unable to administer its own affairs or maintain its brothers. With Simon FitzMary now long dead, there was nobody to watch over it. Worse still, it appears that Bethlem had already acquired the lurid reputation which would endure for centuries. The hospital seems to have been plundered by the bishop of Bethlehem, by the king, by discharged soldiers, tramps and thieves and descended into chaos and dissipation where there should have been discipline, supervision, economy and a ledger.[14] The result was that by 1346, the hospital had suffered a century of failure and was completely destitute. Every day in the past hundred years, a steady stream of the poor and the sick had flowed through Bishopsgate, but such was its dreadful reputation that they hurried past and on to the convent of St Mary Spital, lower down on the right.[15]

Given these appalling circumstances, the brothers threw themselves on the mercy of the City of London. Their appeal met with a favourable response, and on 20 October 1346, the mayor and aldermen of the City of London agreed to take Bethlem under their protection. In return for acting as governors, they were given certain privileges at the hospital, including being remembered in the order's prayers for all time. This ensured that 'by the perishable memorial of written names they might be written in the pages of the heavenly book'.[16] The benefactors were gratified to know that on their anniversaries their names would be recited at early Mass, laid upon the altar, and commended to the mercy of God.

The mayor and the aldermen were not only good businessmen, they were also devout and generous. They contributed to the building of a new chapel, to replace the one which had fallen down during the hospital's period of neglect; they carried out religious observations, lighting candles in the oratory, and the hospital was remembered in their wills. In 1361, the will of one John Nasing, a brewer, specified that the ceremonial knives attached to his girdle be sold, and half the proceeds donated to the 'new work of the church of St Mary de Bedelem [*sic*]'.[17] In 1378, John of Croydon, sheriff and fishmonger, sat down to make his will, giving serious consideration to who would inherit his 'Norfolk bedstead', a top luxury item of the day, and the bed itself, which was embroidered with dolphins in tapestry.[18] Having done this, he left money to the lepers in the 'lazar house' and to the prisoners of Newgate to pray for his soul, the theory being that the greater the suffering of the prisoners, the more effective their prayers. As the priest murmured the Last Rites, John would have had the comfort of knowing his name would live for evermore.

However, just as it seemed as if the future of Bethlem was assured, fresh storm clouds gathered on the horizon. In England, the Black Death of 1348 presaged tragedy for the hospital, as it did for the whole of London and beyond. The angel of death spread his wings to the blast of some battlefield in China, and breathed as he passed over England plague, famine and disaster. A monk of Bethlem went out with hawk and hounds to hunt in Lambeth marshes, and his hounds returned alone. In the chapel, benefactors were struck down in the act of lighting candles to Our Lady of Bethlem. One again, Bethlem faced an uncertain future, but salvation was to come from an unexpected source: the despised, the broken and the lonely: the mad.

MEDIAEVAL MADNESS AND MEDICINE

By the fourteenth century, London clearly needed specific provision for the mad. In 1369, Robert Denton, a chaplain, had obtained a royal licence to found a hospital in honour of the Virgin Mary in the parish of All Hallows Barking, near the Tower. This was intended to be for priests and others, men and women, who 'suddenly fell into a frenzy and lost their memories, until such time as they should recover'. But this plan did not go ahead. Instead, Denton diverted his funds to endow a chantry. Denton may have been advised to do this, given that Bethlem was beginning to serve the purpose instead.

The new arrivals at Bethlem had been transferred from the Stone House, an establishment which became the property of Bethlem in the late 1370s. The Stone House was at Charing Cross, on land owned by Bethlem which had been farmed out in a bid to raise money for the hospital. At that period of London's history, a house built of stone would have belonged to a religious community (the laity lived in houses built of wood and rubble). It may have been a chantry chapel, where Masses would have been said for the

21

soul of Queen Eleanor, wife of Edward I. A cross erected to her memory by her grieving husband stood nearby, the origin of the district's name: 'Chère Reine'. It is possible that the brothers at the Stone House devoted themselves to the care of the insane, because in those days, the fields of St Martin's were regarded as remote enough from the centre of London for the mad not to pose a risk. Other isolation hospitals were nearby, such as the leper houses, which stood on sites later covered by St James's Palace and St Giles, Holborn.

According to the historian John Stow, writing in 1603, the Stone House in St Martin in the Fields was: 'an house wherein sometime were distraught and lunatike people, of what antiquity founded, or by whom, I have not read'. Another source, from 1632, confirms Stow's account: 'it was sometimes employed for the harbouring of mad and distracted persons, before such time as they were removed to the present hospital of Bethlehem, without Bishopsgate'.[1]

Given that the fields of St Martin's were considered suitable for the mad, one wonders why they had to be moved at all. It appears that their relocation was the result of a mediaeval form of 'nimbyism'; according to Stow, 'sometime a king of England, not liking such a kind of people to remain so near his palace, caused them to be removed further off to Bethlem without Bishopsgate'.[2] Richard II ordered the removal of the mad from the Stone House around 1377. A record from 1632 states: 'when the hospital was first employed to the use of distracted persons appeareth not'. The first mention we find of Bethlem being employed so was in the late 1370s at the beginning of the reign of Richard II. An inventory from 1398 included 'four pair of manacles, eleven chains of iron, six locks and keys, and two pair of stocks' – all the equipment associated with the care of the mad at that time – and another source states that in 1403 Bethlem was entrusted with the care of 'six men who had lost their reason' (*sex viri mente capti*).[3]

Other neighbours were also uncomfortable with the proximity of those of disturbed mind. The Stone House was adjacent to the mews where the king's falcons were kept. Sir Simon Burley, master of the king's falcons, had submitted large expense claims for refitting the mews house and for his 'wardrobe'. Was Sir Simon, irritated by the noise after appointing his mews so lavishly, influential in the relocation of the raging inmates, away from him, his falconers and his birds?

A more sympathetic witness to the dramatic appearance of the mad at Bethlem would have been William Langland (c. 1330–c. 1387), who lived in a ramshackle cottage in the Cornhill, not far from Bishopsgate. 'Long Wille' had drifted up to London from the West Midlands, and scratched a living copying out legal documents and singing Masses while he revised his *Vision Concerning Piers the Plowman*. Dreamer, preacher, satirist, eccentric and emaciated in his shabby brown robe, Wille himself was regarded as half mad by many, particularly his wife, Kytte. According to her, his reason waxed and waned until most people took him for a fool, and he became so preoccupied with his writing that he refused to doff the cap to authority – a form of insurrection which could have lethal consequences in the political climate of the time. Sometimes, driven to distraction herself, Kytte actually wished that her husband was already in heaven. But Long Wille empathised with the lunatics of his day:

> They care not for cold, and they reck [care] not of heat; they carry no money, nor even bags to beg with; and they salute no man by the way, reverencing not even a mayor more than another. They are all more or less mad according to the age of the moon. But surely they walk the roads in the spirit and guise of the apostles and disciples of Christ. Does not the Holy Book teach us that we ought to receive into our houses the poor and the wanderer? Ye rich are ready to entertain fools and minstrels, and to put with all they say. Much more should ye welcome and help lunatic lollers [layabouts], who are God's minstrels and merry-mouthed jesters.[4]

Wille's description summarises many contemporary ideas about madness. One preconception, which endured into the nineteenth century, was that the mad constituted a lesser class of humanity. Like brute beasts, they were deemed insensitive to heat or cold, making their physical abuse acceptable. Then there is the reference to the moon (the term 'lunatic' derives from *luna*, the Latin word for moon). Many writers, from antiquity onwards, maintained that the mad were directly affected by the phases of the moon, with the full moon being the cause of the greatest agitation.

A diagnosis of 'madness' covered a broad spectrum of conditions in the mediaeval period. An observer from 1377 would have found it difficult to distinguish between the symptoms of epilepsy or 'the falling sickness', learning difficulties, dementia (caused in some cases by venereal disease) and hydrophobia, a symptom of rabies. There was no public responsibility for the mad, and as a result, the afflicted faced an uncertain future, left to rely upon their families, if they were equal to the task, or throw themselves upon a number of small hospitals, such as Bethlem, where they had to compete for treatment with the poor, the aged and the physically sick.

Many found themselves shunned by society, consigned to a root-less existence. As the historian Andrew Scull has noted, the deranged beggar was a familiar part of the mediaeval landscape, drifting from community to community in search of alms, any livelihood or possessions long lost, along with their sanity.[5] Those that were incarcerated, such as the motley crew shuffling towards Bethlem on that morning in 1377, would have been physically restrained after being accounted a danger to society. These patients were the lucky ones. Others, having committed some heinous crime under the influence of their disorder, would have been summarily executed, and left to rot in a gibbet at the crossroads.

Fear of the mad and distaste for their visible presence co-existed alongside the religious imperative to care for the sick, whether they were sick in mind or body. Andrews reminds us that: 'attitudes generally were mixed. On the one hand, madness and afflictions like epilepsy could provoke a superstitious horror or moral condemnation. On the other, Bethlem's benefactors often displayed a tender care for the inmates' welfare which seems not simply to be a consequence of the benefactors' anxiety to minimise the time they spent in Purgatory.' [6] The valuable contribution made by those caring for the mad received some official recognition, with attendants excused from jury service because they could not leave their patients. In 1436, one William Mawere, citizen and tailor, was exempted from jury service or service on the watch because his duties required him to be 'daily and without intermission in attendance on the poor frenzied and demented creatures who are housed in the hospital of the Blessed Mary of Bedlam'.[7]

*

To the modern reader, the treatment available in mediaeval Bethlem must appear barbaric: a regime of whips, chains, darkness and isolation. But there was a rationale to this approach. According to Bartholomaeus Anglicus, a professor at the University of Paris, since the mad were considered dangerous, 'the medicines of them is, that they be bounde – that they hurt not them selfe & other men'.[8]

The mad also endured periods of isolation, during which it was thought that they would come to their senses. Healers believed that by reducing external sources of stimulation and placing the patient in a dark, quiet room, the maniac would become calm. As late as 1551, the mayor of London sentenced one William Bradye, a merchant, to Bedlam for 'rayling and other frantyk behaviour', ordering that he should 'be held in close confinement and totally *incommunicado*'.[9]

Bradye's treatment represents one example of popular attitudes towards the mentally infirm. For an explanation of this, and other theories, we need to look back into prehistory, to the Bible, and to ancient Greece. The history and treatment of madness across the centuries falls into three basic categories: magical, medical and psychological. In the beginning, madness was regarded as 'magical' in origin, a perception dating back to prehistoric times, when no real distinction existed between medicine, magic and religion. During the Stone Age, the custom developed of trepanning the skull (drilling a hole to allow the evil spirits out), a practice which still found currency in Roman London – the skull of a trepanned man, who survived the operation (judging by the condition of the skull), was recovered from the Thames and is on display at the Museum of London. Cave paintings in Ariège, France, show a strange being with antlers and human feet and hands that has been identified as a shaman or medicine man. In ancient Egypt, circa 2850 BC, patients treated by physician-priests were prescribed sleep therapy, excursions on the Nile and lucky amulets, and sedation took the form of opium. In Mesopotamia in 2000 BC, physician-priests known as the 'asu' dealt especially with mental disturbance and studied dreams, which were regarded as showing the will of the gods.

According to the ancient Greeks, madness was a form of divine retribution. In the words of Euripides, 'those whom the Gods wish to destroy, first they make mad'. To be considered mad in ancient Greece or one of its neighbouring states was most unfortunate. In his *Laws* Book XI (fourth century BC) Plato puts responsibility for care of the mad on to the family, and was one of the first to suggest that 'enemies of the state' should be locked away in a *sōphronistērion* or a 'house of sanity'. This practice became a common method of destroying the credibility of dissidents, and continued throughout history, most recently in the former Soviet Union.[10]

Those born with a perceived mental or physical handicap fared even worse. In Sparta, where racial homogeneity was highly prized, the abandonment of deformed and sickly infants was actually a legal requirement, 'in the belief that the life which nature had not provided with health and strength was of no use either to itself or to the state'.[11] Epileptics, whose disorder was widely believed to have been caused by the gods, were treated by witch doctors, quacks, faith healers and charlatans, 'who sought to alleviate their symptoms by prescribing purifications and incantations along with

26

abstinence from baths, and from many foods unsuitable for the sick'. They were also forbidden to wear black, because it was associated with death, and it was believed epilepsy could be prevented if they did not wear goatskin or place one hand on top of the other or one foot on top of the other.[12]

Hebrew monotheism also dictated that madness, like physical illness, was a punishment from God. Deuteronomy named insanity as one of the many curses that God will inflict on those who do not obey him (along with haemorrhoids, the scab and the itch).[13] Nebuchadnezzar II (King of Babylon 605–562 BC) experienced an episode of insanity which lasted for seven years. The king, who had overseen a magnificent building programme which included the famous Hanging Gardens of Babylon, found himself humbled by God for boasting about his achievements. His punishment took the form of believing he was an ox, a condition known as 'boanthropy', and he lived like a wild animal for seven years, before making a full recovery and being restored to power.

The ancient Greeks initiated diagnostic techniques and treatments that were to survive for centuries. One of the most enduring was the classification of personality types in terms of the four 'Humours', comparable with the practice of ascribing certain character traits to star signs. The difference is, of course, that few twenty-first-century Westerners regard horoscopes as more than a diversion. In ancient Greece, the Humours represented a serious attempt to categorise personality types and the medical conditions associated with them. To function successfully, it was believed that all four Humours had to operate harmoniously – an imbalance of one or the other caused illness. This was not confined to physical ailments. Hippocratic doctors also attempted to treat mental illnesses such as hysteria (the name derives from the Greek *husterikos*). The condition was also known as 'suffocation of the mother'. It was believed that women of childbearing age were driven mad by their own wombs (Greek *hustera*) wandering about their bodies and even choking them, a condition for which constant pregnancy was the only cure.

The Humours consisted of black bile, blood, phlegm and yellow bile. These four Humours matched the four seasons: autumn: black bile; spring: blood; winter: phlegm; and summer: yellow bile. Each of these Humours was associated with one of the universal elements: earth: black bile; air: blood; water: phlegm; fire: yellow bile.

An imbalance of the Humours gave rise to certain mental and physical characteristics. Of these, the melancholic temperament was caused by too much earth, the choleric by too much fire; if you were phlegmatic, you had too much water in your composition, and if you were sanguine, then air predominated. Some vestiges of this classification survive today, with cultural stereotypes of 'choleric', hot-tempered alpha males. Each element was associated with certain qualities: yellow bile was hot and dry, phlegm cold and moist, black bile cold and dry and blood was hot and moist. Melancholy, which has similarities with clinical depression, remains the best known of the Humours and recurs, in different manifestations, throughout the history of madness and its treatment.

Many practitioners in the classical world demonstrated a sympathetic attitude towards madness. Asclepiades (c. 129–c. 40 BC) invented a swinging bed that had a relaxing effect on emotionally disturbed patients and condemned the incarceration of the mad; he believed that all illness was caused by an imbalance of the natural harmony of the body and he advocated natural therapy, taking great care with patients' diet and exercise. Soranus of Ephesus (AD 98–138) seems to have discovered lithium as a cure for manic depression by recommending that severely disturbed patients be treated with the alkaline waters of the town, which contained high levels of lithium salts. A more radical approach consisted of a pioneering form of electric shock treatment: the Greeks used the 'electric torpedo', or eels, as a cure for headaches, believing that 'the touch of a living torpedo stupefied or blunted the acute sense of pain'. An oil was prepared from the dead fish for use when no live ones were available.

The pleasure-loving Romans tended to concentrate on agreeable physical therapies: warm baths, massage and music, although they too pioneered an early form of shock treatment involving electric eels. Among his other achievements, the distinguished lawyer Cicero (106–43 BC) designed an interview format for diagnostic criteria, an assessment tool subsequently used throughout the Roman Empire, then in monasteries until the Reformation.

Unfortunately, these breakthroughs in medical thinking were not always accompanied by sympathetic treatment. In the last years before Christ the enlightened views of the Roman doctors began to decline, and Cornelius Celsus (25 BC–AD 50) recommended starvation, fetters, flogging and shock treatment, during which patients were isolated in total darkness and administered doses of laxatives, the aim being to frighten them back to health.

*

One consequence of the domination of the Christian Church was that the mind and the body came to be regarded as the province of the clerics, with the result that madness and illness were inevitably conceptualised in terms of good and evil. The belief developed not only that madness was caused by evil spirits, but that they could be driven out through beating, immersion in cold water and exorcism, as in the famous example of Christ's encounter with Legion.[14] Legion is portrayed as a mad man whom no chains can hold, and who lives in a graveyard, cutting himself with stones. When addressed by Christ he explains that his name is Legion – 'for we are many!' – because he is possessed by the spirits of seventy demons. At the demons' request, Christ drives them out of Legion's body and into a nearby herd of swine, which then hurl themselves over a cliff into the sea. Legion himself, duly exorcised, is found by the townspeople sitting, clothed and in his right mind.

By the time of the Saxons, beating had become established as a time-honoured method of treatment. According to O'Donoghue, 'our Saxon forefathers found on the Roman Ridgeway a half-naked creature – a clovewort attached by a red thread to his neck [clovewort was believed to 'cure' madness] and they gave the "moon-sick" a good "swingeing" [whipping] with a whip of porpoise hide!'[15]

While the ancient world offered a number of remedies to the mentally ill, the influence of the Christian Church led to less sympathetic treatment. As Christianity gained ground in Europe, the biblical precedent of Legion made exorcism a common response to insanity. A mediaeval exorcist was trained by the Church to distinguish between true demoniac possession and a build-up of black bile (which it was believed could be cured by inducing vomiting). If he is possessed, the patient speaks volubly in a tongue unknown to anybody else, claims he knows the answers to the greatest secrets or demonstrates strength and power far in excess of his normal capabilities; in effect, delusional symptoms, but which were regarded at the period as evidence of evil spirits. The exorcist would have been taught that the demons were artful and might possess the voice of an angel or a devil: he must be forever on his guard, no matter what the patient said. Sometimes, just to embarrass the priest, the demon would even send his patient to sleep. Not surprising, given that exorcism services lasted for hours, and included praying, begging and pleading. The actual ceremony – where the exorcist laid his hand upon the patient's heart or head and made the sign of the cross, and placed one part of his stole around the patient's neck – was brief enough; it was felt that the patient was sufficiently fortified to take communion after hours of prayer and fasting. One radical example of exorcism is described in *The Life and Miracles of St Thomas of Canterbury*, where the unfortunate 'mad Henry of Fordwich' was dragged by his friends to the tomb of St Thomas with his hands tied behind him, struggling and shouting, and there remained all day, but began to recover as the sun went down, and after a night spent in the church returned home, 'perfectly well in his mind'.[16]

In a manuscript account of St Guthlac of Croyland Abbey, near Peterborough, an exorcism is depicted vividly: Guthlac appears to be stooping down and gazing fixedly into the face of the demented Egga, who had been brought to Guthlac by his friends so that his evil spirits may be exorcised. Guthlac takes the girdle from round his own waist and binds it round that of the sufferer. Straight away, the devil himself, 'flecked and spotted, horned and winged', issues from Egga's mouth, to the astonishment of his companions.[17]

By the late sixth century, the mad did at least have their own patron saint, when a shrine sprang up to St Dymphna of Geel, in what is now Belgium. According to legend, the King of Ireland had a gentle and beautiful wife, Odilla, who became a Christian under the influence of Gereberne, a priest. The king and queen had a daughter, Dymphna. A disappointment to her father, young Dymphna was removed and placed in Gereberne's care. Subsequently, on the death of Odilla, the king sent out a search party to find another woman as beautiful as she had been. His men resolved to find Dymphna, who, by this time, had inherited her mother's beauty. When Dymphna met her father, the king denied their relationship and claimed her for his bride. Horrified by this prospect, Dymphna fled with Gereberne. Finally, they settled in the forest of Geel, where Dymphna resolved to devote herself to the religious life. However, her father caught up with her, and, infuriated by her refusal to marry him, attacked her and severed her head. His soldiers decapitated Gereberne. It is claimed that these extraordinary scenes so frightened several lunatics who witnessed them that they became cured. In this way, Dymphna, who had resisted the spirit of evil, became the patron of demented victims; later, miraculous cures were said to have taken place at the scene of her martyrdom, and the spot eventually became a lunatic colony. Commentators have suggested that Dymphna not only wanted to forgive her father for his insane, murderous madness, but wanted to relieve madness in others.[18] This she did: centuries later, the colony at Geel served as an inspiration to some of the most influential doctors and therapists in the history of madness.

*

In addition to being whipped and chained and beaten to rid them of demonic possession, the new arrivals at Bethlem would have endured the vagaries of mediaeval medicine, an inexact science at the best of times. For instance, John of Gaddesden, court physician of Edward II (circa 1320), wrapped smallpox cases in red cloth in the belief that it would prevent scarring. He prescribed pounded beetles for gallstones, and diseases of the spleen were treated with the heads of seven fat bats. Possessed of a great bedside manner, Gaddesden created a magic necklace for epilepsy, and recommended brandy for palsy of the tongue, while ingratiating himself with women by creating perfume, hair colourants and even recipes. Said to have been the original of Chaucer's physician, who 'lov'd gold in special', he made a fortune from treating his wealthy patients.[19]

In 1300, the Rector of St Margaret Lothbury claimed he could cure skin cancer – 'Le Lou' or lupus, from the French *loup* – by treating the afflicted with the skin of four dead wolves which had been imported for the purpose. A garland of betony worn at night was a specific against 'phantasma or delusions' and a head poultice of crushed teasel (a spiky plant with hooked spines) would relieve the symptoms of 'the frenzy'.[20] Another popular belief was that 'a rosted Mous, eaten, doth heale Franticke persons'.[21]

*

Those patients from the Stone House who were capable of examining their surroundings would not have been impressed with their new home. Compared with the stone building in Charing Cross, Bethlem was little more than a ramshackle hovel. We can gain some idea of how it looked from elements of the hospital's fabric, which survived until the sixteenth century. There were the tenements, or lodgings, which had been built on the site of the old monks' refectory. The gateways, east and west, provided further accommodation. The great house included rooms for the master and the secular clergy, while worship took place in the chapel. The churchyard, which had stood nearby since Bethlem was founded in 1247, received the bodies of the chapter, the laity and Bethlem's patients. The patients themselves were accommodated in an infirmary or 'Abraham ward', with cells branching off a main corridor. (An 'Abraham man' was another term for a mad beggar.) By modern standards, provision was modest: patients could expect cribs lined with straw, basic medical treatment and a modest diet of bread, beer and cheese. By 1403, records indicate that there were no more than six insane and three sane patients. Above the infirmary was a dormitory, where the servants slept. It was also a hostel for travellers, though it is difficult to imagine that they got much rest on the nights when a florid patient was rampaging downstairs. Compared with a modern psychiatric hospital, security was non-existent. Patients might have been chained and manacled, but visitors could come and go as they pleased, bringing much-needed items of clothing and food. Bethlem was a religious institution and, as such, the homeless and elderly were permitted to seek refuge there. Up until the sixteenth century, local residents who wanted to use the communal latrine or 'jaques' on Bishopsgate had to walk through the precincts of Bethlem to reach it.

One might have thought that the transfer of the hospital from the Church and the king to the Corporation of London would have stimulated the citizens to rebuild their ancient hospital, but they lacked the motivation, and were content to farm it out to a keeper in part as a private asylum.[22] The keeper was kept in check by three 'surveyors' and the court of aldermen. Sadly, these checks were not always successful, and Bethlem was rocked by the first in a long series of scandals.

Between 1388 and 1403, the janitor Peter Taverner or 'Peter the Porter' became the hospital treasurer. The master of Bethlem had handed over his duties to Peter, including that of the safe keeping of the poor and sick as well as the custody of the alms.[23] The master gradually became aware that the order was in dire financial straits, and invited Henry IV himself to intervene. The royal commission, entitled 'The Visitation of Bethlehem Hospital', carried out by two of Henry IV's royal chaplains in 1403, revealed neglect and financial irregularities. Vestments and ornaments had gone missing from the chapel, Mass was intermittent, many of the monks and nuns had left and the habit of the order, emblazoned with the famous star, was no longer worn. Worst of all, the 'visitation' exposed the fact that all the funds raised by the licensed 'Bedlamites' had gone to line Peter's pockets.

At a series of official hearings, which lasted from March to May 1403, thirty-five charges were laid against Peter, including misappropriation of funds and selling off goods and chattels. Peter had also brought disgrace upon Bethlem by encouraging drinking, gambling and lewd behaviour and consorting with low life – runaway servants, poachers, acrobats, beggars who deliberately maimed their own children, gypsies, tramps and thieves, who vandalised the property and stole everything that they could get their hands on.

As for the poor patients, whom Peter had sworn upon oath to defend when elected to his post, the patients were forced to pay for their own food, despite the fact that it was donated by the public along with the bread, ale, meat, fish and candles sent in daily by the mayor and aldermen. Patients had to buy their own charcoal and wood in the winter, and were even expected to pay their own fees, despite the order's charitable status. It was the patients who suffered most from this appalling regime. If they wanted beer, they had to buy it, at Peter's prices; Peter's wife, described as 'threatening', refused to let them go outside to purchase food or drink. Bethlem was so noisy it was impossible to sleep. Patients were kept awake by the sound of swearing and shouting at the gate of the hospital, where Peter's wife had set up a buttery and sold ale late into the night. Worst of all, the patients received no form of treatment.

Eventually, Peter was charged with stealing: '33 coverlets (red and blue worsted), 34 blankets, 25 sheets, 6 mattresses, 5 brass pans, 1 axe, 1 spade, 3 shovels, 1 pair of tongs, 8 platters, 8 wooden dishes, 2 trivets, 4 tubs, 2 keys to a garden gate, 1 bier, 1 bucket, 1 barrow, 1 cement, 3 tankards [for drawing water], 1 iron skimmer, 1 pillow of serge, 1 table cloth, 1 towel, and 2 pairs of stocks, 4 pairs of iron manacles, 5 other chains of iron, 6 chains of iron with 6 locks'.[24]

In his defence, Peter appears to have run a form of almshouse or home for the children of patients: 'the said Peter has divers patients in his house whom he boards and lodges'.[25] This could either have been a baby farm or a 'Dotheboys Hall' (like the infamous boarding school in Dickens's *Nicholas Nickleby*) or an act of genuine kindness, giving the inmates' offspring somewhere to live. But neither the master nor the royal commissioners were impressed by this state of affairs: 'when poor or sick people come to the hospital to obtain rest . . . they are shut out by the presence of these children, and this seems to be an extraordinary state of affairs, unless such children be sick, or sent there from charitable motives'.[26]

Peter was found guilty and ordered to replace everything that was missing, or face a fine of £100. This was lenient considering he had stolen about £300 from the institution. Peter failed to repent, and so, on 9 May 1403, he was sacked from the office of janitor. But it is unlikely that he went hungry. A resourceful man, Peter had probably set up alternative accommodation elsewhere in London. A tavern, perhaps, or a lodging house, which the locals would have noticed filling up, by degrees, with some rather fine items such as mattresses, bed linen and tankards, where labourers toasted their feet by the fireplace, and the local hangman regaled his fellow drinkers with tales of cut-purses, and the ladies of the night plied their trade, while down in the cellars, those missing iron chains with locks and keys still manacled human flesh and blood.

Peter had gone, but his legacy lived on in the form of further corruption and neglect. In 1411, Parliament presented Henry IV with a petition for hospital reform, alleging that many hospitals had become 'for the most part decayed' and urging that their funds be withdrawn. The petition includes a reference to hospitals which exist 'to maintain those who have lost their wits and memory', a clear reference to Bethlem. But any attempts at reform were overshadowed by Henry's death in 1413, his son's succession, and more pressing issues such as the battle of Agincourt (1415) and its consequences.

When Edward Atherton became master in 1437, his first act was to petition Henry VI, then just a boy of fifteen, to order an inquiry into various scandals and abuses at Bethlem, due to the neglect of former masters.[27] The hospital had once again endured 'pillaging, trespasses and wastings'. Priceless documents had disappeared from the archives, sold to bakers to wrap hot pies, or to the local quack so that he had parchment to scribble down his magic charms. Bethlem was dilapidated: parts of the quadrangle lay in ruins; the tenements were falling down, but no money was available for repairs. The gardens had been stripped of their fruit, and the churchyard (as so often in London at this time) was occupied by market stalls, where hares and rabbits hung down above trays of shimmering fish, and hot pies and hair-ribbons competed for attention alongside herbal remedies and tawdry gimcrack jewellery. Religious observance had deteriorated to the point where Mass was scarcely even celebrated, because the chapel had been desecrated, looted of its devotional metalwork and now served as a shelter for vagrants.

Atherton's appeal clearly met with some success: by 1451, William Gregory, the then Mayor of London, referred to 'A church of Our Lady that is named Bedlem [Bethlem]. And in that place are found many men that have fallen out of their wits. Right well are they cared for in that place, and some are restored to health again, but some are there for ever, for they are incurable. And unto that place many indulgences have been granted, more than they of the place know.'[28] The hospital received many legacies, including forty shillings from Gregory himself after his death in 1465.

Henry VI, to whom Edward Atherton had appealed for help, succumbed to madness himself in 1453. A mild-mannered, obedient and extremely religious man, who had been king since he was six months old, Henry appears to have suffered from a form of schizophrenia. In August 1453, Henry was described as losing his reason and memory, his powers of speech and movement, in an attack of insanity which recurred until his death. This particular episode lasted until Christmas 1454. Henry was treated by his confessor, John Arundell, who was also a doctor and the king's principal physician. The following March the Privy Council authorised Arundell and his colleagues to treat the king according to the traditional principles, including purges, shaving and baths. Arundell demonstrated such sympathy and skill in his treatment of Henry that he was appointed master of Bethlem in 1457.

However, despite all the efforts of Arundell and his team, Henry's condition deteriorated. He suffered from dementia and religious mania, including hallucinations, and between 1464 and 1470 he lay in the Tower of London, dishevelled and neglected. In 1471, allegedly on the orders of Richard, Duke of Gloucester (later Richard III), he was murdered. His tomb at Windsor later became a shrine for mad pilgrims.

Bethlem itself did not escape the Wars of the Roses. Red and white roses grew in its gardens; red and white roses adorned the altar of its chapel. But then the time came when it was dangerous to wear the red, the badge of the House of Lancaster: London supported the white rose of York. In May 1470, the war touched the walls of Bethlem, when Falconbridge launched his Kentish sailors, under the red rose of Henry VI, against Bishop's Gate.[29] Several grand houses were burnt down, and there was an attempt to blow up the gate with gunpowder. Behind the barricades, the quadrangle was full of refugees, and a pall of acrid smoke hung over the hospital. The handful of patients, chained up behind locked doors and barred windows, must have cowered in abject terror as steel clashed and fire crackled so nearby. Among the citizens fighting back against Falconbridge was a neighbour, Alderman John Crosby, who left £100 to rebuild the gate and twenty shillings to be distributed among the 'distract people being then within the hospital of Bedlam in ready money or good wholesome food, be it at one time, or at several times'.[30] It was a practical legacy, anticipating the treatment options of the twentieth century: good wholesome food to restore the body, and ready money for the patient's immediate needs on rehabilitation.

Bethlem also witnessed the final stages of the war: in August 1485, after the Battle of Bosworth when Richard III was slain by Henry Tudor's victorious army, Bethlem watched the mayor and aldermen ride to Shoreditch. Henry VII, escorted by an armed throng, with standards and other trophies, passed by on his way to hear a Te Deum (a service of thanksgiving) at St Paul's. The old order changed at Bethlem, too: on 20 September 1485, a new warden was appointed: Thomas Maudesley, chaplain to Henry VII's mother. The hospital had survived war, pestilence and over a century of silence and disaster. But soon Bethlem would face another challenge: the Reformation.

3

A MAD WORLD, MY MASTERS

By the time of the Reformation, Bethlem had become a unique London institution. As the only hospital devoted to the care of 'distracted persons', it was still run along mediaeval lines, with the master appointed by the Bishop of Bethlem. The last of these, before the Reformation swept away the influence of Rome, was George Boleyn, brother of Anne, appointed in 1529. There had always been a strong link between Bethlem and the Crown, so it is likely that George was appointed through the influence of his famous sibling. It is even possible that Anne visited the hospital, in the days before her marriage, when Henry VIII was still infatuated with her, and courtiers would do anything to make her smile. Anne would have been introduced to some of her brother's deluded subjects, and traded lewd remarks and pleasantries among the filth and straw.

But if George had cultivated Henry in order to advance his career, he paid a high price for his position. On evidence supplied by his wife, who wanted him dead for her own reasons, George was executed for alleged incest with Anne in June 1536, lamenting on the scaffold that he had sinned in preferring the vanities of the world to religious observations. Boleyn was succeeded by another of Henry's favourites, Sir Peter Mewtys, his private secretary and spy master. Sir Peter's tasks included trying to find a French wife for Henry following the execution of Anne Boleyn and assisting in the reception of Anne of Cleves. As a former spy, Sir Peter proved more resilient than his predecessor: after military campaigns at Calais and Edinburgh, he was knighted in 1544.

In 1536, Bethlem's future seemed in doubt once again, when Parliament authorised the dissolution of all religious houses worth less than £200 a year. However, in 1538, the Lord Mayor of London, Sir Richard Gresham, petitioned Henry VIII to intervene. Four religious houses which had been 'founded for the relief and comfort of poor and impotent people unable to help themselves' faced closure: the priory or hospital of St Mary, Bishopsgate, just up the road from Bethlem Hospital; St Bartholomew's; St Thomas's, and the New Abbey, a religious foundation located between East Smithfield and Tower Hill.[1]

Bethlem is not mentioned on this list, possibly because it was considered to be the king's personal property. Gresham was aware that Henry considered his assault on the hospitals, as religious houses, to come from the highest motives. Therefore, Gresham calculated his appeal in these terms: 'they were not founded for the maintenance of canons, priests and monks to live in pleasure' he reminded Henry, suggesting that the clergy had in fact ignored 'the miserable people lying in every street, offending every clean person passing by with their filthy and nasty savours'.[2] Gresham implied that he and his post-Reformation cohorts in the City of London would rescue the hospitals from such mismanagement and come to the aid of the patients.

A year passed without a reply from Henry. Gresham tried again, suggesting that the 'late dissolved houses be made over to them with their rents and revenues'. This petition was ignored. Henry was holding out for a better offer. Finally, on 1 August 1540, the Court of Common Council authorised the mayor and aldermen of

London to make an offer of £700 for houses, churches and cloisters, 'if they can be gotten no cheaper'.[3]

Henry retorted that Gresham was being 'pynchepence' (stingy) and let the matter lie for years, obviously hoping for a higher bid. This went on until 27 December 1546, when Henry eventually agreed to grant St Bartholomew's Hospital and 'the House of Bethlem' to the City of London, along with an endowment, if the City would agree to pay for outstanding maintenance and restoration work. The offer was only just made in time: Henry signed the deeds on his deathbed.

From 1547 to 1556, Bethlehem was administered by the court of aldermen, directly through the 'keeper' of the house, who was compelled to submit his accounts to the chamberlain of the City. By late 1556, however, Bethlem had been transferred to the governors of Christ's Hospital (a school for poor children). But these governors, who were already responsible for the children of Christ's Hospital, struggled to administer it. Eventually, on 27 September 1557, Bethlem was placed under the management of Bridewell, a notorious prison. Those records of Bridewell which survived the conflagration of 1666, when the Great Fire swept through the prison, provide a vivid insight into the London underworld of the time: taverns named 'The Hanging Sword' and 'The Popinjay'; prodigal apprentices gambling the night away; bogus cripples begging in St Paul's Churchyard; and prostitutes being whipped, then dragged round town to 'rough music' – the clatter of bowls and basins by the respectable – while their wealthy clients were ordered to pay towards the repair of Bridewell wharf, or make a much needed contribution to the poor.

*

The royal hospitals were in a sorry state after the Reformation. In their capacity as religious houses, they had been plundered and wrecked on Henry VIII's orders; charitable funding had collapsed and they relied on financial support from the City. To obtain this, a tax was levied on every citizen from 1557. The following year, the hospitals appealed to the newly formed Anglican Church for support. Collections were taken throughout the churches of England and Wales, and a special proctor, authorised by the Crown, was dispatched to the cathedrals of Cambridge, Lincoln and Ely to solicit funds, just as in the old mediaeval days of the Bedlam beggars. Unfortunately, the majority of the money went to St Thomas's, leaving little in the way of funding for Bridewell and even less for Bethlem, making it the poor relation in the family of London hospitals.

There are few references to Bethlem in Bridewell's records, but from those few that do appear we get some idea of what life was like for the patients. The stories include an account of a man charged with sending his wife to Bethlem without cause in 1574. The wife complained that, for six weeks before her committal, she had been tied down in bed by her husband and another woman until she was 'well nigh famished!' In another entry, the governors of Bridewell assessed an unfortunate woman who passed through both institutions. She seemed to be mad, and 'yet was a rogue', and so she was first whipped at Bridewell before being sent to Bethlem.[4] One witness in October 1579 described how he and a couple of his friends stalked his sister and her lover through 'Bedlem' and eventually discovered them in the alley of a garden in Shoreditch, 'abusinge their bodyes'.[5] Another witness testified that a perfidious Mr Lee had promised her two or three angels (a pricey sum) for sleeping with her in her father's house. The deed being done, he had not paid up and had started avoiding her: the previous week, she had seen him in Bethlem, 'and he had run away into a house!'[6]

The fabric of Bethlem remained, despite Henry VIII's depredations. The tenements, built on the site of the old monks' refectory, still stood, as did the east and west gateways. The great house, which included rooms for the master and the secular clergy, was still there. But the chapel had been turned into a foundry, before being demolished in 1575. In the same year, a carpenter and a bricklayer won the contract to build a dozen houses on the site (two storeys high, with a garret above), recycling the old stone, timber and metal in the construction.

A lease granted to the father of Edward Alleyn (1566–1626), the famous Elizabethan actor, mentions two gardens with a chapel enclosed by a brick wall. This was actually the churchyard used by Bethlem from its foundation in 1247 up to the dissolution of the monasteries. In 1569, the Lord Mayor, Sir Thomas Roe, ordered an acre of ground, including this plot of land, to be enclosed as a burial ground for non-parishioners, creating much-needed burial space in an overcrowded city. Among those buried here was Robert Greene, the dramatist (1558–92), who, according to his contemporary Thomas Nashe, departed this life after an overdose of 'Rhenish wine and pickled herring'.

*

One of the tasks of the governors was to conduct regular inspections of the hospital. Conditions during the latter part of the century may be assessed from one 'View of Bethlehem' conducted on 4 December 1598. This gives a list of the twenty patients in residence, the amount charged for each, and the name of the person or parish responsible for paying their fees. It reveals that two men and four women had been sent over from Bridewell, and fourteen were private patients, whose family or friends paid the keeper between one shilling and four pence to five shillings a week for their keep. The keeper, or official in charge, was allowed the use of a house, and was permitted to take private patients, on condition that he received any patients sent to him from Bridewell. Unpaid at first, he was later granted six or seven pence a week per head for these patients, who had no means of their own. Contributors included city companies, St Bartholomew's Hospital, Gray's Inn and the Lord Admiral. Residents on 4 December included a Dutch man who had been confined for four months, a Spaniard, Salvado Mendes (three years), and one member of the queen's chapel who had been there for two months. In the ground-floor ward, paupers with acute mania rubbed shoulders with the rich. Eleven of the twenty cells were occupied by women. The registers of St Botolph's Church, Bishopsgate, reveal that children were born in Bethlem, the mothers being attended by the porter's wife, and female servants were employed directly by the keeper to take care of the wealthier inmates.[7] In 1578, one Mrs Thomson, the wife of Davie Thomson, 'who hath given medicine to the poor at Bedlem', was paid '8s a week to look after two lunatics in Bedlem in romes ther provided for her she to finde them diet and medsens'. She reported she had cured one William Horne, a rich man from North Cray, and also many others.[8] William Shakespeare, who had lived in Bishopsgate, may well have derived his knowledge of love potions and 'noxious philtres' from observing herbalists at work in Bethlem's garden.

During the day, those men and women permitted to leave their cells shared the same exercise yard and corridor, and were allowed to warm themselves by the kitchen fire, the only one in the house. The report, signed by the treasurer and six governors, describes Bethlem in damning tones, condemning it as so loathsome and filthy that it was unfit for human habitation. The hospital stank. It was situated between two open sewers, one of which was regularly choked with excrement and by-products from nearby industrial processes including a hop boiler and a chandler. The inhabitants had no choice but to inhale the poisonous fumes day and night. The gallery and cells became so disgusting under private management that, by 1598, the governors of Bridewell were forced to admit that the hospital was not fit to enter. In 1612, a subsequent inspectorate informed the governors that the gardens to the north of the hospital were blocked with human waste and stinking water, 'which is very noisome to the prisoners'.[9]

The prior inspection of 1607 mentions the names of patients sent by Bridewell, and their nicknames, too. They seem vivid, even after all these years: 'Welsh Harry', 'Black Will', 'Joane of the hospital', 'Old Madam' and the legendary Minnie Barber, who inspired the ballad 'The Maid of Bedlam' and had diverted the visitors, and kept the neighbours awake, for twenty-five years. These are the first of many stereotypes who will feature in accounts of the hospital over the centuries. We may imagine the keeper showing the team round, telling them all about his human menagerie, expressing regret for the filth and squalor. The very fact that the keeper found it necessary to apologise for his poor housekeeping suggests that individuals who were neither friends nor relations were starting to visit Bethlem, though not in vast numbers. Given the hospital's location, on Bishopsgate, near the Tower Menagerie, within easy reach of other entertainments such as the Theatre and the Curtain playhouses and the firework displays at the Artillery Gardens, Bethlem would inevitably feature on the tourist trail. The first reference to an actual visit to 'the shew of Bethlem' dates from 1610, when Lord Percy spent ten shillings on a visit, accompanied by his wife, Lady Penelope, and his two sisters.[10]

*

From this evidence, we can see Bethlem as a physical entity in post-Reformation London: dirty, chaotic, but surviving despite funding problems and filthy wards. At the same time, Bethlem was starting to feature in London's imaginative life, developing an alter ego in the form of 'Bedlam', the Cockney contraction of 'Bethlem', in popular drama. Madness, in all its grotesque manifestations, appealed to the sensibilities of the tragedians, who could manipulate the distinction between the sane and the insane to make satirical comments upon the state of the nation. Thomas Dekker (c. 1570–c. 1632) set entire scenes in 'Bedlam'. Even his bookseller's premises, 'Joseph Hunt's in Bedlam', were in the vicinity. The first use of 'Bedlam' on a title page came in 1615, with the appearance of *Mystical Bedlam* by the Puritan divine Thomas Adams (1580–1653), who took as his text Ecclesiastes 9: 3: 'The heart of the Sonnes of men is full of evil, and madnesse is in their heart while they live.'[11]

In Dekker's *The Honest Whore* (1604), although the Bethlehem Monastery is situated in a fictional Milan, it is obvious to the audience that this is an institution known to every Londoner.

Quarrelling violently among themselves, or abusing their inquisitive visitors, these are familiar figures. Even Dekker's depiction of a deluded patient rings true: one man 'lashes himself into a fury' and then becomes convinced that the people talking to him are actually 'the Turks, who wrecked his ships and his fortunes'.[12]

Dekker also reveals a disturbing theme, which was to recur during the history of Bethlem: a majority of inmates appear to be admitted shortly after coming into money. When asked by one character if there are many gentlemen or courtiers at the hospital, the Sweeper replies: 'O yes, abundance, abundance! Lands no sooner fall into their hands, but straight they run out a' their wits. Farmers' sons come hither like geese, in flocks, and when they ha' sold all their cornfields, here they sit and pick the straws.'[13] Father Anselmo, fictional master of this Bedlam, provides an insight into the phenomenon of Bedlam as entertainment:

> And, though 'twould grieve a soul to see God's image
> So blemish'd and defac'd, yet do they act
> Such antics and such pretty lunacies,
> That spite of sorrow they will make you smile.[14]

For poets and writers, to be considered 'mad' was a form of compliment, hinting not so much at mental instability as divine inspiration. Michael Drayton (1563–1631) praised Christopher Marlowe thus: 'For that fine madness still he did retain, Which rightly should possess a poet's brain.'[15] Shakespeare, of course, observed that 'the lunatick, the lover and the poet are of imagination all compact'[16] and refers to Bedlam twice, in *Henry VI Part 2* and *King Lear*, as well as working a standing joke about the English and madness into *Hamlet*. According to the gravedigger, Hamlet, Prince of Denmark was to be packed off to England because he was mad, and 'shall recover his wits there; or, if 'a do not, 'tis no great matter. 'Twill not be seen in him there: there the men are as mad as he.'[17]

King Lear, meanwhile, of course, constitutes one of the most moving and eloquent studies of madness in the English language. Thwarted Lear, already unhinged enough to relinquish the crown to his daughters, succumbs to dementia while retaining enough insight to realise that he is actually losing his sanity. 'O! Let me not be mad, not mad, sweet Heaven; Keep me in temper; I would not be mad!' he pleads, even as he realises that his wits are slipping away from him, and that he has even been reduced to the indignity of tears.[17] Having lost everything that made him every inch a king – respect, power, his entourage – Lear rails at the storm in impotent rage, a poor, infirm, weak and despised old man:

> Blow, winds, and crack your cheeks! Rage, blow!
> You cataracts and hurricanes, spout
> Till you have drench'd our steeples, drown'd the cocks!
> You sulphurous and thought-executing fires,
> Vaunt-couriers to oak-cleaving thunderbolts,
> Singe my white head! And thou, all-shaking thunder,
> Strike flat the thick rotundity o' the world!
> Crack nature's moulds, all germans [seeds] spill at once,
> That make ungrateful man![19]

With Lear in a hovel in Kent is another madness stereotype, 'Poor Tom', the Bedlam beggar. With straw in his hair and rips in his clothes – or sometimes no clothes at all – 'Tom' was a fantastic and pitiful figure, the subject of a celebrated ballad:

> From the hag and hungry goblin that into rage would rend ye,
> And the spirits that stand by the naked man
> In the book of moons defend you!
> With an host of furious fancies
> Whereof I am commander
> With a burning spear, and a horse of air,
> To the wilderness I wander

> By a knight of ghosts and shadows
> I summoned am to tourney
> Ten leagues beyond the wide world's end
> Methinks it is no journey![20]

Filthy, clad in a blanket, his hair in elf knots, Tom would present himself at a lonely farmhouse with a distressed look and his catch-phrase – 'Poor Tom's a cold', looking as if he had just escaped from his miserable cell. The average farmer's wife, alone in her home, was happy to offer him a piece of bacon or a slice of cheese just to make him go away. But Tom is a vulnerable figure, pitiful and unthreatening. In one verse, he even reassures female listeners that 'Poor Tom will injure nothing.' All he wants is food and clothing. He even has a lover, 'Bess of Bedlam', who is devoted to him:

> To find my Tom of Bedlam ten thousand years I'll travel,
> Mad Maudlin goes with dirty toes to save her shoes from
> gravel.[21]

The 'Poor Tom' of *King Lear* possesses an additional dimension: this 'Poor Tom' is actually Edgar, the son of Lear's comrade, Gloucester. But this is no ordinary beggar. Edgar's dissimulation comes from the best of motives. Disguised as a Bedlamite, his mission is to protect Lear, who was a loyal friend of his father. As he explains this to the audience, Edgar paints a vivid picture of the Bedlamite, the most despised of men:

> I'll grime my face with filth;
> Blanket my loins; elf all my hair in knots;
> And with presented nakedness out-face
> The winds and persecutions of the sky.
> The country gives me proof and precedent
> Of Bedlam beggars, who, with roaring voices,
> Strike in their numb'd and mortified bare arms

Pins, wooden pricks, nails, sprigs of rosemary;
And with this horrible object, from low farms,
Poor pelting villages, sheep-cotes and mills,
Sometime with lunatic bans, sometimes with prayers
Enforce their charity – Poor Turlygod! Poor Tom![22]

'Poor Tom' sets himself the task of embodying the mad stereotype: he is 'Poor Tom' that eats the swimming frog, the toad, the tadpole, cow-dung for salads, swallows the old rat and the ditch-dung and drinks the green mantle of the standing pool. As though this behaviour is not enough, 'Poor Tom' also displays extraordinarily colourful language, full of fantastic visions and pithy epithets. Anyone who has listened to the phenomenon of 'pressure of speech' (a fast, random way of talking, common in cases of mania) will recognise 'Poor Tom's language as clinically accurate: 'The foul fiend haunts poor Tom in the voice of a nightingale. Hopdance cries in Tom's belly for two white herring. Croak not, black angel; I have no food for thee.'[23]

*

Women were assumed to be particularly at risk of madness on physiological grounds, a concept derived from classical antiquity and the theory of hysteria. Mad women feature throughout the drama of this time, most notably Ophelia, who drowns herself after being driven insane by her father's death and her unrequited love for Hamlet. Ophelia is an early manifestation of an enduring female stereotype, that of the beautiful nymphomaniac, her inhibitions removed by madness. Ophelia's later speeches, as one character observes, are a document in madness, full of sexual innuendos: 'Young men will do't if they come to't/ By Cock, they are to blame,' she observes, before quoting endless songs of spurned love and abandoned, deflowered wenches.[24] There is a reference to the herb rue, believed to bring on a natural abortion, and even her name, 'O-feely-her', is crudely suggestive. But even at her most insane, Ophelia is desirable, even as she drowns.

The Duchess of Malfi, meanwhile, in John Webster's play of the same name (1623), is made of sterner stuff. Despite the attempts of her brother, Ferdinand, to drive her mad by surrounding her with Bedlamite lunatics, it is Ferdinand himself who succumbs to insanity. Ferdinand's madness takes the form of lycanthropy or 'wolf madness', a delusion which had men howling around churchyards at night, pale and feral, convinced that they had turned into wolves. Ferdinand's treatment tells us a lot about the contemporary medical response to the condition, later diagnosed as 'porphyria' and characterised by frantic behaviour, sensitivity to ultraviolet rays and ulceration of the skin. His doctor prescribes such mythical cures as a salamander's skin, to prevent sunburn and the white of a cockatrix's egg as a remedy for Ferdinand's photosensitive eyes. Ben Jonson and Thomas Middleton also used Bedlam as a location.

*

As they shambled round on the conducted tour of Bethlem, it is rather tempting to visualise Shakespeare's contemporaries as a gang of ageing reprobates, in down-at-heel boots and dusty hats, peering at the inmates for inspiration before heading for the bowling alley that a resourceful local had set up in the hospital's precincts. However, this activity was not always an unalloyed pleasure: play was frequently interrupted by robbers, mugging participants at knifepoint. But, resigned to their losses, the scribblers and libertines would retire to the nearby White Hart Inn, to feast on the pickled herrings and 'Rhenish wine' that did for poor Robert Greene, and to be joined by 'Taffety Meg', the local whore, and her companions. Recently discharged from Bridewell, Meg was full of tales of a new governor who, far from welcoming her into custody with a whipping, as was customary, had offered sympathetic hospitality to the women in his care. Under this regime change, the ladies of the night were dressed in glorious apparel, and dined in the liveliest company, on crab, lobster and artichoke pies, washed down with gallons of wine.[25]

Nicholas Breton (c. 1545–1626) was a regular visitor to Bethlem. Although he, too, was a man of letters, Breton's motive was not to humiliate the inmates or gain 'copy' for his next book. A depressive, Breton actually felt close to becoming a patient himself. Sympathetic and genuinely religious, he tried to impart his resignation and hopefulness to those whose depression and temptations he understood all too well.

In 'Forte of Fancie' (1584) Breton describes 'Bedlam' as 'foul hole and loathsome den', filled with the raging and the stamping, the fretting and the groaning, to which contemporary writers testified. Breton portrays a roofless, windowless house, open to the wind and rain. In the middle of this house stands a dilapidated bedstead, carved with nightmarish faces. Lying on the bed is madness itself, tossing and turning, with haggard eyes. Beside the bed are instruments, but they are not fit to play: the strings are broken, the lute has a hole in it, and the trumpet is cracked. In this house, the music of life is hushed, for a while, or maybe for ever. It is a terrifying vision:

> Above them all, upon the top of this same hill,
> Dwells madness, master of them all, and witless will.
> He fears no hurt, nor cold, for if with heat he glow,
> The waves of woe will cool him straight, which there by tides
>   do flow.
> For through this forest runs the sea of sorrow sore,
> Whose waves do beat against this fort, that bordereth on the
>   shore;
> In raging, frantic fires he passeth forth the day,
> In strange perplexities, himself tormenting many a way.
> Ready to kill himself and with his hair upright,
> He cried, he would rather die than bide such deep despite.[26]

*

But not every 'Tom o' Bedlam' was genuinely insane. Recognising one way to survive in an indifferent world, opportunists joined the ranks of genuine ex-patients tramping the highways in search of charity. You could even obtain a fake 'beggar's licence' for half a crown at the Griffin, Waltham Cross, from one of London's original fraudsters. Apparently signed by the keeper of Bethlem, this document stated that you had been incarcerated there for the last two years and were now an authorised beggar. Another scam consisted of a brass bracelet bearing an inscription which claimed that its wearer had been licensed to beg by the governors of Bethlem Hospital. It was 1675 before the governors saw fit to issue a statement that they never sent discharged patients out to beg, and that no bracelets or brands were ever attached to patients, during residence or on discharge.

In 1566, the bogus Tom o' Bedlam met his biographer in the form of Thomas Harman, a country gentleman and magistrate who lived near Crayford, Kent.[27] Harman was fascinated by low life: whenever he encountered the underclass, he wormed their stories out of them, and their tricks and customs. One November day in 1566, when he was in Whitefriars, Harman met 'the Counterfeit Crank', who claimed he had been treated in Bedlam for epilepsy. The Crank's story was that he had fallen in a fit in Carmelite Street, the foul lane by the waterside, and nearly bled to death. But Harman became suspicious when The Crank refused a basin of water to clean his face and clothes and asked the beggar his name. How long had he suffered from the falling sickness? Had he been in London long? The Crank introduced himself as Nicholas Jennings, and said he had suffered from the falling sickness for eight years. He had been in London for two years, spending eighteen months in Bethlem. Ascertaining that the keeper of Bethlem was one 'John Smith', Harman immediately sent his servant to verify the man's story. Harman was not surprised when his servant returned with the news that the keeper of Bethlem had never heard of Nicholas Jennings, and that furthermore, no man was allowed to leave unless he was taken away by his friends, and that ex-patients were no longer allowed to beg about the City. Despite being rumbled, The Crank continued to beg round the Temple for the rest of the day, with such success that he relieved the charitable of thirteen shillings. One trick of the trade involved a pig's bladder filled with blood. At noon, The Crank retired to the back of St Clement's Lane and daubed his face and hands with fresh blood and rubbed mud into his breeches and jerkin before presenting himself to the gullible with his hard luck story.

It was a profitable scam: The Crank had a pretty house in Southwark with a well-stocked table and a cupboard full of pewter. This did not stop him, two months later, from begging in White-friars for the price of a bed for the night. This time, he was disguised as an unemployed hatter, in a good black frieze coat, a new pair of white breeches, a fine felt hat on his head, and a shirt of Flanders work worth six shillings. This time, The Crank was not so lucky. Arrested, he was admitted to Bridewell, where he was stripped stark naked, before being pilloried at Cheapside and then whipped at a cart's tail through London. This was not the end of it: The Crank was then forced to carry a banner, with his name and offence displayed upon it, through the streets to his own front door, before returning to Bridewell to serve his sentence. At length he was freed, on the condition that he would work for a living in future. A portrait of The Crank, in all his abject humiliation, was displayed at Bridewell as a warning.

*

One of Bethlem's most famous neighbours, Sir Thomas More (1478–1535), lived at Crosby Hall, Bishopsgate between 1516 and 1523, and frequently sauntered across the newly cobbled street past Bedlam Gate. The famous statesman and author of *Utopia* recorded many observations on the Dystopia located next door. In 'Four Last Things' (c. 1522), More alludes to an incident to which he played eyewitness. 'Think not that everything is pleasant that men for madness laugh at. For thou shalt in Bedlam see one laughing at the knocking of his head against a post, and yet there is little pleasure therein. But what will ye say if ye see the sage fool laugh, when he hath done his neighbour wrong, for which he shall weep for ever hereafter?'[28]

In his *Apology* (1533) More tells us about a man who, after falling into a frenzy, was taken into Bethlem, where, through beating and correction, he eventually came to his senses. Set at liberty, however, he began to succumb to madness once again, and took to wandering into church during Mass and causing a disturbance. The worst manifestation of this came during the Elevation of the Host. If he saw a woman kneeling before the altar rail, lost in her prayers, he would creep up behind her and tip her skirts over her head. This must have been particularly disconcerting, given that knickers had yet to be invented. The perpetrator was given short shrift for his anti-social behaviour: he was taken by the constables and tied to a tree in the street, where he was beaten with rods in front of the entire town, a treatment which, according to Sir Thomas, effectively cured him of his madness.

Not only did More espouse this brutal cure for madness, but he also accepted the conventional explanation that madness was caused by evil spirits. When his neighbour, Sir Thomas Wentworth, reported that his 12-year-old daughter appeared to be suffering from demonic possession, More was convinced that she had been 'tormented by our ghostly enemy the Devil, raving with despising and blasphemy of God'.[29] More's pronouncement is proof of the fact that the concept of 'witchcraft' had a powerful grip upon the popular imagination. We have already seen how, during the mediaeval period, the mind and body were regarded as the province of the clerics, and madness and illness were conceptualised in terms of good and evil. We have also learned that madness was assumed to be a form of demonic possession, which responded to exorcism as a treatment. By the fourteenth and fifteenth centuries this explanation had expanded to embrace witchcraft. Not only were the mad possessed by the devil – they were in league with him. Elizabeth Sawyer's life was dramatised as *The Witch of Edmonton*. In her confession to the clergyman Henry Goodcole, she admitted that the devil first came to her when she was 'cursing, swearing, and blaspheming. This sacrilege assured the Devil that she was of his party.'[30] Almost all the mentally ill were considered witches or sorcerers, or bewitched.

Witch hunts became an expression of the scapegoat culture, with witches taking the blame for the Black Death and the threats to the Church represented by crop failure, plague and civil war. In their ignorance, citizens assumed that illness and disease were caused by God, or evil spells by their enemies, and held witches accountable for all ills, from the milk turning sour and bread failing to rise through to impotence, ailing livestock and child mortality. Popular hysteria about witchcraft reached its apotheosis with the publication of Jacob Sprenger and Heinrich Kramer's *Malleus Maleficarum* ('The Witches' Hammer') in 1487. This notorious bestseller chronicled the lurid crimes of witches in pornographic detail and was swiftly appropriated by the Inquisition, joining the Bible to enforce the message that all women – not just witches – were evil, and responsible for man's fall from grace. The witch was a social parasite, a member of a secret organisation which rivalled the Church, and adept at every form of crime and perversion. Bizarre accounts circulated of victims disgorging the most extraordinary objects under the influence of magic spells. According to the historian Cornelius Gemma, one Katherine Gualter suffered from such strange passions and convulsions that 'three men could not sometimes hold her'; she purged a live eel (which later, conveniently, vanished), and vomited copiously for fourteen days, bringing up, among other items, 'great balls of hair, pieces of wood, pigeons' dung, parchment, goose dung, glass and brass'. This was accompanied by paroxysms of laughter, weeping and ecstasies. Gemma's comment, 'this I saw with horror', seems like a bit of an understatement.[31]

In one notorious account, Sprenger and Kraemer even claimed that witches possessed the power to remove a man's genitals, collecting 'as many as twenty or thirty members together', and putting them in a bird's nest, or a box, 'where they move themselves like living members and eat oats and corn, as has been seen by many as it is a matter of common report. One witness reported that when he had lost his member, he approached a known witch to ask her to restore it to him. She told the afflicted man to climb a certain tree, and that he might take which he liked out of a nest in which there were several members. And when he tried to take a big one, the witch said: you must not take that one, adding, because it belongs to a parish priest.'[32]

The most suspect women were widows and spinsters, those who lived alone: according to the witch-finders, their crimes included killing and eating children and orgiastic sex with the devil, who came equipped with a twenty-three-inch member for the purpose. Once caught, these unfortunate women were stripped and shaved and underwent a cavity search for 'the mark of the witch', a catch-all phrase which covered moles, birthmarks or scars. So-called witches were then tortured, a procedure that included beating, thumbscrews and gang rape, until a 'confession' was wrung out of them, a practice which led one commentator to observe that 'they are racked and tortured, so they can hardly stand or hold themselves from confession. In which case I doubt but that the Pope would blaspheme Christ, and curse his mother for a peacock.'[33]

One of the most notorious ordeals was ducking, the water trial in which the victim was thrown trussed up into a pond to sink and drown, if innocent, or float if guilty. If she were unfortunate enough to survive this test, the 'witch' faced death by hanging or being burnt at the stake.

It is impossible to be certain exactly how many 'witches' were condemned and killed. Records were not always kept, and estimates vary between hundreds of thousands to many millions. It seems that many more women died than men: the historian Wallace Notestein suggested in 1911 that the ratio was around twenty to one. In certain cases, young children were arraigned and murdered. With their vile ideology and endless pronouncements from 'witch-finders', the psychiatrist Thomas Szasz compared the witch hunts with the Spanish Inquisition or the Nazi persecution of the Jews.

Reginald Scot, who had seen many so-called witches brought before him in his capacity as a Justice of the Peace in Kent, was among the first to suggest that an element of insanity informed the diagnosis of the 'witch' and the 'bewitched'. He surmised that many 'bewitched' people were suffering from a disordered brain, rather than enchantment. Careful observation convinced him that the accused and the accusers were not bewitched at all, but mad, arguing that a belief in witchcraft was 'contrarie to reason, scripture and nature'. Witches, argued Scot, were not possessed by the devil at all, merely delusional, and suffered from 'not witchcraft but melancholie'.[34] The allegations against the poor old women brought before him mostly consisted of frivolous guesswork, motivated by spite. There was no objective way in which it could be proved that an old lady had soured the milk, or caused crops to fail.

Scot gave as an example an account of 'One Ade Davie, the wife of Simon Davie', who developed a sad, pensive mood, and eventually confessed to her husband that she had sold her soul to the devil.[35] Simon reassured his wife, reminding her that she could never have done so, as her soul belonged to Christ, who had already redeemed it 'and deerlie paid for it, even with his bloud, which he shed upon the crosse'. Ade replied that she *had* bewitched him, and his children. Simon still refused to accept this, but decided to stay up late that night, to meet the devil when he arrived to possess Ade, according to his bargain. Suddenly, about midnight, there was a tremendous rumbling noise under the bedroom window, and they both became convinced the devil was outside, waiting to come in. They prayed, loudly and fervently, and the noise eventually stopped. But Ade remained melancholy for days afterwards, refusing to leave the house. If she looked out of the window and saw somebody carrying firewood, she screamed, convinced they were coming to burn her. And all this, Scot reminds us, although she had not actually hurt anyone – except herself. Ordered to rest, Ade eventually recovered, and acknowledged that this incident, which today we might regard as a breakdown, had developed 'through melancholie'. What about the rumbling, feared to be the sound of the devil downstairs? On the night that the devil was due to take his turn with Ade, an injured sheep had taken refuge by the wall of the house, underneath the bedroom window, and a dog had come along and devoured it.

Scot's enlightened attitude represented a real psychiatric advance; he identified a large group of the mad who were eventually rescued from theological speculation and persecution, and treated in the realm of the natural sciences as objects of medical and psychological study. But progress was slow, and persecution continued over the following centuries, as 'witches' proved an irresistible target for the fanatical religious fundamentalists. Reginald Scot was attacked by James I in *Daemonologie* (1597), with the future king slating 'the one called Scot an Englishman' and maintaining that 'such assaultes of Sathan are most certainly practised & that the instruments thereof, merits most severly to be punished'.[36] In *Basilikon Doron* (1599) he wrote: 'witchcraft takes its place with wilful murder, incest, sodomy, poisoning and false coining as horrible crimes that yee are bound in conscience neuer to forgiue'.[37]

It is tempting to conclude that witches were, indeed, mad, suffering from delusions and the effects of naturally occurring hallucinogenic substances such as ergot of rye and fly agaric. The psychologist Jane Ussher has argued that judging 'witches' as harmless but insane constituted another method of undermining their credibility. Ussher concluded that 'witches' were persecuted because their knowledge of herbal medicine, particularly with regard to childbirth and abortion, represented a threat to the clerical establishment.

Whatever his limitations regarding the treatment of so-called witches, James I had a benevolent impact on the history of Bethlem. In 1618, the king ordered an investigation into conditions at the hospital. The then keeper, Thomas Jenner, was made the subject of an inquiry at the Guildhall. Unfortunately, details about Jenner, which would have been written in the court books between 1610 and 1617, are unavailable as the books covering that period are missing. However, we can gain some impression of Jenner's character from the charges levelled against him. It was alleged that he was 'unskilful in the practice of medicine' and therefore 'unfit for the duties of his position', a criticism suggesting that the governors understood the need for the hospital to be run by a bona fide doctor rather than a gaoler. There were also allegations of cruelty and neglect. James humanely reminded the commissioners that the mad should be 'treated with all the care necessary to their state by the rules of medicine'; he instructed the commissioners to 'dislodge any person who lacks the necessary skill, and to raise Bethlehem to the level of St Bartholomew's and St Thomas's'.[38] In Jenner's place, the commission urged the king to appoint 'a faithful and skilful man to set over the house of Bethlem'. This man, a regius professor of medicine, was 'our beloved servant, Helkiah Crooke'.

4

MYSTICAL BEDLAM

Dr Helkiah Crooke (1576–1648) took up the post of third medical superintendent at Bethlem during desperate times. Conditions at the hospital were poor and 'Bedlam' had entered the English language as a byword for pandemonium. But conditions *outside* were little better. Throughout Bethlem's fourth century, England was a sick country, driving all to madness, particularly the poor, who lived in appalling conditions. Unemployment produced thousands of beggars, there was no police force and it was too dangerous to go out at night without arms or an escort.[1] Alcoholism proliferated: there were no licensing hours and spirits, wine and beer were extremely cheap. In some London streets every third house was a tavern. And gambling fever was at an all-time high, with a huge and addictive lottery run by the state.[2] In addition, a dense criminal underworld and teeming slums drove many Londoners to madness and despair. According to Robert Burton, author of *The Anatomy of Melancholy* (1621), life in England was enough to drive people mad: 'You shall see many discontents, common grievances, complaints, poverty, barbarism, beggary, plagues, wars, rebellions, seditions, mutinies, contentions, idleness, riot, epicurism, the land lie untilled, waste, full of bogs, fens, deserts &c., cities decayed, base and poor towns, villages depopulated, the people squalid, ugly, uncivil; that kingdom, that country, must needs be discontent, melancholy, hath a sick body, and had need to be reformed.'[3]

Crooke seemed well equipped to face the challenge. A graduate of Cambridge and Leyden universities, he had been appointed physician to James I in 1604. In 1615, he wrote *Mikrokosmographia*, a book on anatomy dedicated to James with a sycophantic reference to how much 'foreign nations loved and admired the encyclopaedic learning of the most literary of kings'. A second edition (published 1631) was dedicated to Charles I, which could be interpreted as evidence of further obsequiousness or a pragmatic bid to ensure royal patronage. The frontispiece of *Mikrokosmographia* shows Dr Crooke as a sombre figure with a long face and a pointed beard, delivering a lecture on the brain to students and professors at the College of Barber-Surgeons, near St Paul's Cathedral.

Crooke was elected keeper of Bedlam on 13 April 1619, after king and courtiers had lobbied Bridewell, which still controlled Bethlem, on his behalf. He knew everyone in London worth knowing and, potentially, could secure a successful and even prosperous future for the hospital. Crooke's first action was to usher in a sweeping programme of reforms, beginning with a demand to free Bethlem from the control of Bridewell, quite rightly asserting that it had not flourished since the union of the two in 1557.

However, this move made James suspicious. He assumed that the City of London was trying to take Bethlem out of royal jurisdiction. Perhaps because of this, Crooke swiftly lost interest in the hospital. His subsequent lack of personal supervision over his staff inevitably resulted in a catalogue of abuse. A broadsheet appeared in 1620 entitled 'The Petition of the Poor Distracted People in the House of Bedlem', representing an attempt to bring attention to their plight. In the same year, a father complained to the governors about his daughter's treatment, stating that 'for want of proper attention', his daughter's foot was rotting away.[4] In 1622, charges were brought against the servants for cruelty towards one patient, Sir William Clifton.

By the end of 1625, Dr Crooke was only appearing at the hospital on 'quarter days', to complete his accounts on the four days when patients' bills were due. This represented a violation of the conditions of his appointment, which required him to serve in person. It also appeared that Dr Crooke was making no effort to cure 'the distracted persons' in his charge, and that fees and other money were going straight into his bulging pockets. When, in 1631, two governors decided to pay a surprise visit to Bethlem, they found the patients starving. There had been nothing to eat for days apart from a few small scraps, and the previous Sunday there had been nothing except 5 pounds of cheese to divide among thirty inmates. They were cold, too: the porter's wife monopolised the fire in the kitchen, and refused to let the patients come near it.[5]

Notwithstanding the allowance he received from the parishes and friends of 'divers of the distracted persons', Crooke also demanded an extra fee, of between fifteen and twenty shillings, for each patient admitted[6] and refused to reveal what he had done with any legacies received. As a result of Crooke's embezzlement and neglect, Bethlem became the scene of such scandals that Charles I was constrained to have them investigated by two commissions, which revealed, on 10 October 1632 and 1 April 1633 respectively, that land had been sold off and that Crooke had exploited hospital finances for his own gain. When pressed by an auditor from the Board of Trade, Crooke begged for more time; daringly evasive, he produced a conjectural balance sheet and even claimed that the hospital owed *him* for eggs and butter supplied to the patients from his own farm in Essex. In turn, the auditors estimated that Crooke made at least £100 a year from the hospital. He was eventually dismissed in 1634, and forced to resign from the Royal College of Physicians. Crooke lived on until 1648, vigorously campaigning for his reinstatement and compensation.

Despite being corrupt and embezzling funds from the hospital,

Crooke had the occasional success, particularly if a patient intrigued him. One such case was that of Edmund Francklin of Bedford. A contemporary account is notable for a description of Edmund's florid behaviour and also constitutes one of the first examples of a 'psychiatrist' visiting a patient at home and having him committed. Normally, patients were referred to Bethlem by the magistrates, or presented to the governors by their families, who agreed to pay their fees. In this example, the patient is actually visited at home and then forcibly removed to Bethlem.

Edmund's behaviour had been violent and outrageous on several occasions over the previous two years. Convinced he was God, he claimed to have killed his father and two of his sisters and boasted that he would murder his remaining brothers before he was done. He broke glass windows, threw valuable household items into the fire and the pond, and, instead of eating his food, would mangle it up and throw it to the dogs. Events came to a head in November 1629, when Edmund attacked a dinner guest, Mr Roper, when he challenged Edmund's claim to be God. This followed an incident the previous Easter, when Edmund battered his brother with an iron winch, threw a rock at him and threatened to cut his throat. Concerned for their own safety and the future of the estate, Edmund's brothers applied to the governors of Bethlem, agreeing that they would pay Dr Crooke £200 a year for the 'Physick, Diet, Clothes, Lodging, washinge and all things necessary for the said Edmunde' if he could only be admitted. Dr Crooke came up to Bedford from London with his coach and horses and three men in attendance. The coach arrived at seven o'clock in the morning, as the servants were bustling about the house. Finding Edmund in bed, they begged him to get dressed and break his fast, and come to London with them. Considering Edmund's previous behaviour they might have predicted a scene, but Edmund submitted meekly, and was taken away to Crooke's house, 'where he was fairly intreated and well used & carefully provided of a good Lodging and wholesome and good dyet, according to the Quality of his person and the nature of his Infirmity'.[7]

Crooke's medical competence was never questioned. It was his dishonesty which led to his dismissal. But Crooke's removal from office at least represented an attempt on the part of the governors to improve standards at the hospital. Medicine was beginning to emerge as a profession in its own right, with practitioners keen to maintain their professional reputation. The College of Physicians had extensive power over the profession and protected its reputation by prosecuting irregular practitioners. One of the earliest accounts of a 'quack' being indicted for 'malpractices on the mad' dates from the annals of the College of Physicians of London, 13 January 1614. William Sheperd appeared before the Marshal, and confessed that he was a quack practising on mad people. When pressed by Dr Thomas Moudeford, the President, for a distinction between mad men and sane, he said: 'they are not all of one kinde, but all of ye foure humours, and those burnt'. When questioned further, 'but how is flegme burnt? And what is it? And what author hath he for it?' Sheperd could not respond. He stood accused of practising on 'the wife of John Newbery, a chandler, of whom he received 10*li*. And covenanted upon cure 10*li*. More. How he manacled, sore hurt her finger and face, and miserably misused, but cured not.' Sheperd was asked to wait while the college attended to more serious business. But 'fearing that he would be recalled and cast into prison, he took to his heels'.[8]

There were other minor scandals after the dismissal of Dr Crooke; more than once, the governors were perturbed by the inordinate quantity of soap supplied to the patients, or had grave suspicions about the dozens of wooden platters supposed to be lost or destroyed.[9] This, in turn, drove the governors to extreme behaviour. On one occasion, 'Joane, a patient' was dumped at the door of her friends' house, where they threatened to leave her, unless her arrears of half a crown a week were paid there and then. Rather than take in poor filthy, lousy, demented Joane, her friends swiftly paid up.

With the dismissal of Crooke, the office of keeper became obsolete, and a dynasty of stewards succeeded him. The first of these was

Richard Langley, whose arrival coincided with the appointment of a prototype matron. Up until this point, the wife of the porter had traditionally fulfilled the role, in a casual and unpaid capacity. Her duties consisted of supervising female servants, overseeing the laundry and the kitchen and caring for the female patients when required. An attempt to formalise this arrangement was made in July 1633, when Elizabeth, the wife of the new porter Humphrey Withers, took on the role of matron. Her duties included assisting in the bathing and bleeding of male and female patients.[10]

Sadly, the new appointment was not a success. Relations soon deteriorated between the Witherses and Richard Langley. By the end of the year, Withers was telling the court of governors that he wanted to resign and had a better offer elsewhere (with the almoner of the City of London). It emerged that the Langleys had committed abuses 'in words, blowes, assaults and fowle carriages' against him.[11] Withers also alleged that the Langleys appropriated the takings from the visitors, and purloined the provisions intended for the patients. It appears that the steward and his wife lived off the pickings: this included food and drink donated to the patients by friends and family, and by London's merchants. When nothing came in, the patients starved. The court awarded Withers £10, and suspended Langley, and not without reason. The Langleys were notoriously heavy drinkers. Neighbours testified that Langley and his wife were 'unquiet, uncivil and ungoverned people'. Eleanor Davies, Lady Audley, a patient at Bethlem in 1636, placed in the Langleys' lodgings rather than a cell on account of her noble birth, complained to the court of governors that her hosts regularly woke her up, stumbling home after midnight, both far gone in drink. The Witherses, meanwhile, developed a reputation for extortion and embezzlement,[12] shutting out visitors if they did not think they had contributed enough to the poor box. Humphrey Withers was later disciplined for absenteeism – he and other servants were found guilty of adjourning to the nearby White Hart tavern with leftovers from the patients' plates, 'and abiding there to tipple and disorder themselves and neglect their service and staying out late in the evening'.[13]

When Withers died in 1654, the court of governors retained the destitute Mrs Withers, though whether she could function effectively as a matron by this stage is doubtful. She appears to have become a chronic alcoholic. The court records of 1655, 1657 and 1662 refer to 'the Widow Withers not behaving herself in an orderly manner'. Two basketmen or attendants, the widow's drinking buddies, were sacked for being drunk on duty. The then porter, John Hopkins, was instructed to lock her up in one of the rooms appointed for 'Lunatique persons' if there were further incidents. Elizabeth Withers disappears from the records after 1662, perhaps dying as a patient in her own hospital. But Elizabeth was something of an exception: female servants tended to behave better and stay longer than their male counterparts,[14] while basketmen were regularly found guilty of misconduct. Between 1633 and 1700 fifteen of the forty-three basketmen mentioned in hospital records were discharged, and their average length of service was five years, as compared with around eleven years for the women. Records are not always explicit about the nature of the offences that led to them being sacked. Anthony Dadsworth, in 1652, was dismissed for 'abusive carriages and misbehaviour', while Roland Wolly left in 1675 branded as 'a person of evill fame and of a dishonest Conversacon': the reader's attitude changes when we learn that a year earlier, he had been attacked so violently by a patient that he required surgery.[15] In an institution where male basketmen attended female patients, sexual assault was inevitable. In the 1680s, Edward Langden was fired for impregnating a patient while his colleague, William Jones, was complicit in a cover-up. The governors were horrified by 'the greate miscarriages lately committed in Bethlem', and the incident eventually led to the segregation of male and female patients.

*

While Bethlem remained a ramshackle hovel, still struggling to survive in Bishopsgate, one aspect of madness was beginning to receive serious intellectual consideration. This element was 'melancholy', a state analogous to our contemporary diagnosis of clinical depression, but imbued with considerable cultural significance. Classical writers such as Aretaeus of Cappadocia had described a set of symptoms which would strike a chord with any modern reader, telling of stern, dejected sufferers, dull or unreasonably torpid, peevish, sleepless and paranoid. In extreme cases, victims avoid the haunts of men and want to die. The condition was caused, the ancients believed, by an excess of black bile, and its name derived from the Greek words *melon* (black) and *colim* (humour). The development of printing and increasing preoccupation with scientific investigation and spiritual matters combined to produce a sudden increase in books about melancholy during the Jacobean period. These ranged from the theological treatise to the prototype self-help manual, although it is difficult to distinguish between the genres as melancholy was considered as much a spiritual condition as an organic one.

Timothy Bright's *Treatise on Melancholie* (1586) went into two editions in the first year of publication. Written for his 'Melancholicke Friend: M', it was designed to 'discourse of the nature of melancholie, what causeth it, what effectes it worketh, how cured, and farther to lay open, whatsoeuer may serue for the knowledge thereof'. Bright distinguishes between melancholy caused by physiological disorders and despair arising from mental or spiritual anguish.[16] One is a disease of the body, and can be treated by a doctor of medicine; the other is a disease of the soul, and needs the attentions of a doctor of divinity. Bright assumes the dual role of physician and divine.

As a physician, Bright believes that the root cause of physiological melancholy is bad diet, and recommends that the first step is to abstain from certain foods and drinks, including beets, cabbages, dates, olives, bread of fine unleavened flour, pork, beef, quail, peacocks, fresh-water fish, red wine, beer and ale.[17] And the cause of melancholy is not purely physiological: 'M' suffered from dreadful feelings of guilt and anxiety. Despite constant prayer and supplication, he feared the wrath of God and eternal damnation.[18] For this, 'M' requires a physician of the soul. The effect of the body upon the soul could only be compared with the sound of a badly tuned lute to a musician, or a rough pen in the hands of a skilled writer – annoying but not really damaging. M's only recourse, Bright urges, is to throw himself upon the mercy of God, and the knowledge that Christ died for his sins. 'You say you are a great sinner: what then? Is not the mercie of God greater? Is there anie ende of his compassion?'[19] Bright's advice is compassionate, urging the wretched M to stop castigating himself and reminding him that a form of unconditional positive regard is available, albeit in a metaphysical form.

Fifteen years later, in 1601, Thomas Wright's *The Passions of the Minde* was devoted to showing man how wretched he had become through his inability to control his passions. This study, designed to help man know himself in all his depravity, emphasised sin rather than salvation, claiming that the animal passions prevented reason, rebelled against virtue and, like 'thornie briars sprung from the infected roote of original sinne', caused mental and physical ill health.[20] Despite its punitive message, the book went into further editions in 1604, 1620, 1621 and 1628, suggesting that the seventeenth-century reader was a glutton for punishment.

The Puritan divine Thomas Adams, who had been the first to use 'Bedlam' on the title page of his *Mystical Bedlam*, divided madness into 'corporeal and spirituall, That obsesseth the braine, this the Heart'. Further subcategories include those who are lucid enough to know that they are the victims of *'imagination & phantasie,* those who hallucinate but cannot distinguish between reality and delusion and another classification of patients so hurt in both *imagination* and *reason*, they necessarily therewithal doe lose their memories' – they suffer from dementia.[21] Like Bright before him, Adams puts his faith in a heavenly rather than an earthly physician and his pre-scription is a simple one: open your Bible.

Wright and Bright are long forgotten, consulted only by the his-torian, but one book, Robert Burton's *Anatomy of Melancholy* (1621),

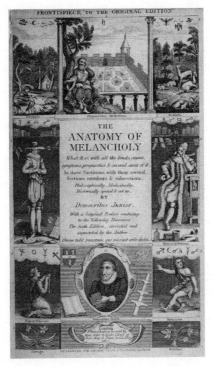

Robert Burton's Anatomy of Melancholy *– the first real self-help book.*

continues to fascinate us. This eccentric but compulsive tome, with its distinctive prose style and confessional air, has rarely been out of print. No less an authority than Samuel Johnson attested that: 'there is great spirit and great power in what Burton says, when he writes from his own mind'.[22]

Born into an ancient and genteel family at Lindley, in Leicestershire, in 1577, Robert Burton went up to 'Brazen Nose' College, Oxford, in 1593, and became a fellow of Christ Church in 1599. Burton soon gained a reputation as a formidable scholar, and he was excellent company, popular with dons and undergraduates alike. An avid reader, his speech glittered with fascinating anecdotes and classical allusions, the fashionable style at the university, then as now. But, at some point in his late twenties, Burton succumbed to profound depression. His response to this 'horrid disorder' was to write a book about it. *The Anatomy of Melancholy* starts from the conventional premise that melancholy is punishment for original sin, but also represents the culmination of the classical tradition, bringing together centuries of knowledge and reflection on the condition.

Like a surgeon, Burton sets about the task of 'anatomising' melancholy, *what it is, with all the kinds, causes, symptoms, prognostics & several cures of it, Philosophically, Medicinally, Historically opened & cut up.* Burton's alter ego is 'Democritus Junior', in honour of the philosopher Democritus of Abdera. Le Blond's engraving for the third edition shows the original Democritus, who first dissected living creatures to locate the source of melancholy, sitting under a tree, knife and book in hand, surrounded by the dissected corpses of cats, dogs and other creatures.

There are also vignettes of the different causes of melancholy: loneliness, or 'solitariness', represented by owls hovering in shady bowers; *Inamorato*, represented by a forlorn young man clutching a batch of poetry, hat pulled down low over his eyes (a symbol of lovesickness at the time). Then comes *Hypochondriachus*, surrounded by fresh supplies of lotions and potions newly arrived from the apothecary, and Superstition (complete with rosary beads, which Burton, as an Anglican priest, disdained as the trappings of popery). Burton was one of the first commentators on madness to recognise the condition of religious mania, condemning it as 'a vast, infinite Ocean full of incredible madness and folly . . . with swift currents and contrary tides, full of fearful monsters, uncouth shapes, roaring waves, tempests, and Siren calms, Halcyonian Seas, unspeakable misery'.[23]

Tough on Dissenters, dismissing them as 'Anabaptists, Brownists and Barrowists, rude, illiterate, capricious base fellows',[24] Burton reserves his greatest contempt for the Roman Catholic Church, stating that the biggest cause of religious melancholy was 'that High Priest of *Rome*, the dam of that monstrous and superstitious brood, the bull-bellowing Pope, which now rageth in the West, that three-headed *Cerberus*'.[25] Priests were 'the Devil's own agents'.[26]

Given the temper of the times, with its climate of treason, this is predictable: after the various unsuccessful conspiracies against Elizabeth I, the Armada and the Gunpowder Plot of 1605, Roman Catholics were regarded by many as terrorist sympathisers. Statesmen such as Lord Edward Coke viewed Recusants (those who refused to conform to the Church of England) as a serious threat, blaming Elizabeth's previously moderate policy towards Roman Catholics as the cause of 'manifold intended invasions against her whole kingdome, the forreine practises, the internall publike rebellions, the priuate plots and machinations, poisonings, murthers and all sorts of deuises, fomented from *Rome*'.[27] It was with the aim of drawing a distinction between honest, law-abiding Catholics and militant extremists that, in 1606, James I formulated an Oath of Allegiance:

> to be taken by my Subiects, whereby they should make a cleare profession of their resolution, faithfully to persist in their obedience vnto mee, according to their naturall allegiance; To the end that I might hereby make a separation, not onely betweene all my good Subiects in generall, and vnfaithful Traitors, that intended to withdraw themselues from my obedience; But specially to make a separation betweene so many of my Subiects, who although they were otherwise Popishly affected, yet retained in their hearts the print of their naturall dutie to their Soueraigne.

This differentiated between those 'carried away with the like fanaticall zeale that the Powder-Traitors were' and law-abiding 'quietly minded Papists'.[28]

Mania is depicted as *Maniacus*, roaring and bound naked in chains, an object lesson for any readers who consider themselves immune to this terrifying and pitiful condition:

Observe him; for as in a glass,
Thine angry portraiture it was.
His picture keeps still in thy presence;
'Twixt him and thee, there's no difference.

One cure for the condition is shown, in the form of Borage and Hellebore, 'sovereign plants to purge the veins of melancholy, and cheer the heart', and Burton himself appears at the foot of the page, although he insists that this was at the request of his publisher, rather than an act of vanity. This aside is typical of Burton's confessional tone and somewhat defensive attitude. He fears his critics will complain: 'that I have read many books, but to little purpose, for want of good method, I have confusedly tumbled over divers authors in our Libraries, with small profit for want of art, order, memory or judgement'[29] or that his book is 'a rhapsody of rags gathered together from several dung-hills, excrements of authors, toys and fopperies, confusedly tumbled out, without art, invention, judgement, wit',[30] but Burton does himself a disservice. We are carried along by 'his skills as a raconteur, remarkable erudition and a real literary skill'.[31]

Burton makes it quite clear that the 'distinguished' nature of melancholy makes it superior to other forms of madness, as evidence of a refined nature. It is melancholy, after all, which afflicts scholars and poets: 'Melancholy men of all others are most witty.'[32] Despite the drawbacks of the condition, his ambivalent attitude prefigures that of many modern depressives, who regard the disease as an essential component of their character, even their creativity.

Burton follows Bright, Wright and Adams in many ways, as in the discussions of diet, sleep and climate and their relation to the disease; of the body–mind or body–soul relationship, and of the perturbations of the mind. On a practical level, *The Anatomy of Melancholy* functions as a medical textbook, containing hundreds of herbal remedies and pragmatic advice on the virtues of keeping busy and avoiding rumination: 'be not solitary, be not idle'. As we would expect, given Burton's religious vocation, he also exhorts his readers to turn to God for solace and salvation. Medical intervention alone is insufficient. Burton also reminds us that the experience of melancholy in its various forms is inevitable for us all, and we should learn to accept that life is 'like a Chequer table, black & white men; families, cities, have their falls and wanes'.[33] '[F]rom these melancholy dispositions no man living is free, no *Stoik*, none so wise, none so happy, none so patient, so generous, so godly, so divine, that can vindicate himself; so well-composed, but more or less, some time or other, he feels the smart of it. Melancholy in this sense is the character of Mortality.'[34] 'And he that knows not this, & is not armed to endure it, is not fit to live in this world.'[35]

Burton's own defence mechanism derived from Diogenes, the Stoic philosopher who strolled into town to seek distraction. Nothing amused Burton more than to walk down to the river and hear the boatmen swearing at each other, which rarely failed to throw him into fits of laughter.[36]

One other aspect of *The Anatomy of Melancholy*, which distinguishes it from previous authors, is Burton's acknowledgement that the pressures of contemporary life drive many to despair, acknowledging the role of the state and Church in causing melancholy. Even if we do not suffer from religious mania, unrequited love, loneliness or jealousy, most readers can identify with Burton's account of information overload over three centuries before the invention of the internet, an extraordinary broadside which is worth quoting in full:

I hear new news every day, and those ordinary rumours of war, plagues, fires, inundations, thefts, murders, massacres, meteors, comets, spectrums, prodigies, apparitions, of towns taken cities besieged in *France, Germany, Turkey, Persia, Poland &c.* daily musters and preparations, and such like, which these tempestuous times afford, battles fought, so many men slain, monomachies, shipwrecks, piracies, and sea-fights, peace, leagues, stratagems, and fresh alarms. A vast confusion of vows, wishes, actions, edicts, petitions, lawsuits, pleas, laws, proclamations, complaints, grievances, are daily brought to our ears. New books every day, pamphlets, currantoes, stories, whole catalogues of volumes of all sorts, new paradoxes, opinions, schisms, heresies, controversies in philosophy, religion &c. Now come tidings of weddings, maskings, mummeries, entertainments, jubilees, embassies, tilts and tournaments, trophies, triumphs, revels, sports, plays; then again, as in a new shifted scene, treasons, cheating tricks, robberies, enormous villanies in all kinds, funerals, burials, deaths of Princes, new discoveries, expeditions; now comical then tragical matters. To-day we hear of new Lords and officers created, to-morrow of some great men deposed, and then again of fresh honours conferred; one is let loose, another imprisoned; one purchaseth, another breaketh; he thrives, his neighbour turns bankrupt; now plenty, then again dearth and famine; one runs, another rides, wrangles, laughs, weeps &c. Thus I daily hear, and such like, both private and public news.[37]

And that way, Burton reminds us, that way madness lies . . .

Burton passed away in his rooms at Christ Church in January 1640. The fact that he died at or very near the time that he had predicted in his own horoscope led to rumours in college that, 'being an exact [punctilious] mathematician, a curious calculator of nativities [horoscopes], rather than there should be a mistake in the calculation, he sent up his soul to heaven through a slip about his neck'.[38] Burton's epitaph, composed a few months before his death, appears to bear this out, although the authorities must have ruled out any suggestion of suicide since he was buried in consecrated ground, in Christ Church Cathedral, on 27 January 1640, and given 'a comely monument, with his bust painted to the life'[39] and bearing this inscription:

> *Paucis notus, paucioribus ignotus,*
> *Hic jacet Democritus Junior,*
> *Cui vitam dedit et mortem*
> *Melancholia*

Known to few, unknown to even fewer,
Here lies Democritus Junior,
To whom Melancholia
Gave life and death.

The epitaph is typical of Burton's teasing, gently ironic style, with its deliberate paradox about his pseudonym, Democritus, which earned him fame but was known by so few as being him.

There were really three Burtons, the scholar, the stylist and the psychiatrist. As a scholar, Burton gave the world an encyclopaedia of melancholy, plagiarised by John Milton for *Il Penseroso*, the dramatist John Ford, who used it as a series of case histories on which to base his plays, and by Laurence Sterne, who aped its digressive, meandering style in *Tristram Shandy*. As a writer, Burton was described by Charles Lamb as a 'fantastic old great man', a quaint literary stylist inviting the reader into an old museum of musty antiquities, as though he were entering a forgotten chamber where the skeletons of seventeenth-century spiders are still poised upon undisturbed cobwebs.[40] And last of all, there is Burton the psychiatrist. *The Anatomy of Melancholy* was regarded by Sir William Osler, Regius Professor of Medicine at Oxford (1905–19), as the greatest medical treatise every written by a layman.[41]

*

While Burton's musings on melancholy began to gain a following, Bethlem was about to face the challenge of the Civil War. In 1638, Charles I granted Bethlem to the City of London. He gave over the hospital to the governorship of the City, and reminded the governors that they had an obligation to the poor, and should not let out the hospital land for long leases at small rents. This was part of a deal between Charles and the City. The king was raising money for a war against Scotland. He granted the City its ancient privileges in return for £12,000. But the clouds were again gathering around London. In 1641, Charles on his return from Scotland had been greeted by an escort of devoted cavaliers at the house in Hoxton of the hospital's president, Sir George Whitmore, then the Lord Mayor of London. In their company, the king and his queen had ridden past Bethlehem Hospital on their way to the Guildhall. Within a year Sir George Whitmore lay in prison as a Royalist 'malignant', the portcullis had been lowered at Bishopsgate, and the road over against the hospital was fortified with chains and posts.[42] The Civil War had an economic impact on Bethlem. The treasurer, Rawlins, unable to balance his accounts, ended up handing over the title deeds of his mansion in Fulham, worth £700, to the governors. The governors themselves, meanwhile, experienced increased difficulty in collecting their rents. The tenancy of the mediaeval Staple Hall was sequestrated, making the tenant unable to pay the rent for two years. Many of the buildings adjacent to the hospital had become so derelict they could only be home to lewd and dangerous characters.[43]

One leaseholder, the landlord of the Goat tavern at Charing Cross, successfully pleaded to the court of governors that he was unable to pay full rent because property prices in his neighbourhood had fallen at least one-half in value since the king left Whitehall and all his trade had been diverted to the fashionable new quarter of Covent Garden. Previous historians have speculated as to whether prisoners of war were interned in Bethlem, but it seems unlikely that there was sufficient room. It is more likely, however, that soldiers who had become insane were admitted.[44] In 1644, Parliament exempted the royal hospitals from certain taxes, 'in consideration of many sick and wounded soldiers being supported in them, while their revenues are much diminished in these dead and troublous times'.[45] Over at Bridewell, disbanded soldiers and prisoners of war were considered a nuisance, because of their habit of smoking tobacco in a straw-strewn basement.

There are other references to the years of revolution in the court books: the king's coat of arms was removed and a ballad-singer was shorn of his cavalier locks. And some of the names which crop up on the court books, distributing Bibles to the apprentices or checking the bills, are the same names which signed the death warrant of Charles Stuart: Lord Packe, Sir R. Browne, Alderman Fowke.

The influence of Puritanism, with its emphasis on personal social responsibility for the sick and the poor, led to some changes for the better at Bethlem. Conditions improved during the period 1644–77. In June 1643, the court of governors ordered the hospital to be enlarged as quickly as possible, and contracted workmen to carry out redevelopment. Over the following year, accommodation was provided for twenty additional patients. In 1652, £5 a year was earmarked for clothing the destitute, so that gowns, coats, shirts and smocks could be provided for 'the poor lunaticks, who have no friends to take care of them'. However, some things did not change. In 1657, the diarist John Evelyn strolled into the ward after dining with an old friend, and saw prisoners in chains.[46] The younger generation, less engrained with Puritanism, began to amuse themselves on Sunday mornings with an hour in Bethlem, taunting the more voluble patients and plying them with alcohol. The only solution to such abuses in public institutions was perpetual vigilance. Therefore, in order to retain their improved reputation, and protect the patients, the governors devised a system of surprise inspections. The court books have the following entries:

18 July 1646: Ordered that no officer or servant shall give any blows or ill-language to any of the mad folks on pain of losing his place.

16 May 1655: Such governors as can, or live near, are entreated to go as often as possible to see how the lunatics are used, and how officers and servants behave themselves.

12 June 1657: Ordered that the porter keep the doors locked every Lord's Day and days of public fasting or thanksgiving; no body to enter on any pretence, except to call in personal assistance and no strong drink to be brought in except on the orders of the doctor;

and no man to walk about, and the men and women to be kept asunder, and the governors to consider how best the men and women may be lodged and kept asunder'.[47]

*

Puritanism may have led to improvements at Bethlem, but it was not always a benevolent influence. At this period, the hospital became the home of many a religious maniac or 'Enthusiast'. The ancient Greeks originally used this term to denote possession by the gods – deities such as Apollo or Dionysus – reaching its most extreme in the wild celebrations of the Bacchantes. However, by the seventeenth century, an 'Enthusiast' was one who demonstrated extreme religious fervour. Many reported hallucinations and the conviction that they were in contact with a higher power, symptoms which would now be associated with temporal lobe epilepsy and schizoid episodes. In 1655, the author Meric Casaubon referred to this condition as 'enthusiasme, as it is an effect of nature: [it has an organic origin] but is mistaken by many for either divine inspiration, or diabolical possession'.[48] Casaubon argued that this form of madness led genuine spiritual conviction into disrepute: 'to embrace a Cloud, or a Fogge for a Deitie; it is done by many, but it is a foul mistake'.[49]

Religious enthusiasm represented a real danger to those with fragile and delicate minds. During the late sixteenth and early seventeenth centuries, the Bible was often expounded by preachers or prophets who were, or had been, clinically insane. George Fox, the founder of Quakerism, was one example, having undergone considerable mental anguish as a young man. 'Frequently in the night I walked mournfully about by myself, for I was a man of sorrows in the times of the first workings of the Lord in me,' Fox confessed in his journal of 1647, [50] while in 1666 John Bunyan, the author of *Pilgrim's Progress*, was plunged into deep despair by such a strong compulsion to blasphemy that he thought he might have to 'leap with my head downward, into some muckill-hole or other to keep my mouth from speaking'.[51] As late as 1788, one visitor to Bedlam noted this inmate:

Across us stalk'd a man who had no other covering than a blanket, neither would he wear any other; 'because (as he told us) Adam was cloath'd in flesh, but for himself he was a Pre-Adamite'. I told our guide this man was too mad to be trusted loose. 'Ah, dear!' (he replied, shaking his head), 'Why, Sir, there are several people so fond of his doctrine, that we should lose taking pounds if we were to shut him up. Sir, there are several females come to him to be converted; and we are apt to believe that his doctrine is like a chapel of ease to Methodism.'[52]

*

George Fox and John Bunyan recovered sufficiently to leave a written legacy. Others were not so fortunate. One such was the Colchester weaver Richard Farnham, one of those prophets who identify themselves with characters in the Bible, and are unable (for they are victims either of mental delusion or of crude literalism) to distinguish between the actual and the figurative. In 1636, Farnham, claiming to be one of the 'anointed witnesses' of the Book of Revelation, prophesied the imminent end of the world, because England is full of 'abominations, idolatries and whoredoms'. He would be slain in the streets of Jerusalem, he claimed, receive the 'gift of the holy tongue' to make himself understood and rise again on the third day as priest and king.[53]

These delusions were inspired by the mystic visions of John the Divine. Farnham took as an example the action of Hosea, who was commanded by God to marry an unfaithful woman, or to retain a wife who had become unfaithful, to humiliate himself. However, in seventeenth-century Colchester, the 'whore' took the form of Mrs Haddington, 'a woman of fine parts', according to *False Prophets Discovered* (1642). Mr Haddington, a sailor, was away in the Far East. When he returned from sea, he promptly indicted his wife for bigamy: 'He laid his wife in Newgate, where she was arraigned and condemned for having two husbands.' Eventually, the courts decided that 'the seaman should have his wife again, who, accordingly, took her and lay with her in prison'. Mrs Haddington was released into her husband's custody, and there it might have ended – except that once he had gone back to sea, Mrs Haddington took to visiting Farnham for sex 'in Newbrideswell, where he was a prisoner'. Apparently, Mrs Haddington was 'content to lose the glory of being esteemed an honest woman and to be accounted a wife of whoredoms that she might on occasion, as she did conceive, the fulfilling of the prophecy'.

While the governors of Newgate were loath to part with him in March 1638, by June of the same year they were begging Archbishop Laud to take him away. Once in Bethlem, Farnham gathered round him a number of acolytes and prophesied the coming of a great plague, to which he would be immune. He claimed that the dread disease, which had haunted England since the twelfth century, had no power over him. 'The plague shall not come nigh thy dwelling,' he told his followers.[54] Dr Meverall, physician of the hospital from 1634 to 1648, asked by the governors to report on the case, recommended Farnham's discharge on probation.

Despite his convictions, Farnham sickened in late 1641, and died at a disciple's house in the following January, presumably to his own surprise as much as anybody else's. His right-hand man, John Bull, died ten days later. Farnham's followers, however, refused to admit he was dead. Hysterical and deluded, they maintained for weeks after that Farnham was resurrected on 8 January 1642, and continued to drink a toast to the dead man.

Meverall, meanwhile, had his own claim to fame in the death stakes. At the age of twenty-three, the young doctor succumbed to an attack of smallpox, and every aperture in his sick room was carefully closed up. He became unconscious due to lack of oxygen, and was assumed to have died. It was not until his body was being prepared for burial that he was exposed to fresh air, and came to his senses just in time to escape being buried alive.[55]

Other 'Enthusiasts' of the time included 'Robins the Ranter', who claimed to be God and said he could raise the dead, and pioneers of Quakerism who ran around naked as a sign against insincerity. These included Tannye, who called himself 'The Lord's High Priest' and organised a trip to Jerusalem to rebuild the temple. Instead of reaching the Holy City, poor Tannye, who may have been suffering from epilepsy, got no further than Bethlem Hospital, where he died in 1677, and was buried in Bedlam Yard. Other free-thinkers buried at Bethlem were Ludovic Muggleton (1609–98), founder of the Muggletonians, millenarists who believed in a Second Coming of Christ, and John Lilburne (1615–57), notable for his disapproval of the government, regardless as to who was in power. 'Agin it all, he could even start a fight with himself.' Wits at the time suggested that Lilburne lay so uneasy in his grave that he disturbed the eternal rest of the Roman soldiers and mediaeval friars buried far beneath him.[56]

One other famous inmate was Oliver Cromwell's porter, Daniel (1648–67). Daniel was admitted to Bethlehem Hospital in 1665. Once the authorities had ascertained that he was incurably insane, they permitted him to collect a library of books and pamphlets, which included a large Bible presented to him by Nell Gwyn, mistress of Charles II. Moreover, they did not complain when Daniel preached to his admirers from his window at the east end of the building. Sober matrons, clutching their Bibles and listening reverentially, were often to be seen gathered on the grass plot beneath his cell.

*

Another of Bethlem's most celebrated patients was the self-styled prophetess Lady Audley (1590–1652), otherwise known as Eleanor Davies. Before admission to Bedlam, Eleanor had already been incarcerated for publishing her tactless prediction of the fate awaiting Charles I. Rather in the style of modern devotees of Nostradamus, Eleanor claimed that the account of Belshazzar's feast, in the Book of Daniel, prefigured Charles's death. In the original version, Belshazzar, King of the Chaldeans, was hosting a drunken feast for over 1,000 men on the night before an important battle. While his father, Nabonidus, was rallying the troops, who faced certain annihilation from the Medes and Persians, Belshazzar was encouraging his followers to drink to every god they could think of, out of the ceremonial vessels stolen from the Jewish temple at Jerusalem, thus profaning them. Suddenly, to Belshazzar's horror, a hand materialised out of nowhere: 'In the same hour came forth fingers of a man's hand, and wrote over against the candlestick upon the plaster of the wall of the king's palace'; Belshazzar was so terrified that 'the joints of his loins were loosened and his knees smote one against another', although he could not understand what it said. Eventually, Daniel, the interpreter of dreams, was sent for, and explained that the words read: 'MENE, MENE, TEKEL, UPHARSIN: God hath numbered thy kingdom and finished it. Thou art weighed in the balance and found wanting. Thy kingdom is divided, and given to the Persians.' That night, Belshazzar was killed in battle.[57]

According to Eleanor, 'Belchaser' becomes 'Be Charles'. The ancient 'Medes' are the Medici, and the 'Caldeans' (or Chaldeans) are interpreted as the Caledonians, or Scots.

Eleanor was the fifth daughter of George Touchet, Lord Audley and Earl of Castlehaven. Her brother was the notorious Mervyn Touchet, who was beheaded on Tower Hill on 14 May 1631 for alleged rape and buggery, although subsequent investigations suggested that he was incapable of the former and that the latter was a consensual act with his footman, Florence, who confessed under torture. Some weeks after Mervyn's execution, Florence was hanged.

An educated woman, Eleanor impressed contemporaries with her intellectual gifts. A portrait from the early 1600s shows a pensive, blue-eyed beauty, with finely arched brows, pale red curls and a determined mouth. In 1608 Eleanor married Sir John Davies, attorney general for Ireland, and a renowned poet. Eleanor had two children with Sir John, one of whom drowned. Her daughter, Lucy, survived to marry Ferdinando, sixth Earl of Huntingdon.

It was in 1625 that Eleanor began to fancy herself a prophetess, and 'took to the study of Daniel to the neglect of her household duties' as Bethlem's historian O'Donoghue rather chauvinistically observed.[58] Anagramming was a popular fad at the time, and when she found that John Davies was an anagram of 'Jove's hand' Eleanor became convinced that he would be dead within a year. Eleanor immediately donned widow's weeds, while her husband responded sardonically: 'I pray you weep not while I am alive, and I will give you leave to laugh when I am dead.' Eleanor had the last word, though: Sir John died a year later, on 8 December 1626.

Between 1625 and 1633, Eleanor's obsession grew. Juggling the letters of her own name, she claimed that 'Eleanor Davies' was an anagram of 'Reveal, O Daniel'. Eleanor gained a reputation at court, having prophesied the murder of the Duke of Buckingham in 1628, but her reputation turned against her with the publication of the Belshazzar predictions in 1633, and she was tried at an ecclesiastical court at Whitehall for treason against the king.

Two judges deemed Eleanor insane. 'Send her to Bedlam!' advised the Bishop of Rochester. But Heylin, Laud's chaplain, humiliated her by concocting an anagram from the letters 'Dame Eleanor Davies'. As the court laughed out loud, he demonstrated that Eleanor's name spelt out 'Never so mad a ladie!' Eleanor was fined £3,000 and imprisoned, without writing materials, in the Gate-House, Westminster, until the fine was paid. This took two years. Upon release, Eleanor went to Litchfield, where she gathered around her a circle of admiring women. Eleanor's behaviour, however, became increasingly bizarre. Disapproving of the Laudian reforms at the cathedral, which involved fencing off the communion table and turning it into an altar, she defaced the hangings by pouring hot tar over them, sat on the bishop's throne and declared herself Primate and Metropolitan Bishop.[59] This led to her committal to Bethlem on 17 December 1636, where she was placed, not in a cell, but in the household of the steward, Mr Langley. As we know, she complained about the Langleys' rowdy behaviour, but it seems that her own was not much better. On 16 August 1637 Langley told the court of governors that he wanted Eleanor out of his house. Then it emerged in court that Langley's wife 'hath used ill words' to Eleanor, for which Langley was admonished.

In April 1638 Eleanor was transferred to the Tower of London, presumably because of her allegedly treacherous activities. After her release, Eleanor described her removal to the Tower as 'an exchange of the grave for hell – such were the blasphemies and the noisome scenes'. Upon discharge, Eleanor was stripped of all her possessions, and, although her then husband, Sir Archibald Douglas, had died while she was inside, she was not even told where he had been buried. Eleanor also resented the stigma associated with admission, in that it would 'make her ever incapable of anie complaint but ever held or taken to be person non compos mentis to the perpetuall blott and infame of her familie and posteritie'.[60]

After being released, the 'Blessed Ladie', as Eleanor liked to style herself, published a dozen or so rambling treatises. She attempted to send a 'testimony' of her prophecies to Charles I, who burnt it in front of his courtiers. Four years later, she sent a tract to Oliver Cromwell. This was entitled *The Armed Commissioner* and based on the biblical text 'Behold, He cometh with ten thousand of His saints.' Cromwell's response was typically dry: 'I'm afraid we're not all saints,' he remarked.[61] In her final effort, a tract entitled *The Gatehouse Salutation*, Eleanor looked back over her confinements in symbolic and surprisingly positive terms, with Bedlam becoming Bethlehem, Eleanor as the Virgin Mary, undergoing labour – in this case, imprisonment – but in the hope and expectation of entering heaven:

> So Gates and Prison Doors be no
> More shut
> The King of glory comes, your
> Souls lift up.[62]

Eleanor died in 1652, and was buried beside her first husband, Sir John Davies.

As Bethlem historian David Russell observes, Eleanor's behaviour has attracted different interpretations. Despite derisive comments, the recently canonised St Peter Dumoulin described her as 'learned above her sex, humble below her fortune, having a mind so great and noble, that prosperity could not make it amiss, nor her deepest adversity cause it to shrink'.[63] The medical historian Roy Porter considered Eleanor to be a victim of psychiatric abuse, and other writers have regarded her as an early feminist.

*

Meanwhile, life unfolded beyond the walls of Bethlem, sometimes mirrored by events inside. In February 1660, a Lady Monck visited the hospital, and received this greeting from one of the 'phanatiques':

> Most noble lady, now we see
> The world turns round as well as we.
> Whilst you adorn this place we know
> No greater happiness below,
> Than to behold the sweet delight
> Of him that will restore our right,
> Let George know we are not so mad,
> But we can love an honest lad.[64]

These words were spoken to the wife of Sir George Monck, instrumental in the restoration of the monarchy. On 29 May 1660, the 'honest lad' – Charles II – paraded through London to Whitehall, along streets strewn with flowers. But the celebrations did not last. Five years later, Daniel the Porter claimed he had seen an angel in white unsheathing the sword of pestilence over a guilty city, as the Great Plague lapped against the walls of Bethlem as it swept through London and killed 100,000 people. The registers of St Botolph's, the parish church, do not contain records of the mortality rate at the hospital. It is likely that, at the outset, before the burial ground became overcrowded, patients would have been interred in the hospital's own cemetery. In 1863, when the North London Railway broke down the brick wall and invaded the pleasant gardens which were enclosed within it to build Broad Street Station (now closed), immense heaps of bones were carted away. In 1911, the engineers of the London Underground, on their way to Liverpool Street Station, bored into layers and layers of skulls closely packed: the victims of the sweating sickness or of other plagues were probably interred here.[65]

A year later, in 1666, the Great Fire of London swept through Bridewell, devouring the rooms in which king and queen, cardinal and captains had once paraded. But Bethlem and its ruinous tenements were spared. Thanks to Pepys, who had requested that the king order buildings to be demolished to create a fire break, Bishopsgate ward was hardly scorched. Matthews, the porter, had prepared for the worst by moving everything he could to a place of safety. One can only imagine the panic and confusion in Bethlem on the morning of 5 September: tenants pouring out of the neighbouring houses, some labouring under burdens of possessions, and the patients stubbornly struggling with their rescuers, until an east wind carried the flames westwards and the hospital was out of danger. Matthews, for his trouble, was awarded £4 by a grateful court of governors.

For three years after the fire, the governors were obliged to sit at Bethlem, no other accommodation being available. During these years, the governors were of necessity brought into much closer touch with the hospital, and realised more vividly, with a new London rising up round them, how inadequate the accommodation was. On 24 January 1674 they passed a resolution that the 'hospital-house was old, weak, ruinous, and so small and strait for keeping the great number applying for admission that it ought to be removed and rebuilt elsewhere on some site grantable by the city'.[66] Bethlem needed a new home.

5

THE 'PALACE BEAUTIFUL'

Unlike the ramshackle hovel in Bishopsgate, New Bethlem was to be a 'palace beautiful'. Intended to excite the admiration of contemporaries and foreign visitors, it would be built at Moorfields, near a stretch of the ancient London Wall, which ran west from Moorgate. The Romans had drained the moor and fen, but in mediaeval times the district had reverted to marshland, dappled with sheets of water during the summer. In winter, apprentices skimmed the frozen marsh on primitive bone skates. As one of the largest open spaces in London, Moorfields doubled as a recreation ground and a refugee camp for those left homeless after the Great Fire of 1666. Though not for long: once the land was acquired for development, the destitute were unceremoniously moved on, to seek refuge in the East End.

The land was donated by the City of London in 1674, under the auspices of former Lord Mayor Sir William Turner, president of the associated hospitals of Bridewell and Bethlem from 1669 to 1689. Turner was a wealthy bachelor, noted for his industry and generosity (he paid his cook the same rate as his chaplain). A cousin of Samuel Pepys, he began life as a draper. But Turner was not without his peccadilloes: a magistrate, he considered it his civic duty to witness every prostitute he sentenced being flogged at Bridewell, moving one commentator to observe: 'Oh, Bridewell! What a shame thy walls reproaches. Poor Molls are whipp'd, while rich ones ride in coaches!'[1]

The land itself measured 720 feet east to west from the postern, Blomfield Street to Moorgate, and its breadth was 80 feet from London Wall northward. It had a 999-year lease, running from Michaelmas Day (29 September), 1674, at a rent of a shilling a year, and was given on condition that it should be used for no other purpose than that of a lunatic asylum. According to Stow's *Survey of London*, an inscription in the entrance hall stated that the building was completed within fifteen months, between April 1675 and July 1676,[2] at a cost of £17,000, raised by donations and loans. However, the diaries of Bethlem's architect, Robert Hooke (1635–1703), which contain over 100 references to the hospital over a period of four years, indicate that a great deal of preliminary work took place beforehand, and the chapel (for the edification of the staff) was completed at a later date: Hooke was still consulting on the design specification for it in January 1678.[3]

Robert Hooke was a polymath, one of the most brilliant men of his generation. A gifted mathematician, he anticipated Newton in his scientific investigations and invented an early form of microscope. As surveyor to Sir Christopher Wren, Hooke's achievements included the Royal Observatory at Greenwich and the Royal College of Physicians. Indeed, Hooke was considered in many circles to have been the equal of Wren, and worthy of greater recognition. 'Mr Hooke,' wrote Samuel Pepys, recalling a shy man with a crooked, emaciated figure, 'is the most, though he promises the least, of any man I know.'

Hooke's references to Bethlem begin with a site visit to Moorfields on 14 April 1674, accompanied by the hospital's physician, Dr Thomas Allen. By 3 July, Hooke had presented two drawings to the court of governors for the: 'New House for

Lunatikes intended to be erected betweene Moorgate and the Posterne next London Wall where there wilbe ground enough for One Hundred & Twenty Roomes for the Lunatikes & Officers being about Fower Hundred & Twenty foote long'.[4] After seeing a pasteboard model of the proposed building, the governors opted for a 'single building, and not double'.[5] This design, which consisted of one row of rooms, plus galleries, running from a single corridor, was popular at the time for colleges and hospitals, as it allowed the construction of separate rooms or cells. It was an ideal design for the new hospital as the layout would admit light and fresh air, regarded as beneficial for the mad. The location allowed generous provision for exercise yards, 'reserved for the use and refresh' of patients, where they could walk and take the air. Massive walls, 680 feet long, 70 feet wide, would surround the hospital, and would be 14 feet high round the exercise yards 'to prevent the Escape of Lunatikes'. The front wall, however, was to be no more than 8 feet high. Patients were not to be allowed at the front of the building. Apertures in the wall allowed glimpses of the hospital's spectacular 500-foot façade. Hooke's design was in the French tradition, similar to the Tuileries or the Louvre, and consisted of stone pavilions with steep roofs, the tallest one in the middle and two at each end, linked by brick wings a storey lower. According to *The Survey of London*, the central pavilion boasted 'a large Cupolo with a gilded Ball, and a Vane at the Top of it, and a Clock within, and three fair Dials without'.[6] No expense was spared, although Hooke reports 'A great Huff' from the committee on 19 July when he held out for stone for the pavilions, as opposed to brick dressed with stone, the cheaper option, which was used for the wings.

The 1720 edition of *The Survey of London* explained that: 'The interior of the new hospital consists chiefly of Two Galleries, one over the other, each 193 Yards long, 13 Foot high, and 16 Foot broad; not including the Cells for the Patients, which are 12 Foot deep.'[7] Stevenson describes Bethlem as consisting of a 'shell around two galleries, one on top of the other, running the full length of the building'. [8] The design derived from the Elizabethan English country house, where galleries provided space for families to promenade during bad weather. At Bethlem, self-contained galleries offered an area for non-violent patients to exercise and socialise with their visitors. The servants' quarters were in the dormer attics, with their Dutch-style windows, while the kitchen was in the basement. Other basements were rented to the East India Company, for the storage of pepper. Edward Barkham left £6,000 worth of prime Lincolnshire farmland to build provision for 'pauper lunatics'. The proceeds were used to build and maintain incurable wards. The first, for men, was built in the autumn of 1725, with a ward added to the east, or Bishopsgate end. In 1733, a corresponding west wing was constructed for women.

Bethlem, 1812. With a view of the ancient London wall; note the tiny hands stretching out of the windows.

At the back of the galleries, on both floors, were the individual cells, initially thirty-eight on each side of the gallery, which looked out at London Wall. An etching of 'Parts of London-Wall and Bethlem Hospital' published in 1815 shows the north view of New Bethlem. In the foreground is the ancient Roman fortification with its shabby stonework and straggling vegetation. To indicate scale, a beggar forages on the pavement while the monumental edifice of the hospital rears above him, with its massive chimney stacks and barred windows. From one window hangs a ragged sheet or gown; from that of its neighbour extends a tiny hand, dangling a toy windmill in a poignant gesture of futility.

The project did not run smoothly. By January 1675, Hooke recorded that 'Sir T Player ordered me to agree about Levelling the walk and Re-mounting the trees.' On 9 April 1675, he mentioned a visit to 'the Bedlam Committee who after some bickering left the matter of the stairs to me'. By 29 August 1676, he notes: 'King at Bedlam', implying that his majesty has officially opened the hospital.[9]

Perhaps because it was built so fast, the quality of materials was challenged by one governor, Sir William Bolton, who suggested that the cement was not up to standard. A surveyor was called in who maintained that the bricks and workmanship were good, although the cement was rather thin.[10] On the strength of this report, on 4 December 1674, the governors decided to remove Sir William Bolton from the building committee, on the grounds that his remarks had 'wronged the committee and the bricklayer'; they also recommended that the court of governors should keep quiet about this incident, suggesting that 'such a matter should not be blazoned abroad'. Sir William had not been a popular member of the committee: a notorious gossip, he delighted in spreading scandalous rumours about his fellow governors and was 'troublesome and vexatious to the public government for his own private and sinister ends'.[11] These consisted of embezzling money raised to aid survivors of the Great Fire, for which he was convicted in 1675. But, as the authorities subsequently realised, Bolton was right about the bricks.

*

Staff and patients migrated to their new home in the last week of July 1676. On 21 July, the court of governors ordered fifteen new bedsteads, and on 26 July sexual segregation was declared, with men occupying the lower gallery and women the upper, separated by a metal grille. The admission procedure followed the pattern developed at the hospital's previous site, although now Bethlem had the capacity for a far greater number of patients: 140, as opposed to the two dozen at Bishopsgate. Prospective patients were brought in on a Saturday to be viewed by the committee and the physician. If he or she was judged 'a fit object' for the hospital then a warrant was drawn up by the clerk of the hospital, to be signed by the president (or the Treasurer in his absence), for the patient to be admitted. Those putting forward the patient had to give Bethlem a bond, signed by two people, guaranteeing that he or she would be removed on discharge and that burial charges would be paid for if they died in hospital. (The first mortality at the new hospital came on 2 August, when 'Thos. Tymes, the first lunatic in New Bedlam [was] buryed' at St Stephen's, Coleman Street.)

Families and friends were expected to provide clothing. On 'cure and discharge' the patient was summoned before the committee of governors and the physician, who examined them and decided if they were fit to leave. 'The time of cure is uncertain,' wrote John Strype in 1720. 'Some have been cured in a Month, Two or Three: Some continue distracted many Years. To the Question, Whether there be more Men or Women Lunatick kept here, the Answer was, there have been no Inequality of Number observed as to the Sexes.'

Rising day by day above the remains of London Wall, New Bedlam proved an astonishing spectacle. After the Royal Exchange and St Paul's, it was the biggest public building project in London for over half a century, and the first new hospital since the Savoy, off the Strand, in 1519. Bethlem's magnificent new home had a political

View of BETHLEM HOSPITAL, Moorefields.

The first visual record of 'New Bethlem' by Robert White, August 1677.

purpose: the hospital represented another manifestation of London
rising like a phoenix from the ashes of the Civil War, the Plague and
the Great Fire. It embodied Sir Christopher Wren's statement that:
'Architecture has its Political Use; Publick Buildings being the
Ornament of a Country.' Architecture, Wren declared, had a vital
role in establishing national pride and 'makes the People love their
Native Country'.[12] As an architectural marvel, Bethlem appeared in
at least thirty-six tourist guides in 1681.

Within a month of the hospital opening, one anonymous poet
had confessed that this 'Suburb Wonder' would make anyone mad
to be inside,[13] while the diarist John Evelyn considered it 'magnifi-
cently built, and most sweetly placed in Moorfields'[14] and another
commentator mused: 'The Outside is a perfect Mockery to the
Inside, and Admits of two Amusing Queries, Whether the Persons
that ordered the Building of it, or those that inhabit it, were the
maddest? And, whether the name and thing be not as disagreeable
as harp and harrow.'[15] As an architectural marvel and a testimony to
public health, New Bethlem became the latest craze, another source
of amusement on holidays, alongside the travelling fairs and puppet
shows of Moorfields.

The new hospital was so popular that a riot flared up during Whitsun 1677, when crowds of visitors flocked to the gates, resulting in an altercation between Digby, Lord Gerard, a 15-year-old toff who had driven over with his mother, and a 'strapping virago', whom Digby made the mistake of addressing as 'my good woman', asking her to step aside. The 'good woman' promptly thumped Digby, while her husband pushed him down the steps. Acting in his own defence, or so he claimed, young Digby drew his sword, but accidentally stabbed the porter in the gut instead. As Digby and his mother retreated into their carriage, the mob roared 'kill him!' and 'tear him to pieces!' and bombarded the coach with brickbats, while a rescue party of constables was swept away in the confusion. Eventually, Sir William Turner appeared to restore order, dragging mother and son from their vehicle and into the building, while the 'Bedlamis'd multitude' melted away.[16]

If we look at the earliest visual record of New Bethlem, produced by Robert White in August 1677 (see page 93), we can follow in the foot-

The 'Brainless Brothers': Acute Mania (in chains) and Dementia appeared over the gateway to 'New Bedlam' in Moorfields.

steps of the earliest visitors. The engraving shows a long, straight wall pierced by the entrance gates and by three apertures of open iron-work (later filled in) on either side of them at regular intervals. Four steps led up to the large gates, which swung from stone piers, and there were wicket gates for visitors on either side of the double gates. On the piers of the wicket gate ramped the lion and the unicorn of Charles II's royal standard, reminding the visitor that this was a royal hospital. And the nature of the hospital itself was left in no doubt by the two colossal figures sprawled 12 feet overhead on the stone piers of the great gate, in a style reminiscent of Michelangelo's *Night and Morning* in Florence. These massive statues, carved in Portland stone, represented the two forms of madness: dementia and acute mania. The tense, chained figure of Acute Mania embodied anger and menace (he was said to be modelled on Daniel, Cromwell's porter). Meanwhile, poor Dementia sprawled aimlessly opposite, his blank expression signifying the cerebral deterioration associated with terti-ary syphilis. These grim insignia of Bedlam's corporate identity were immortalised a century later by Thomas Fitzgerald, a poet who became a patient at Bethlem. 'Rattling his Chains the Wretch all raving lies, And roars, and foams; and earth and Heav'n defies' is a vivid description of Acute Mania, while Dementia is portrayed as sit-ting for ever, 'moping on the Ground'.[17]

In *The Dunciad*, Pope states that 'o'er the gates, by his famed father's hand, Great Cibber's brazen, brainless brothers stand'.[18] *The Survey of London* attributed the statues to Caius Gabriel Cibber, father of Colley, the dramatist. Larger than life (erect, the figures would stand 7 feet tall), the statues are now on display at the Bethlem museum. Oppressive and pitiful in their depiction of mad-ness and despair, they dominate the room, a powerful reminder of the concept of 'Bedlam'.

After these brooding figures had made their impression, the vis-itor was ushered into a forecourt of grass plots and carved walks, the better to take in the extraordinary vision of the 'palace beauti-ful'. Four semicircular steps led up to the main entrance under the iron balcony. Beyond this door were the 'Penny Gates', with alms boxes where visitors placed their entrance money – a penny or two. These alms boxes consisted of two disconcertingly lifelike figures, male and female, dressed as gypsies and painted Bethlem's trademark blue. In their time, this pair received thousands of pounds for charity. Watching over them was the porter, in his gown of blue, bearing a staff with a silver head, engraved with acanthus leaves. A forbidding figure, the porter ensured that all visitors paid their dues; he never carried any change. A notice nearby instructed: 'PRAY REMEMBER THE POOR *LUNATICKS*, AND PUT YOUR CHARITY INTO THE BOX WITH YOUR OWN HANDS.'

The passage beyond the 'Penny Gates' opened out into a large hall, right and left of which on each storey were the entrances to the galleries, with gates of open ironwork keeping the most violent patients in their place. To the right of the hall at its north end was the office of the steward; to the left, the consulting room where the physician and apothecary saw patients on their admission and discharge. The hall was decorated with marble tablets in memory of benefactors, and from the back a staircase led up to the court room, dominated by a portrait of Henry VIII, a significant figure in the hospital's development, where the court of governors met on Saturdays.

The patients' cells opened out on to the galleries. These bleak rooms had narrow, unglazed windows or 'lunettes' (shaped like a crescent moon) that let in the highly regarded light and air, but also kept the patients perpetually cold. This, too, was deliberate: chilly conditions were believed to clear the head, and the belief persisted among many experts that the mad were insensitive to their surroundings. One doctor, visiting Bethlem, observed:

In general, insane persons endure hunger, cold, nakedness and want of sleep with amazing perseverance, and impunity: in the maniac the muscular strength is prodigiously increased. During

the exacerbation most are restless, and most are costive [consti-
pated, hence the relentless laxatives]. Some obstinately refuse all
food and medicine, and are drenched [given medicine] by compulsion as horses taking physic: which in time renders them
more docile. Some, if indulged, are ravenous and insatiable as
wolves.[19]

*

The New Bethlem inevitably featured in the popular press and
literature of the time, and gradually another set of stereotypes
emerged, culminating in Hogarth's terrifying final frame of *The
Rake's Progress*, which we will examine in more detail later in this
chapter. We owe many of the earliest accounts of New Bedlam to
one Ned Ward, the landlord of a nearby tavern. Writing as 'The
London Spy', Ward chronicled the underbelly of city life with
tabloid enthusiasm, slamming the new hospital as 'a costly college
for a crack-brained society' and suggesting that City leaders had
spent a fortune on the building because they feared for their own
sanity and wanted to ensure that there would be somewhere decent
for their own reception when the time came.

In one of his many trips to Bethlem, Ward tells us that 'the spec-
tators were bad of all ranks, qualities, colours, and sizes'. The
hospital was a notorious pickup joint: 'There was a Jack to every
Jill: people came in singly and went out in pairs. And all I can say of
Bedlam is that it is a hospital for the sick, a promenade of rogues,
and a dry walk for loiterers.'[20] Patients were actually robbed of food
and clothes on many occasions, by professional thieves. Pickpockets
circulated, plucking the purses of the unwary. Meanwhile, the
inmates rattled their chains and battered on the doors of their cells
for attention; or belted out a ballad in return for a glass of gin, with
their fellow inmates roaring along with the choruses. Nuts, fruit
and cheesecake were sold in the galleries and the 'basketmen' or
keepers in their sky-blue coats doubled as fairground barkers,
parading their charges like performing bears. The popular novelist
William Harrison Ainsworth drew on Ward's descriptions for his

vivid portrait of Bedlam in *Jack Sheppard* (1839) when the eponymous anti-hero, a notorious highwayman, visits his insane mother while on the run. The first thing Jack notices is the noise; he is stunned by the deafening clamour on all sides. Some lunatics rattled their chains, others shrieked or sang, some beat with frantic violence against the doors. In fact, it was the most dreadful sound he had ever heard. Several of the wards had been thrown open, and as Jack passed, he could not help glancing at the wretched inmates. He spotted a terrific figure gnashing his teeth, and howling like a wild beast, and a demented huntsman, who had fractured his skull whilst out hunting, and was perpetually 'hallooing after hounds'. And in the middle of it all, several groups of visitors strolled from cell to cell, laughing and joking, tourists for whom this misery was nothing more than entertainment.

Jack eventually found his mother, a complete wreck of her former self, cowering in a corner on a heap of straw. Her eyes glistened in the darkness like flames, and seemed to penetrate his very soul. A piece of old blanket was fastened across her shoulders, and she had no other clothing except for a petticoat. Her arms and legs were skeletal, and her pinched, ghastly white face bore the unmistakable stamp of madness. Her head had been shaved, and a piece of cloth was wrapped round her skull, with straws stuck in it. Her fingernails were as long as the talons of a bird, and, worst of all, she was fastened to the wall by a chain, riveted to an iron belt round her waist. The walls of her cell, which was about 6 feet long by 4 feet wide, were scrawled with fantastic designs, fragments of poetry, short sentences and names – the work of its former occupants, and of its present inmate.[21]

This harrowing description is typical of the stereotypes of madness operating at the time. Bethlem might have been relocated, but its terrifying alter ego, a culmination of popular anecdotes and jokes at the expense of eccentric residents, had accompanied it to the new location. These stereotypes, developing from previous images of 'Bedlam' in its Bishopsgate incarnation, began to circulate within weeks of the 'palace beautiful' opening its doors. Many were based upon real people: for instance scholars, victims of immoderate study and penny-pinching poverty like John Thamar, a musician and fellow of St John's College, Cambridge, which paid six shillings a week for 'dyet and attendance during his stay in the hospital of New Bethlem for the cure of his present distraction'.[22] Other destitute academics included Francis Wordis and John Shaxton, taken on sufferance as they had no friends and no means.[23] John Thamar did not recover: he died on 13 May 1700, and was buried in the Bethlem burial ground two days later. A broadsheet of the day depicts other recognisable figures from the world of madness, including those driven to distraction by romantic attachment: a deluded lover who fancies that his cruel mistress is still nearby and a rejected, demented woman, scrawling love letters to her inconstant sweetheart on the wall of her cell.

The Irish satirist Jonathan Swift (1667–1745) was inevitably drawn to this palace of madness. His association with Bethlem began with a visit, described in one of his 'Letters to Stella'. On 9 December 1710, Swift 'set out at ten o'clock to the Tower, and saw the lions; then to Bedlam; then dined at the chop-house behind the Exchange; and concluded the night at the Puppet Show. The ladies were in mobs [caps]; how do you call it? Undressed; and it was the rainiest day that ever dripped.'[24]

Swift was elected a governor on 26 February 1714, and used his position to nominate one 'Beaumont' for admission in 1722: 'Beaumont is mad in London riding through the streets on his Irish horse with the rabble after him, and throwing his money about the street. I have sent to the secretary of the governors of Bedlam to have him sent there, for you know I have the honour to be a governor.'[25] Swift was inspired by the spectacles he witnessed when strolling the noisy, stinking galleries. In *A Tale of a Tub* (1704) he devoted a section to 'a digression concerning the use and improvement of madness in a commonwealth'. Given most great empire builders and religious and political leaders had been clinically mad,

Swift argued, would it not be worth appointing commissioners who would scout Bedlam for appropriately insane people to command regiments, carry out scientific experiments and rage and brawl in the law courts or political elections? Here is a patient screaming his head off and tearing his straw to pieces: why not give him a regiment and send him off to Flanders? In another cell an obsessional patient demonstrates awesome foresight and insight: 'He walks daily in one pace, and entreats your penny with due gravity and ceremony: talks much of hard times and taxes: bars up the wooden shutters of his cell regularly at eight o'clock: dreams of fires and shoplifters and customers. Why deprive the City of such an ideal tradesman? Let him out!'[26] When the incurable wards were established, Swift begged to be admitted. If incurable fools, incurable rogues, incurable liars, the incurably vain or envious were eligible then surely he, Jonathan Swift, the 'incurable scribbler' was eligible to become a patient?[27] Swift's request for asylum in Bedlam was not merely ironic: he suffered from Ménière's Disease and was driven to distraction by the symptoms of vertigo, nausea and memory loss. Despite a reputation for misanthropy, Swift resolved to leave his money to build a Bedlam in Dublin; and, composing his own epitaph in 1740, declared:

> He gave the little wealth he had
> To build a house for fools and mad,
> And shewed by one satiric touch
> No nation wanted it so much:
> That kingdom [Ireland] he hath left his debtor:
> I wish it soon may have a better.[28]

The 'house for fools and mad' was actually St Patrick's Asylum in Dublin, the first mental hospital to be built in Ireland.

*

Swift's observations of Bedlam and the society outside it remain among the most vivid ever written. But the most enduring image of

Bedlam is that created by William Hogarth (1697–1764) in the final, eighth frame of *The Rake's Progress* (series painted 1733, engravings made 1735). The image of Tom Rakewell, collapsed upon the floor, driven to madness by debauchery and surrounded by a cast of grotesques, has defined 'Bedlam' for generations. The scene shows the incurable ward with its cells and staircase, accurate in every detail including the iron grille at the head of the staircase, which had been installed in 1729 to divide incurable from curable patients. In the foreground lies Thomas Rakewell, an eighteenth-century 'Tom o' Bedlam', who had reached the last stage in his journey via the Fleet Prison (where he had been incarcerated for debt). Reclining in a pose reminiscent of the maniacal 'brainless brother', Tom lies on the floor. His head has been shaved by the hospital barber, in accordance with eighteenth-century medical practice, and one of the keepers, in blue livery, is manacling his ankles. Poor Tom is abject; he is grimacing and the black plaster on his chest indicates that he has been 'blooded', meaning that leeches have been applied to suck out his ill-humours. His only friend is Sarah Young, a former lover whom he deserted; the steward is gently attempting to prise away his patient from her well-meaning grasp. As Tom suffers his final humiliation, the other incurables are depicted as oblivious to his torment, each wrapped up in a solitary world of their own. The broken-hearted lover sits on the stairs, deaf to the spaniel barking at him; the deluded 'pope', with his mitre and crosier, intones lines from the Mass interminably. The fiddler – musicians were long rumoured to be susceptible to madness – has a sheet of music over his head in lieu of a hat and the astronomer stares at invisible stars through a rolled-up paper while a demented tailor squats before him on the floor, hands tangled in a tape measure. Behind the door stands a deluded geographer, who has scrawled impossible globes upon the wall (although some commentators have taken this to be a portrait of Hogarth himself, and there is a facial resemblance). Through the open doors of two cells we see, first, a religious maniac, cringing from a crucifix illuminated by sunrays streaming through the bars of his cell; he is turning away, wringing his hands in a frenzy, as though to say 'I am not worthy'. In the second cell, a 'king' sits naked on his 'throne' – in reality a chamber pot. A keeper doubtless placed that crown of straw upon his head and a broken broomstick, like a sceptre, in his hand. The 'king' is either urinating – steam appears to be rising – or exposing himself, much to the voyeuristic delight of a fashionable lady and her maid. The lady peeps through the sticks of her fan, as if too genteel to witness the scene directly, while her maid, less of a hypocrite, leers frankly through the cell door.

'Pirate' versions of Hogarth's etching soon emerged, featuring variations of these stock madmen. One includes a political pamphleteer, driven crazy by the ingratitude of his party: he is casting a glance at a female patient who is staring at her own grim reflection in a mirror, lamenting her lost looks. And Hogarth himself was not immune to parody. When he published his *Analysis of Beauty* (1753), in which the artist maintained that the serpentine or curving line was the most aesthetically pleasing, rival cartoonists consigned Hogarth to the incurable ward, wearing a crown of straw and an ink pot on his head, the chain round his ankle curving into the 'line of beauty'.

Hogarth's 'Bedlam' may be the most notorious image of the hospital, but the artist's motives were laudable. The same year, 1733, the female incurable ward opened. *The Rake's Progress* raised funds for the hospital by attracting extra visitors and publicising the plight of the mad; this engraving appeared in a subscription book being circulated throughout London.[29] Hogarth was a generous supporter of London's hospitals. In 1736 he painted *The Good Samaritan* and *The Pool of Bethesda* for St Bartholomew's; he also provided paintings for the Foundling Hospital in 1746.

Visiting days did not appeal to everyone. The poet Abraham Cowley (1618–67) toured Bethlem on several occasions and confessed himself disgusted by the experience: 'I returned not only melancholy, but sick with the sight. To weigh the matter justly, the

102

total deprivation of reason is less deplorable than the total deprava-
tion of it in the thousands I meet abroad.'[30] As early as 1695, the
philosopher Thomas Tryon (1634–1703), one of the founders of the
vegetarian movement, issued a plea to the governors of New
Bethlem, 'one of the Prime Ornaments of the City of London, and
a Noble Monument of Charity', to restrain their officers from
'admitting such Swarms of People, of all Ages and Degrees, for only
a little paltry Profit to come in there, and with their noise, and vain
questions to disturb the poor Souls; as especially such, as do Resort
hither on Holy-dayes, and such spare time, when for several hours
(almost all day long) they can never be at any quiet'.[31]

It was inhumane, said Tryon, to make a show of these unhappy
objects of charity, by exposing naked inmates of either sex to 'the
Idle Curiosity of every vain Boy, petulant Wench, or Drunken
Companion'. Subjected to the impertinent questions of this staring rabble, what chance had the distracted person of recovery?
What they required, instead, was peace and quiet, a 'clean spare
diet' and visits from 'grave, sober, people' whose company would
provide a more efficient cure than any of the medicines currently
available.[32]

But visiting days continued and not merely to gratify the
voyeurism of the holiday crowds. The public exhibition of the
patients encouraged charity, and added around £400 a year to the
hospital's coffers. As one of the sights of London and a functioning
mental hospital, Bethlem was rooted in the community. Visitors
may have come to mock, but their entrance money contributed to
the inmates' welfare and reflected the sentiments of Robert Burton
in *The Anatomy of Melancholy*: 'But see the madman rage down-
right, with furious looks, a ghastly sight . . . His picture keeps still
in thy presence; 'Twixt him and thee, there's no difference.'

*

Another famous writer associated with Bethlem was Samuel Pepys
(1633–1703), not only for his great friendship with its architect,
Robert Hooke. Pepys's diaries record several references to the

hospital. He drank at the nearby Chequers pub, and the Goat tavern, and was a governor of Bethlem. In 1662, he had used his influence for the benefit of the freezing patients when a hearth-tax of two shillings a chimney threatened the hospital and the shivering patients, for no fire was to be lit there, except in the kitchen. Pepys interceded and the hospital was exempted from payment. Pepys was also instrumental in admitting a former employee, one James Carkesse, a clerk in the Naval Office, whom Pepys had sacked in 1666 for fraud. Over the next decade, Carkesse developed religious mania, professing to be a minister of God and claiming that he had a divine mission to reduce Dissenters in the Church. Extremely violent on admission, Carkesse broke the windows of the coach he was travelling in, and had to be locked up in a windowless cell by two strong men, where he lay in the straw like a fly in amber. Carkesse never fully recovered, but, during periods of remission, wrote a verse sequence entitled *Lucida intervalla* (1679) or 'Lucid Intervals', the medical term for the rational periods between acute attacks of madness. The book represented an attempt to convince the authorities of his sanity, but unfortunately Carkesse chose to do this by taking issue with his doctor, referring to him in print as 'Sir Madquack!' Sir Madquack was actually Dr Thomas Allen, one of the finest mental health practitioners in London. Dr Allen had first treated Carkesse at his private establishment, Finsbury Madhouse, even sending in his cat, 'Catmore', to eliminate the rats and mice that swarmed in his cell.[33] As the authorities refused to declare Carkesse sane until he had stopped writing the poetry in which he lampooned his doctor for running Bethlem and a private madhouse ('both *Bedlams* does haunt, like the *Louse*'[34]), Carkesse seems to have reached something of an impasse. He attracted a stream of regular visitors, including ladies from court, who brought him quill pens, a sixpence, apricots and a wig. In return, they received a flattering poem, written in their honour. Carkesse even claimed to have been visited by Nell Gwynn, whom he admired because, like Carkesse, she was a Protestant. He dedicated *Lucida intervalla* to her lover,

Charles II. Carkesse was eventually deemed cured, and released from Bethlem in November 1678.

Carkesse might have dismissed Dr Allen as 'Dr Madquack' and claimed that he was scarcely fit to dissect an oyster, but Dr Allen emerges as an enlightened physician who refused to let other doctors experiment on his patients. This was a common practice at the time, on the grounds that the chronic insane were a lost cause and therefore suitable research subjects. The experiment described here, conducted by members of the Royal Society, shows us just what Dr Allen was protecting his patients from. When, in 1667, a technique had been developed for transfusing blood from animal to animal, the next logical step was to choose a lunatic for the first attempt to transfuse animal blood into man. When Robert Hooke, the scientific genius who had designed the new hospital, asked Dr Allen if they could try out the technique 'upon some mad person of Bethlem', Dr Allen refused.[35] Instead, the researchers recruited a Mr Arthur Coga and the 'Experiment of Transfusion of sheep's blood into man' was performed on 23 November 1667 at Arundel House, headquarters of the Royal Society, by two learned physicians, Dr Richard Lower and Dr Edmund King. A similar experiment had been carried out a year earlier in Paris on a 'madman' who subsequently died.

Coga, a frantic little man who had previously been a dissident preacher, was hired for twenty shillings to have twelve ounces of sheep's blood transfused into his body, a procedure that, they estimated, would take 'a minute's time by a watch'. Some doctors thought this would have a good effect upon the patient as it would cool his blood and reduce his manic behaviour. Astonishingly, Coga survived the experience and was able to express his thanks to the Royal Society – in Latin, although King later admitted that Coga was still a little cracked in the head.

Dr Allen believed in protecting his own patients from such radical methods, but he was a pragmatist who had no scruples regarding dissection. Once dead, his patients became legitimate specimens and he conducted a number of autopsies to determine the possible physical cause of madness. The first recorded post-mortem of a patient at Bethlem appeared in 1676. Published by Richard Wiseman, sergeant-surgeon to Charles I, master of the Barber-Surgeons Company, it focused on the state of the pineal gland (which Descartes had pronounced the seat of the soul). Wiseman dissected 'one that in Bedlam was observed to sit upright with his back to a wall without speaking or opening his Eyes for many months, onely some odd mimicall gestures he used. Upon his death he was opened by order of Doctour Thomas Allen, Physician of the place. An oedematous Tumour was found to occupy all the upper part of the Cerebrum between it and the Pia mater.' The patient clearly had a brain tumour. Dr Allen's successor, Dr Edward Tyson, wrote up an autopsy on the head of a madman, who had died at Bethlem, which had contained two or three small bladders of water and referred to an anecdote about a fellow of a Cambridge college, a good poet and mathematician, 'who after his death was found to have no part of his brain sound, but all wasted away to a small matter, and like a lump of putrefaction; and that when he was alive he had no other symptom than that he could not endure the heat of the sun on his head'.[36]

*

While Dr Allen and his colleagues were literally anatomising melancholy and madness, other practitioners were springing up with techniques which we would now recognise as physiotherapy and hypnotherapy. One of the most remarkable examples was the arrival in London of Valentine Greatraks or 'The Stroker'. Greatraks came over from Ireland in 1666 on an impulse, convinced that the gift of healing had been bestowed upon him. Greatraks's method, as his name suggests, consisted of stroking the affected parts. His successes caused a stir in medical circles and he was eventually summoned to Whitehall by Charles II and ordered to give a demonstration of his powers on three patients from St Bartholomew's. Greatraks's gift was considered divine, in the biblical tradition of healing by touch.

Fellows of the Royal Society, including the scientific pioneer Robert Boyle, testified to his powers, which seem to have consisted of curing neurotic, hysterical or hypochondriac patients. Boyle saw Greatraks cure a man who could not move his hand, it being to his thinking dead, and recover another who was paralysed down his entire left side.

Among others, Greatraks cured Joseph Warden, a fat sailor debilitated with pain after seeing action against the Dutch. Greatraks stroked Warden from hip to toe, 'with alacrity and heartiness, until his pains were driven out at his toes ends, and the man walkt lustily to and fro in the Garden, professing his apprehensions of being able to do so for another ten miles, carrying his crutches over his shoulders the while'. Other success stories included soldiers from the Tower of London, ships' carpenters, and other victims of lameness, deafness and various infirmities, such as Anne Rose, a widow from Minories, who had suffered a severe migraine for over twenty years that made her life a misery. But, once Greatraks laid his hand upon her head and gently rubbed it, the pain 'flew to her breast and stomack, and made her wondrous faint and sick', but, after those parts had been stroked, she went into an attack of hiccoughs which lasted for an hour before she was fully restored, void of all pain, to her unspeakable joy and comfort.

Gentleman scientists from the Royal Society were inspired to study Greatraks's methods. On one memorable occasion the Right Honourable the Lord Viscount Faulconbridge conducted an experiment upon John Jacomb, of George Alley in Southwark, whose exquisite and continual pains had been lured out of his shoulder joints by the gentle touch of Greatraks's hand, and went to the end of his fingers, which turned completely numb. So dead were they, that Faulconbridge was able to thrust a pin an inch long into his fingers without response from the subject, who was covered with a hood, and without producing blood. After a second attempt, which achieved no reaction, Greatraks gently rubbed the man's fingers. Faulconbridge had only to touch Jacomb with the tip of the pin to provoke a sharp cry and a flow of blood from the man, who later professed himself to be free from all pain. Greatraks told him that he was welcome to come back if the pain returned, but, perhaps understandably after undergoing this aristocratic attempt at medical intervention, Jacomb never appeared again.[37] In hindsight, it is tempting to conclude that these remarkable cures came about as a form of 'faith healing', and that the patients who made such a spectacular recovery did so simply because their symptoms were entirely psychosomatic. These methods would not stand up to modern scientific analysis and the case histories are entirely anecdotal. However, one could argue that Greatraks and Faulconbridge were anticipating Sigmund Freud's theories of hysterical paralysis: physical manifestations of mental trauma which could be resolved with sufficient sympathetic attention from a sensitive, benevolent authority figure.

Meanwhile, Bethlem's architect Robert Hooke advocated another form of therapy for the mad: Hooke extolled the benefits of a substance then known as Indian hemp or marijuana. Hooke's apologia for this drug may strike a chord with modern readers:[38]

It is a certain Plant which grows very common in *India*, and the Vertues, or Quality thereof, are there very well known; and the Use thereof (tho' the Effects are very strange, and, at first hearing, frightful enough) is very general and frequent; and the Person, from whom I receiv'd it, hath made very many Trials of it, on himself, with very good Effect. 'Tis call'd, by the Moors, *Gange*; by the Chingalese *Comsa*, and by the Portugals, *Bangue*. The Dose of it is about as much as may fill a common Tobacco-Pipe, the Leaves and Seeds being dried first, and pretty finely powdered. This Powder being chewed and swallowed, or washed down, by a small Cup of Water, doth, in a short Time, quite take away the Memory and Understanding; so that the Patient understands not, nor remembereth any Thing that he seeth, heareth, or doth, in that Extasie, but becomes, as it were, a mere Natural, being unable to speak a Word of Sense; yet is he very merry, and laughs, and sings, and speaks Words without Coherence, not knowing what he saith or doth; yet is he not giddy, or drunk, but walks and dances, and sheweth many odd Tricks; after a little Time he falls asleep, and sleepeth very soundly and quietly; and when he wakes, he finds himself mightily refresh'd, and exceeding hungry. And that which troubled his Stomach, or Head, before he took it, is perfectly carried off without leaving any ill Symptom, as Giddiness, Pain in the Head or Stomach, or Defect of Memory of any Thing (besides of what happened) during the Time of its Operation.[38]

For this reason, Hooke suggests, hemp might be 'of considerable Use for Lunaticks, or for other Distempers of the Head and Stomach, for that it seemeth to put a Man into a Dream, or make him asleep, while yet he seems to be awake, but at last ends in a profound Sleep, which rectifies all; whereas Lunaticks are much in the same Estate, but cannot obtain that, which should, and in all Probability would, cure them, and that is a profound and quiet Sleep.'[39]

Having tried it himself, Hooke assures us with the conviction of a grizzled old stoner that 'What I have hear produced, is so well known and experimented by Thousands; and the Person that brought it has so often experimented it himself, that there is no Cause of Fear, tho' possibly there may be of Laughter.'

*

When Dr Madquack, or Thomas Allen, retired from Bethlem in 1684, he was succeeded as visiting physician by Dr Edward Tyson (1650–1708). An anatomist like his predecessor, Tyson published monographs on the strange animals, including porpoises and chimpanzees, which travellers brought to his house to be dissected. Dark and laconic, this erudite 'man of parts', as the historian Strype described him, was often to be found browsing the second-hand bookstalls which lined the walls outside Bethlem. Tyson oversaw a period of therapeutic optimism, when the intention of Bethlem was to cure the poor distracted lunatics. His most significant medical breakthrough was the observation that many of his patients, when admitted, were physically, as well as mentally, ill. Some had lost the use of limbs, or their toes had become gangrenous. Others were suffering from disfiguring skin diseases, or dropsy; some patients suffered such severe ulcers that amputation was required. Tyson realised that the cure of patients' physical ailments would have to precede any attempts at restoring their sanity. He requested that hot baths, nutritious food and appropriate medical treatment should be available for patients with physical symptoms, and developed an aftercare system whereby discharged patients were offered clothes and money. Tyson even opened an outpatients' department, where they might continue to receive treatment. Tyson estimated that he cured two-thirds of the patients treated over the course of twenty years, so it comes as no surprise that patients preferred conditions at Bethlem to those of the private madhouse or their own home, and that he had a long waiting list.

Tyson also revived the ancient theory of bathing as a treatment, believing it to be an excellent cure for suicidal despair: 'In the Heat of the Weather, a very convenient Bathing Place, to cool and wash them, and is of great Service in airing their Lunacy; and it is easily made a hot Bath for restoring their Limbs when numbed, or cleansing and preserving them from Scurvey, or other cutaneous Distempers.'[40]

One of Tyson's most famous patients was the dramatist Nathaniel Lee, who was under his care from 11 November 1684 to 23 April 1688. Dashing and handsome, Lee came down from Cambridge intending to take London by storm. But for all his dark good looks and commanding voice, Lee was a lousy actor. Undeterred, he turned his attention to writing, penning a series of classical spectaculars such as *Oedipus* and *The Rival Queens* (1677) and collaborating with Dryden and Purcell. One of the original libertines, Lee was a notorious drinker. On one occasion, he overstayed his welcome at the home of his patron, the Earl of Pembroke, in a single-handed attempt to empty the cellars. Lee's appetite for drink contributed to the breakdown which saw him incarcerated in Bethlem in 1684, his fees paid by the Board of Green Cloth, an organisation which carried responsibility for the court within a twelve-mile radius of wherever the court was sitting, and which sent forty-one patients to Bethlem between 1670 and 1750.[41] Lee endured many indignities, the worst being the loss of his fine head of hair, shaved for blistering. This technique, designed to divert the morbid humours from the brain, consisted of applying irritants to the skin. The most popular (although not with the patients) 'vesi-catories' or blister-raising agents were cantharides or powdered Spanish fly and mustard powders. The humours were thought to be eliminated through the serum of the blisters and through the pus, which inevitably formed as they became infected. The pain was agonising, but Lee kept on working. When his friend Dryden came to visit, and asked innocently if Lee now found it easy to write like a madman, Lee shot back: 'it is not so easy to write like a madman: but it is very easy indeed to write like a fool!'[42]

Lee was eventually discharged, and attempted to live on a pension of twenty shillings a year and his royalties. But he produced nothing new and was drinking heavily again, despite the best efforts of Dr Tyson. The link between wine and death in *The Rival Queens* reads like a premonition: 'The rage of wine is drowned in gushing blood,' he wrote, as the hero dies a slow death from a poisoned chalice. The end came in 1692, when Lee was forty-three and had undergone a further stint at Bethlem:

'Misfortunes and drink were the occasion: he was under the regime of a milk diet for the last week of his life; but getting one evening out of his physician's reach, he drank so hard, that he dropped down in the street, and was run over by a coach. His body was laid in a bulk near Trunkit's, the perfumer's, at Temple Bar, till it was owned.'[43] Lee was buried at St Clement Dane's, and his portrait still hangs in the Garrick Club.

With hindsight, one wonders whether Lee should even have been in Bethlem, although Tyson's sympathetic treatment undoubtedly prolonged his life. Lee told another playwright, William Wycherley, that 'he ought no more to be in Bethlem for Want of Sense, than other Mad Libertines and Poets abroad, or any Sober Fools whatever'.[44] But in the end he felt powerless in the face of his addiction and the authorities, as expressed in his famous observation that: 'They said I was mad: and I said they were mad: damn them, they outvoted me!'[45] Lee may also be immortalised, in a cryptic fashion, in Hogarth's famous engraving of Bedlam: carved into the wall, above the prostrate figure of poor Tom Rakewell, the letters LE are clearly visible: an oblique reference to poor Nathaniel?

Tyson himself died on 1 August 1708, at the age of fifty-eight. Elkanah Settle, a London poet, composed a 'Threnody on the Death of Dr Edward Tyson', which describes the physician's sudden and painless departure from life: death so loved him, Settle claimed, 'that he plucked every thorn from the roses on which he pillowed the physician's head for his last long sleep'.[46] His monument bore the inscription: 'He was to the last hour of his life the devoted physician of Bethlehem Hospital.' Richard Hale was elected Tyson's successor in 1708. Despite being 'stern of feature', he was regarded as a kind and sympathetic man, who considered 'company very beneficial to the patients', especially those suffering from depression. An early advocate of music therapy, Hale even recommended that a band at the hospital would aid recovery.

Unfortunately, Hale was the last of the therapeutic optimists. In 1728, James Monro was appointed, the first of a dynasty which was to rule Bethlem for the next four generations, during which the hospital would experience further notoriety. Meanwhile, London itself seemed about to embrace madness.

6

THE MIRROR OF MADNESS

Londoners were rudely awakened on the morning of 8 March 1750 – by an earthquake. The quake, which had been preceded by a previous movement on 8 February, convinced the religious that this was a warning from God. Charles Wesley issued a sermon, and the Bishop of London circulated a pastoral letter, to the effect that only a national act of repentance could save this depraved nation from divine retribution.

The event brought out the incipient maniac in everybody. After a Life Guardsman ran about town prophesying that a third earthquake would swallow up London and Westminster one lunar month ahead, on 4 April 1750, panic set in. From 1 April, the roads out of London were crowded with pedestrians and coaches, fleeing the 'City of Destruction' and the wrath to come. The politician and author Horace Walpole ridiculed this outburst of mass hysteria:

Several women have made earthquake gowns, *i.e.* warm gowns to sit in out of doors all night. Others go this evening to an inn ten miles out of town, where they are to play brag till 5 o'clock in the morning, and then come back, I suppose, to look for the bones of

113

their husbands and families under the rubbish. Dick Leveson, on his way home the other night, knocked at several doors, and in a watchman's voice cried: 'Past four o'clock, and a dreadful earthquake!'

A day before the impending earthquake, the Life Guard was found in a state of delirium, and dispatched to Bethlem. His colonel sent for the guardsman's wife and asked if her husband had ever suffered from madness before, but she maintained that he was quite in his right mind.[1] According to the *Whitehall Evening Post* of 31 March, the guardsman was Swiss, heir to a fortune, and regularly subject to bouts of religious madness. He believed that he himself had caused the earthquake, by virtue of the fact that he possessed a ball of fire in his body, and a 'sword which will cut devils in two!'[2] His arrest did nothing to stop the panic, and it is unlikely that anyone in Bethlem slept on the night of 3 April, when the blast of the exploding guardsman might trigger the crack of doom at any moment. People were on the move all night long. Outside Bethlem, the dark fields were illuminated as numerous families shivered before flickering bonfires, surrounded by their possessions. And then Thursday morning dawned, as punctual as ever, and they shuffled away home, damp with dew and full of relief.

The fright and flight was captured by a contemporary cartoonist, in the style of Hogarth. The engraving, entitled *The Military Prophet: A Flight from Providence*, shows the crowd passing along Piccadilly at the top of St James's Street. The Life Guardsman is on a horse, urging on the panic-stricken crowd and waving his 'Sword of Prophecy'. Two women are reading his 'Prophecy', sold to them by a broadsheet vendor anxious to turn a quick penny. A carriage and four horses await a decrepit old gentleman and his buxom young wife, who is already eyeing up a younger man. Other characters include an itinerant gin-seller, certain to make a killing on a day which took a toll on everybody's nerves. One curious feature of this cartoon is that the crowd is heading towards the City of London,

Westminster and St Paul's, rather than out of it – to do so, the crowd would need to be travelling in the opposite direction, to Covent Garden. This could have been a genuine error on the part of the cartoonist – or a further illustration of the stupidity of this crazed crowd.

The London earthquake was just the latest episode in the city's apparent descent into madness. As far as their European neighbours were concerned, the English had not shaken off their reputation for insanity or '*la maladie anglaise*'. (The English, by way of retaliation, referred to syphilis as 'the French disease'.) But what were the causes? Why were the English and Londoners, in particular, credited with a condition ranging from harmless eccentricity to demoniacal mania?

Towards the end of the eighteenth century, the majority of press and Parliament appeared clinically insane, with the religious enthusiasts a narrow second and an ongoing dispute between the 'hacks' (journalists) and the poets as to who was maddest. A 1763 version of Hogarth's famous engraving even depicted Britannia herself as a lunatic. The image of the warrior queen, as it appeared on the coin of the realm, is drawn on the corridor wall, with Britannia looking particularly distracted.

One explanation for the apparent increase in the prevalence of insanity was the change in the size and structure of the population.[3] During the reign of George III (1760–1820), the total population of England and Wales rose from approximately 7 to 12 million, and it continued to rise rapidly thereafter. The combination of this rise in the population with the widespread economic changes that accompanied the Industrial Revolution led to a vast increase in the number of paupers. The substitution of machinery for hand labour led to increasing discontent and distress, aggravated, in turn, by such factors as the Corn Laws, imposed at the end of the Napoleonic war in 1815, which stated that no foreign corn could be imported into England until the domestic product reached a price of eighty shillings per quarter. As a consequence, food prices soared, the manufacturing market was depressed and the poor, unable to grow their own food, suffered the most, venting their frustration with outbreaks of rioting.

By the close of the eighteenth century, workhouses and Bridewells (houses of correction modelled on the original one in London) were taking in mad people and idiots, or as the historian Andrew Scull refers to them, 'vagrants and beggars who could not be convicted of any crime save that of wandering abroad or refusing to work', as well as the more dangerous and troublesome lunatics.[4] Workhouses, which had been established on an experimental basis in a few towns in the 1630s, had spread rapidly after the successful example of the Bristol workhouse in 1696. By the middle of the eighteenth century, almost every market town had its own workhouse.[5] They were desperate places, despite the good intentions of their founders, 'dumping grounds for the decrepit and dependent of all descriptions'. Defoe counted twenty-seven public gaols and 125 'tolerated prisons' (institutions for deviants) in 1724, commenting that 'there are in London, notwithstanding we are a nation of liberty, more public and private prisons, and houses of confinement, than in any city in Europe, perhaps as many as in all the capital cities of Europe put together'.[6]

Experts blamed everything from social progress to women drinking and even diet. Writing about 'the English Malady' in 1733, George Cheyne (1671–1743) contended that illness, both physical and mental, was the product of affluence: heavy drinking, gluttony and late nights wrecked the constitution and contributed to attacks of 'the nerves', the eighteenth-century equivalent of 'neurotic'. An early proponent of the 'you are what you eat' school, Cheyne qualified in Aberdeen and arrived in London in 1702. With no accreditation from the Royal College of Physicians he was regarded as little better than a quack, but he did manage to get himself elected to the Royal Society. Desperate to network with other, influential doctors and well-connected patients, he took to drinking heavily and developed a reputation as a bon viveur and man about town. This strategy meant career success but had severe consequences: constitutionally large, Cheyne got even bigger. By 1705 he was 'excessively fat, short-breath'd, Lethargic and Listless'.[7] Realising that his life was at risk, he moved to the country and sobered up, his flesh melting away like a snowball in summer. Years of yo-yo dieting followed, until he fixed on an all-milk plan that restored him to being 'Lank, Fleet and Nimble'.[8] But this did not last. By 1720 Cheyne was drinking three bottles of wine a day and had blown up to thirty-two stone. Walking became so difficult that a servant had to follow him round with a stool; he developed gout and ulcers on his legs and he took large quantities of opium, even though he realised it was a slow poison. It was not until he tried a vegetarian regime and gave up alcohol that he began a slow and successful recovery and established a flourishing practice. Careful to draw a distinction between the raving poor who filled the workhouses, and the 'worried well', Cheyne contributed to the notion that 'to be truly fashionable, it was necessary to display at least a little mental abnormality or emotional anxiety: distinction required a touch of *difference*'.[9] Madness was a different experience for the upper classes: when, he asked, did you last see a country yokel suffering from a fit of the vapours?[10]

When he visited England in 1765, P. J. Grosley, a distinguished French scholar, became so fascinated by 'the English Melancholy', a propensity to suicide and great numbers of madmen and lunatics that he devoted whole chapters to them. Grosley attributed the English Melancholy to the mixture of fogs, beef and beer aggravated by the rigours of Nonconformity and the tedium of the English Sunday. Even the principal festivals of the year, elsewhere joyous occasions, brought only an increase in sadness. Nature was too powerful for laws; even the stone balustrade which obstructed his view of the Thames had not prevented the citizens of London precipitating themselves into their river in considerable numbers.[11] Dr Arnold, the enlightened proprietor of a madhouse in Leicestershire, noted that madness seemed peculiar to the English and again attributed it

to affluence: 'In Scotland, where the inhabitants in general are neither opulent nor luxurious, Insanity, as I am informed, is very rare:
nor is it more frequent in the poorer, and less cultivated parts of
Wales. I can see no other way of accounting for this vast increase of
the disorder, than by attributing it to the present universal diffusion
of wealth and luxury.'[12]

Another French author, Lacombe, concluded a visit to Bethlem in
1784 with the observation that the English temperament would cease
to be 'gloomy, melancholy and taciturn' if only people started drinking wine again, as they had done in mediaeval times. Plant vines, he
declared, encourage dancing on Sundays and the nation would be
happy and sociable, and Bethlem would be empty.[13]

As to those wild, wanton women drinkers, their tipple of choice,
regarded as the source of all evil by many commentators, was tea. In
his *Observations on Maniacal Disorders* (1792), William Pargeter condemned the frequent and immoderate use of tea. 'With what
additional force must the practice and pursuit of the foregoing evils
operate on female constitutions, whose frame and contexture are so
delicate and tender . . . in this age, it is easier to meet with a *mad*,
than an *healthy* woman of *fashion*.'[14]

Another anecdotal cause of madness was self-abuse. Inevitably, a
key text on the vice became a best-seller. *Onania: or, The Heinous Sin
of Self-Pollution* by 'Anonymous' (1730) proved remarkably popular
and went into fifteen editions. First promoted, rather appropriately,
by a 'Mr Crouch', the book warns of 'Frightful Consequences (in
both SEXES)' and contains 'Spiritual and Physical ADVICE to those
who have already injur'd themselves by this abominable Practice'.

The book advised that 'that unnatural Practice, by which Persons
of either Sex may defile their own Bodies, without the Assistance of
others, whilst yielding to filthy Imaginations' caused gonorrhoea,
impotence and sterility, as well as some frightening physical characteristics including 'meagre Jaws, pale Looks, feeble Hams, and Legs
without Calves' as the unfortunate victim became 'a Jest to others,
and a Torment to themselves'. One patient relates: 'My Memory has

entirely fail'd me. I am dull, sleepy and melancholy. I feel Pain in my Arms, small of my Back, and Loins. I fear my Nerves are some way affected. I find my Body full of pimples!' The cure? 'Repentance, Conversion and Amendment' backed up – inevitably – by a specific 'powder' made and sold by the author.[15]

Other perceived explanations for madness, according to Bethlem's apothecary, John Gozna, included 'Misfortunes, Troubles, Disappointments, Grief' (206 patients), 'Religion and Methodism' (90), 'Love' (74) and 'Study' (15), all of which fall well within the established explanations for madness. As does 'Childbed' (79 patients). It is more disturbing to note that 'small pox' and 'ulcers and scabs dried up' were considered a cause.[16]

*

The intellectual progress of the Enlightenment ensured that madness became a fit object for scientific speculation and public discussion. Advances were also being made in medical practice, and the concept developed of establishing charitable institutions for the sick. In London, these included Westminster Hospital (1719), Guy's (1721) and the London Hospital (1740). In 1728, wards for 'chronic lunatics' were opened at Guy's. St Luke's Hospital, set up as an alternative to Bethlem, opened in 1751. Other establishments followed in Newcastle and Manchester. In 1796, the Society of Friends (Quakers) opened the small but massively influential Retreat at York, an institution which was to set new standards for the care and treatment of the insane. Another development was the specialism of 'mad doctoring' with self-styled experts proclaiming new therapies which ranged from the sublime to the ridiculous to the abjectly cruel. The mad themselves, while never consulted about their treatment or conditions, emerged as objects of pity rather than dangerous brutes or victims of demoniacal possession. As to whether they could be cured, or merely contained: this was to constitute one of the greatest medical debates of the century between two of Bethlem's greatest 'mad doctors', John Monro and his progressive colleague William Battie.

*

Another consequence of London's rising levels of insanity was the private madhouse. Originally, these institutions were an extension of the practice of billeting affluent patients in a doctor's own home – as in the example of Helkiah Crooke, who, as we have learned, took Edmund Francklin in as a private patient after he was 'found a lunatic' in 1630. Given that Bethlem, in its Bishopsgate days, was too small to accommodate many, and was really designed for paupers, private madhouses were inevitable. Otherwise, what was to become of Londoners such as the man described by John Vicars, who was 'so distracted, that it was held fit to have him away to *Bedlam*' only to be saved by his friends who rescued him from 'the common condition of the Madmen there' so that he was instead 'kept private in the house of one that endeavours the cure of such persons'?[17]

Private madhouses developed as a solution to caring for lunatics from the more affluent classes. Traditionally, these people were boarded out to be cared for individually by medical men or clergymen. In 1679, for instance, Anne Grenville, the youngest daughter of the Bishop of Durham, was placed in the charge of a Worcester physician who was 'famous for the ordering of distempered persons'. There were also 'houses for lunatics' in Clerkenwell and Lambeth. These enterprises were not always successful: in 1661, the Reverend John Ashbourne, who kept a small madhouse in Suffolk, was murdered by one of his own patients.

One of the earliest madhouse keepers was John Archer, who published *Every Man his Own Doctor* including a treatise 'of melancholly and distraction, with government in cure' in 1673. Archer, who described himself as a doctor, was little better than a quack and possessed no proper medical training. He did, however, offer to 'accommodate those who had lost the use of Reason' and boasted of secure and delightful conditions with 'excellent Air nere the City'. In 1674, a handbill advertised a madhouse on Clerkenwell Green established by James Newton, 'a faithful expert in these distempers, who had cured some that have been twelve years Madd and others that have been sixteen years Melancholy'. The madhouse was the old

Manor House in Clerkenwell which had belonged to the Earls of Northampton. The advertisement contains accounts of previous patients, now happily cured, including a man who believed himself to be Charles II (cured within six days) and a woman covered in sores after being tied to her bed for months, a common but desperate remedy in the days before effective sedation, who was cured within three weeks.[18]

Clerkenwell madhouse appears in the 1720 edition of Stow's *Survey*, situated at the top of Woods Close where St John's Street ran into Islington Road, and was possibly the first madhouse to feature on a map of London. In 1754 it was taken over by William Battie and subsequently passed to John Monro in 1776. His son, Thomas Monro, relinquished it in 1803, when it became a boarding school.

One of the most famous victims of incarceration in a private madhouse was Alexander Cruden (1701–70), whose account of his experiences contributed to the growing public concern over the fate of the mad. The fact that he was a patient of Dr Monro of Bethlem only added to the scandal. *The London-citizen Exceedingly Injured: or a British inquisition display'd, in an account of the unparallel'd case of a citizen of London, bookseller to the late Queen, who was sent to a private madhouse* appeared in 1739 and included 'an Account of the said CITIZEN'S barbarous Treatment in *Wright's* Private Madhouse on *Bethnal-Green* for nine Weeks and six Days, and of his rational and patient Behaviour, whilst *Chained, Handcuffed, Strait-Waistcoated* and *Imprisoned* . . .'[19]

A tiny, eccentric but brilliant Scot, Cruden suffered a life-long battle with madness. According to Scull, he stalked a young woman in his native Aberdeen so relentlessly that he had to be put in prison. Another episode occurred on the completion of his famous *Concordance* (a reference book for the Bible still in use today). The pamphlet of 1739 is a vivid depiction of his allegedly false incarceration in Bethnal Green madhouse, recounted in the third person as 'Mr C', 'with all the sensitive though detached attention to detail of a paranoid personality'.[20]

Cruden's ordeal began on 23 March 1739, when 'Mr C' was decoyed into a coach on the grounds that a Mr Wightman wanted to see him at his lodgings in Spring Gardens, Vauxhall. Robert Wightman suspected Cruden of stalking a wealthy gentlewoman, and perhaps regarded him as a rival for her affections.[21] Mr C soon realised that his coach was travelling in the wrong direction – up the Strand via Ludgate Hill, instead of along Chancery Lane, and he demanded to know if he was being taken to Bethlem. The coachman admitted that he had been ordered to take Mr C to Wright's private madhouse on Bethnal Green. When they arrived, Mr C was put in the custody of John Davis, the under-keeper, and locked in a room. That night Davis told him that, as he was in a madhouse, he must expect to be treated like a madman, 'and submit to have the Chain on the bedstead lock'd upon his Leg'.[22] The following day, he was visited by the apothecary, who took his pulse and administered 'physick' prescribed by Dr Monro. Mr C prudently submitted to the treatment, having observed that 'if Prisoners in this Madhouse refuse to take what is ordered them, there is a terrible iron Instrument put into their mouths to hold down their tongues, and to force the physick down their throats'. The 'physick' – a strong laxative – took effect at three o'clock in the morning, but when Mr C begged for help, Davis refused to acknowledge his needs and, instead, reminded the prisoner that he was his keeper. Instead of providing a chamber pot, the keeper added to Mr C's misery by handcuffing him and leaving him to his disgusting fate.

On the Saturday, the apothecary ordered Davis to put Mr C into a 'Strait-Wastecoat'; this garment was made of strong 'Tick' (tough stripy material used for mattresses and pillows), with long sleeves that extended beyond his fingers. The keeper clasped the prisoner's arms upon his chest, and his hands around his sides towards his back, securing his hands tightly with large strong strings of tape.[23]

The following Tuesday, 28 March, Mr C was allowed out of his room and into the 'publick parlour' with the other patients. The straitjacket was taken off, but he was handcuffed and chained to the chimney corner by one leg. The company of the other patients soon proved so disagreeable that Mr C begged to be taken back to his room, where he remained straitjacketed and chained to the bed. The only way he could get into bed that night was by entering at the bed's foot: the chain did not extend far enough for him to get into bed in the conventional manner.

On the Thursday, Dr Monro came to visit Mr C for the first time. Understandably, the patient expostulated about his barbaric treatment, but the doctor's only response was to order blooding of his left foot, 'which took away so much blood that the foot was for some months after benumm'd'.[24] When Dr Monro returned the following Thursday, Davis unchained Mr C. And Mr C again complained about his treatment. 'But Monro, like a bird upon the wing, made only a standing visit, and he was chained up again as soon as Monro had departed.' During Monro's third visit, on 13 April, Mr C demanded an explanation for the fact that Monro had prescribed to him six days before they actually met, and asked why he took a case history from Wightman, the keeper of the madhouse, rather than from Mr C himself. To which Monro retorted that Mr Wightman knew what he was doing.

When Monro visited Mr C on 20 April, Mr C again complained about his unjust treatment and argued that he had never been mad. The doctor left without a reply. This was the fourth, and last, visit he received from Dr Monro.

Mr C was still in the madhouse on 27 May. He was chained to his bed day and night during hot weather, and terrified by the prospect of being sent to Bethlem. He had been provided with a knife with which to eat his food, and devised a plan to secure his escape by sawing through the bedstead. Over the following days, he worked on the bed 'till his Shirt was almost as wet as if dipt in water' until the job was finished at four o' clock on the afternoon of 30 May. But Mr C did not escape immediately. He bided his time, requesting a shave from one of the keepers, then settling down for a few hours' sleep.

Wednesday, 31 May, was Mr C's birthday. He woke early, prayed, then 'held his chain in his hand still fastened to his leg', but managed to get out of the window into the garden. He mounted the garden wall with considerable difficulty, losing one of his slippers in the process, then jumped down into the back alley, just before the clock struck two. Mr C headed for Mile End, but his left foot was so injured from landing on the gravel that he had to put his other slipper over it. From Mile End, he went to Whitechapel, where a kindly soldier took pity on him and tried to get him a coach, with no success. Then Mr C and the soldier walked to Aldgate, where a watchman spotted his chain and raised the alert, following them to Leadenhall Street, where he was arrested. When they took Mr C to Aldgate watch-house (a precursor of the police station) and he told them his story, he was treated with sympathy and offered refreshment. But the authorities also sent a watchman to Bethnal Green, to get their account of events, which led to Davis and 'two more of their bull-dogs' arriving at the watch-house with handcuffs to recapture Mr C. The constable, to his eternal credit, observing Mr C's lucid and rational manner, refused to allow them to take him back. Instead, a meeting was arranged between the keepers and the Lord Mayor at the Grocers' Hall. Mr C subsequently appeared before the Lord Mayor, in chains, to show just how badly he had been treated, and gave him 'a just and full account of his illegal and barbarous Imprisonment'.[25]

This was not, sadly, Cruden's last experience of the madhouse. In 1753 he was confined in Duffield's madhouse, Chelsea, and, as the years progressed, he developed symptoms consistent with paranoid schizophrenia and megalomania, promoting himself from a 'corrector of the press' (today's equivalent would be a newspaper sub-editor) to a moral guardian who, he believed, should be offered a government job as 'Alexander the Great, Corrector of the Morals of the Nation'. After an abortive attempt to stand for Parliament, he became a figure of fun and was found dead at his lodgings in 1770, rigor mortis having set in as he knelt at prayer.

There are many aspects of Cruden's account of his treatment which demand further investigation, particularly his references to Dr Monro. By today's standards, Monro's practice of prescribing without examining his patient first, and only interviewing the patient seven days after he had been admitted, appears extraordinary. In fact, Monro was only following common practice. Practitioners at this period did not identify specific diseases through their symptoms and then prescribe a cure. Instead, they resorted to an arsenal of treatments which were regarded as defeating bodily dysfunction. This scattergun approach included the classic purges, leechings and 'powders, whose secrets were known only to their compounders'.[26] Doctors believed that, if insanity was only a disease of the brain, then these methods must work as well on lunatics as they did on those suffering more obvious symptoms of physical illness.

As Scull points out, Cruden's account may have been biased, not least because he regarded the Monros as Jacobites (political campaigners intent on returning Stuart kings to the throne of England and Scotland). Rather than seeking common ground with his fellow Scots, he was keen to discredit the family on the grounds of supposed Catholic sympathies. And there was another reason, hidden for 250 years but revealed by Scull after considerable research: Cruden was deeply ashamed by his apparent lapses of sanity, and concealed the fact that, on 17 December 1743, he was admitted to Bethlem, remaining there until 3 March 1744.

Cruden was not the only victim of false imprisonment. Many private madhouses became 'mansions of misery', run by private speculators looking for easy profits and unfettered by legal restrictions.[27] In 1728, campaigning journalist Daniel Defoe condemned such institutions, particularly when they served as dumping grounds for discarded wives. He painted a grim picture of beautiful, virtuous ladies, their babies torn from their arms, condemned to the madhouse so that their husbands could install a new mistress. 'If they are not mad when they go into these cursed Houses, they are soon made so by the barbarous Usage they there suffer.' Women of spirit fared worst: if they stood up for themselves, they were even more likely to be whipped, chained and starved. It was enough to drive any soul 'stark staring mad, though before they were never so much in their right Senses'.[28] Sensational accounts of legal battles circulated throughout the latter part of the eighteenth century. In 1772, the proprietors of Bethnal Green madhouse went on trial for the illegal confinement of a Mrs Ewbank, placed there by a husband who beat her up and seized her children. Mrs Ewbank's graphic account had her dragged screaming to the madhouse and threatened with disembowelment if she resisted. Mrs Ewbank was eventually rescued from Bethnal Green by her family, and subsequently took her husband to court. During the trial, details emerged of another patient who had befriended her, a Mrs Mills, also committed by her husband and subsequently abused by the proprietors and staff. Mrs Mills claimed she had been handcuffed and chained, called a 'bitch' in a 'house for mad bitches' and threatened with having her head shaved. These incidents were not the last of their kind: madhouses continued to be used as a form of social control for troublesome wives throughout the nineteenth century.[29]

Public concern regarding private madhouses reached such a pitch that in 1754, Sir Colin Firebrace MP asked the Royal College of Physicians to consider a bill in which it was recommended that the college should take responsibility for vetting and regulating such establishments. The college rejected the proposal as too difficult to implement, and it was a further twenty years before legislation was introduced, although evidence was piling up. In 1763, a select committee was set up following widespread concern after the publication of an article in the *Gentleman's Magazine* 33. The inquiry was limited in scope, however, and confined to only two London madhouses. It was not until 1774 that the first Act for regulating madhouses reached the statute book. This act made provision for the inspection and licensing of private madhouses in London and Westminster and within a radius of seven miles thereof, by five commissioners appointed by the Royal College of Physicians. The drawback of this scheme was that it did nothing to alleviate the plight of pauper lunatics, and had little influence over the provincial madhouses, although it was proposed that these be inspected by a team consisting of Justices of the Peace and a medical practitioner.

Although Bethlem had elected medical directors since 1615, James Monro was its first true specialist in madness. As Scull notes, it was not until this point that the concept of a 'particular occupation group' with scientific expertise in dealing with lunacy had emerged. This perspective 'viewed the madman as exhibiting a defective *human* mechanism, and which therefore saw this condition as at least potentially remediable'. This in its turn gave rise to a professional class which specialised in dealing with the mad. 'During his tenure as physician to Bethlem, James Monro was almost the only doctor in and around London who specialised in "treating" the mentally ill. Once the trend had been set, however, the increasing reliance on private madhouses and charity asylums as a means of coping with insanity prompted a quickening of medical interest and involvement in this area and medical men saw the potential of this lucrative new market.'[30] Scull, in his fascinating study of the Monro dynasty, refers to John Monro (James's son) as an 'undertaker of the mind', drawing an analogy between mad doctors and undertakers as an emerging occupational group, catering to the grimmer requirements of the new middle class.

At this point, the medical profession consisted of three distinct categories: physicians, surgeons and apothecaries. Physicians possessed a medical degree and treated the upper classes. In London, they were members of the Royal College of Physicians, as it was then known, but their careers often depended more on social networking than practical skills. Surgeons were somewhat déclassé; entry was via apprenticeship and they had only recently severed their links with the barber's shop. Apothecaries catered to the middle and lower classes. Apprenticed and unregulated, they ranged from quacks to highly competent practitioners. Those doctors who entered the mad trade came from all three backgrounds. Although it is tempting to think that treating the mad was the last refuge for charlatans, 'some of the most educated and literate doctors turned to the study and treatment of the insane'.[31]

James Monro, who was involved in one of the first pioneering experiments in smallpox inoculation, was the second son of Alexander Monro DD, principal of Edinburgh University. James, who had moved to London in search of professional advancement, was condemned as a 'Jacobite' by Cruden, an allegation symptomatic of Cruden's paranoia. The 'Jacobite' slur was a common accusation against Scots seeking their fortune down south. In fact, although his father had been a Jacobite, James Monro was actually High Anglican and as such clearly a member of the Establishment, accepted without comment by the court and the Tories on the board of governors.

The Monros owned private madhouses in Hackney and Clerkenwell and were visiting physicians to others including Bethnal Green and Chelsea. A casebook of 1766 from Brooke House Hackney (which was in continuous use as a private asylum from 1759 until destroyed by enemy action in 1940) reveals that John Monro, James's son, had over 100 patients. The private madhouses were not cheap. Joseph Girdler, sergeant-at-law of the Inner Temple, complained in 1733 that his father's estate was being devoured by the mad doctors, with Dr James Monro demanding £130 for treatment, while Girdler thought him not worth a quarter of that sum. These fees were by no means exceptional.[32]

Dr John Monro was a therapeutic pessimist. 'Madness is a distemper of such a nature, that very little of real use can be said concerning it; the immediate causes will for ever disappoint our search, and the cure of that disorder depends on *management* as much as *medicine*.'[33] This view was not endorsed by his colleague, William Battie (1703–76). A classical scholar, Battie had turned his attention to medicine at Cambridge (Horace Walpole was among his anatomy students). Battie first became interested in insanity in 1742, when he paid a subscription of £50 to become a governor of Bethlem. Battie's *Treatise on Madness* (1758) reveals the great insight that 'madness' was not simply one universal condition. Instead, he devised a simple method of classifying the state into two sorts, 'original' – without organic cause – and 'consequential' – following brain damage and injury.

Most controversial of all, Battie condemned existing treatments which only exacerbated madness, including opium, which was no more a cure for madness than it was for smallpox, and surgery, saying the lancet, when applied to a feeble and convulsed lunatic, was as destructive as the sword. Battie also recognised that patients often recovered spontaneously, without treatment, or even when treatment was stopped. Battie also believed that madness was curable and that, one day, a treatment would become available for the calamity of madness. Medical cures had been discovered for other conditions – 'Mercury in the Venereal infection, Opium in pain' – and it was anticipated that one day 'the peculiar antidote of Madness reserved in Nature's store would be discovered'.[34]

Battie's approach marked a dividing line between the old and the new approach to mental illness and inspired the foundation of several psychiatric hospitals and a series of textbooks. An accomplished author (he had edited Aristotle and published treatises on physiology), Battie maintained that a doctor's duties included teaching his medical students and, even more importantly, writing up his research for the benefit of future generations. As a result, 'theoretical discussion gave way to case histories and preoccupation with physical treatments to "regimen" and "management" from which developed the "moral treatment" of the nineteenth century'.[35]

Another controversial aspect of Battie's *Treatise* saw him accusing James Monro of refusing to take on medical students at Bethlem or publish accounts of his treatment methods, and criticising its culture of a few select physicians keeping the patients to themselves, as well as opening the hospital to the impertinent curiosity of sightseers at a penny a time.

John Monro retaliated with his *Remarks on Dr Battie's Treatise* (the first book on madness to be published by Bethlem although there had been physicians there for 200 years). Satirical, in the spirit of the times, the book sported the Horatian motto '*O Major, tandem parkas, Insane, minori*' ('O greater madman pray have mercy on a lesser one') and consisted of a series of rebuttals of Battie's arguments. Madness cannot be cured, stated Monro. The condition was the result of 'a vitiated judgment' and would respond to 'coercion, restraints and physical treatments'.[36] Monro also questioned the need to produce textbooks and teaching materials, implying that Battie's treatise was a form of vanity: 'My own inclination would never have led me to appear in print.'[37] He also defended the conventional treatment methods in operation at Bethlem, particularly emetics and purging, and claimed he had never seen a patient alarmed by the procedure: 'I should be very sorry to find any one frightened from the use of such an efficacious remedy by it's being called a *shocking operation, the consequence of a morbid convulsion.* I never saw or heard of the bad effect of vomits, in my practice . . . *Bleeding* and *purging* are both requisite to the cure of madness.'[38]

The disagreement between Monro and Battie was not just a medical dispute: it was a clash of personalities, between John Monro, the suave doctor about town, with his carriage and his silver-topped cane, and the earnest, academic Battie. Scull has also suggested that Monro's attack on Battie had another personal dimension, as James Monro had died recently and John felt compelled to defend his father's memory.

Despite their mutual antipathy, Monro and Battie later sat together on committees at Bethlem. On one occasion, they even seemed to have felt a professional obligation to close ranks against an accusation of medical malpractice. When a former patient called Wood sued Monro for illegal detention in a madhouse on the grounds that he had never been insane, and was about to win his case, Battie arrived in court and by judicious questioning made the patient reveal his delusional system and so saved his colleague. The case was later used as an example in legal texts and referred to, as Lord Erskine did when defending James Hadfield in 1800, to

ST.LUKE'S HOSPITAL.
Old Street Road

St Luke's Hospital for Lunaticks, founded 1751.

illustrate that delusions might be concealed during an ordinary cross-examination but would be revealed when the cross-examination was carried out by an expert psychiatric interviewer.

Battie went on to become president of the Royal College of Physicians and his *Treatise* proved massively influential. Most significant of all, he founded St Luke's Hospital for Lunaticks, becoming its first physician when it opened in 1751. He also opened a private madhouse at Islington Road and took over Newton's madhouse in Clerkenwell Close. Devoting himself to the study of madness, Battie developed into the leading 'mad doctor' of his day. At his death, his estate was estimated at between £100,000 and £200,000. One thousand patients, including Kit Smart, the poet, and Alexander Cruden passed through his hands, of whom over half were discharged as 'cured'. His experience as a governor of Bethlem had convinced Battie of the need to improve the conditions and treatment of the mad. Battie also recognised the need for qualified staff – 'there must be Servants peculiarly qualified, and every Patient must have a separate Room, and Diet, most of them, equal to Persons in Health' – and argued that the process of recovery generally required 'several Months, and often a whole Year before a Cure is completed'. Unlike Bethlem, St Luke's would be the first teaching hospital for 'mad doctors'.[39] In February 1753, the governors passed a resolution 'that it will be for the Publick Good and for the Credit of this Charity that the Physician be at Liberty to take Pupils'. This was the first instance of an attempt to teach students by actual observation of the phenomena of madness. Although later historians have pointed out that even St Luke's resorted to some 'hoary old techniques', including the ancient method of substituting one extreme sensation for its opposite and using fear to cast out anger.[40] One of the most significant aspects of the foundation of St Luke's was the decision 'that the patients shall not be exposed to public view'.[41]

At Bethlem, meanwhile, visiting days were still in full swing, with the mad providing a peep show for London's lowlifes. *The World* reported in 1753: 'It was in the Easter week, when, to my great surprise, I found a hundred people at least, who, having paid their two-pence apiece, were suffered, unattended, to run rioting up and down the wards, making sport and diversion of the miserable inhabitants.'[42] Such voyeuristic scenes were not confined to Bethlem. According to *Diaries of a Lady of Quality* the Duke of Marlborough, when in a state of complete imbecility, was actually exhibited by his servants to all who chose to give an additional fee, after having stared at all the magnificence of Blenheim.[43]

Nevertheless, a different attitude towards the insane was emerging among the intellectual elite and the genteel middle classes. As Scull says, the mad were 'no longer seen as "brutes" but as objects of pity, who required aid, not derision'. Samuel Richardson compared touring Bethlem with attending a public execution at Tyburn. The appeal of the peep show was fading fast. But it was not until 1766 that the court of governors decided to close Bethlem to the public view. By 1769, no man apart from a governor was permitted access to the women's side, a male visitor being allowed to see a female patient only in the committee room, and with a nurse present. Finally, on 11 November 1770, Dr John Monro ordered that admittance should for the future be by ticket only, and that accredited visitors be accompanied by keepers or nurses.

*

There are conflicting accounts of Bethlem during the Monro regime. While contemporary journalists such as Ned Ward provide sensational and voyeuristic descriptions of visiting days, other sources suggest that conditions were a great deal better than elsewhere. A committee book from 1767, for instance, ordered: 'That for the future no patient in this Hospital be permitted to have in his cell any box with a lock or key and that the Basketmen and Gallery maids do immediately diligently search all the patients and their cells for any razors pen knives or other offensive instruments of that kind and that they do secure the same to prevent the patients doing any mischief to themselves or others therewith.'

On 21 December 1771, the committee instructed that 'every man who has been a patient in this Hospital and is discharged from it either sick or incurable shall be stripped and examined by the Basketmen to see that he be sent out from the Hospital clean and free from vermin. And in likewise manner every woman patient.'

In 1778, it was 'the opinion of this Committee that the Feet of every Patient in Chains or Straw be carefully examin'd, well rubb'd and covered with Flannel by the respective Basket Man or Gallery Maid every night and Morning during the Winter Season and if necessary that immediate Notice be given to the Surgeon'. Later that same year, the committee recommended that every patient be stripped on arrival – not for some barbaric sadistic reason but because it had come to their attention that many patients were being admitted with 'wounds and sores of which their friends neglect to call notice' and that in such cases the surgeon of the hospital needed to be informed immediately.[44]

P. J. Grosley, visiting in 1765, found a cheerful tea party in progress and was invited to join in:

> The president of the assembly was the daughter of a French refugee, and with great good humour gave me the history of her companions: their malady was occasioned either by love or religious enthusiasm. I took the liberty to inquire the cause of her own trouble. She, thereupon, told me a long story, by which I could discover nothing but a great affection for France. Before I entered the hall I inquired whether I could be there with safety, and was assured that I could. This was the gayest and most noisy of all the coteries I had seen in London.[45]

However, Bethlem still had its critics. John Wesley, the founder of Methodism, noted an account from a 'poore woman' which he would never forget. Mrs Shaw's son, Peter, then about nineteen or twenty, fell into 'great unease' upon hearing a sermon by a Mr Wheatley. Mrs Shaw thought Peter was ill, and wanted to send for a physician, but Peter only wanted to see Mr Wheatley, who was duly summoned. After asking a few questions, Wheatley concluded that the boy was mad. 'Get a coach, and carry him to Dr Monro. Use my name. I have sent several such to him.' Mrs Shaw took Peter to Monro's house. When the doctor entered, Peter stood up and said, 'Sir, Mr Wheatley has sent me to you.' Monro asked: 'Is Mr Wheatley your minister?' and asked Peter to put out his tongue. Then, without asking any questions, he told Mrs Shaw to choose her apothecary, and he would prescribe. Next day, according to Dr Monro's orders, they blooded Peter, confined him to a dark room and put a strong blister on each arm, with another all over his head. This treatment continued for six weeks, by which time Peter was so weak he could scarcely stand but remained as mad as before, constantly singing, praying or giving thanks. At this point, Mrs Shaw dismissed the doctor and the apothecary and let her son be 'beside himself' in peace. This led Wesley to remark on the 'inexcusable negligence' of most physicians. 'They prescribe drug upon drug, without knowing a jot of the matter concerning the root of the disorder. And without knowing this they cannot cure, though they can murder, the patient.' Reflecting on the case of a woman who had constant stomach pain, he concluded that her symptoms resulted from bereavement, 'fretting the death of her son. And what availed medicines while that fretting continued? Why, then, do not all physicians consider how far bodily disorders are caused or influenced by the mind?'[46]

Rumours abounded as to other abuses at Bethlem. Tobias Smollett, a surgeon before he turned novelist, commented that 'if you saw a person with a Friday face and a body very thin, you might at once conclude that he had that day come out of Bethlehem or a hospital'. A steward, who was blinded by a fire at the hospital in 1754, died £1,000 in debt to the governors on account of the supplies that he had stolen; one of the governors, Thomas Horne, was expelled in 1777 for taking anything he liked from the buttery over a period of six months, including 'joints, milk, bread, beer, cheese, butter and vomits [emetics]'.[47] Journalists such as 'The Country Spy' and 'Low Life' noted that patients often seemed terrified of their nurses, regarding them with 'a cowed and frightened look', and they were popularly supposed to help dying patients on their way by removing their pillows, while they rifled through the pockets of the soon-to-be-deceased for small change or a snuffbox. Keen to get the inside story, the Country Spy took a crowd of nurses out to a nearby tavern, and portrayed them as 'a swearing, bullying, set of viragoes', who dressed to the nines on high days and holidays: 'she apes the gentlewoman in wearing silk, but the clumsy piece of mortality looks more like an oyster woman, though bedizened to the best advantage'.[48] By contrast, an anonymous French visitor in 1788 praised the 'orderliness, method and cleanliness of the London hospitals',[49] while a compatriot noted the sympathetic treatment meted out to the patients:

I stayed for some time in Bedlam. The poor creatures there are not chained up in dark cellars, stretched on damp ground, nor reclining on cold paving stones, when a moment of reason succeeds to delirium. When they seem to be awakening from a long dream, there is nothing to recall their pitiable condition – no bolt, no bars. The doors are open, their rooms wainscoted, and long airy corridors give them a chance to exercise. A cleanliness, hardly conceivable unless seen, reigns in this hospital. Five or six men maintain this cleanliness, assisted by the patients themselves, when they begin to come to themselves, who are rewarded by small presents.[50]

*

An extraordinary number of leading politicians were mad, by any standards, and a similar instability characterised the leading intellectuals of the day. From Samuel Johnson to William Blake, from Fox to Pitt, insanity seems an inevitable by-product of public and cultural life. A French visitor to Bethlem in 1788 claimed that she saw among the patients 'great men, scholars and philosophers, and shuddered to think that the fall of a slate, an accidental stumble, or a bullet fired by a child might bring to Bedlam a Lord Chatham, a Locke, or even a Newton'.[51] William Pitt the Elder (1708–78), first Earl of Chatham, actually succumbed to madness in 1767. Pitt had suffered acute and recurring attacks of gout from 1766, but a side effect of his medication caused him to become exceptionally irascible. Between 1767–8, the sound of a child's voice or a casual reference to a parliamentary debate was enough to drive him into a frenzy. Suffering from melancholia, he retreated to two rooms in Pitt House, Hampstead, where he would sit all day, leaning on the table and refusing to speak to anyone. The anteroom was equipped with a hatch, where his meals were left on a tray. He would only retrieve them once his servant had gone downstairs.[52]

Allegations of madness proved irresistible to the political cartoonists William Gillray and Thomas Rowlandson, who seized on these anecdotes with relish. According to these caricaturists, Pitt the Younger, Fox and Burke all belonged in Bethlem. In the election of 1783, Pitt defeated Fox and his followers, who had previously held the majority. Fox is reported to have gone raving mad as a result, and Gillray's cartoon *The Incurable* shows him in a straitjacket, being confined to the incurable ward of Bethlem on the orders of Dr Monro.[53]

Burke was thought to have conducted the prosecution of Warren Hastings so viciously that in *Cooling His Brains* (1789), Gillray has consigned him to a cell in Bethlem, where he is shown chained to the floor by heavy fetters, on which are spelt out the verdict of Parliament on his vehement invective. His head is being shaved, but the barber on this occasion is Major Scott, Warren Hastings's agent. Burke is venting a stream of abuse, as he realises that the king is officially receiving the 'monster' responsible for the judicial murder of Nundcomar, an Indian prince hanged in 1788 at the age of seventy.

In *A Peep into Bedlam*, Rowlandson shows 'Peter Pindar' (John Wolcot), the Grub Street hack who ridiculed the private life of George III in *The Lousiad* and *Ode upon Ode* which are lying on the floor. Pindar is shown in the pose of the mad scribbler, a common Bedlam stereotype. Opposite sits Edmund Burke, regarded by his enemies as little more than a madman. Shaved and naked to the waist, he tramples copies of Tom Paine's *Rights of Man* and clutches a rosary, implying that he was a Roman Catholic like his mother, and aligning him in the popular consciousness with the religious maniac. The caricature dates from around 1794, when Burke was condemning the French Revolution. 'Peggy of Bedlam' completes the picture, looming over the pair to crown them with crowns of straw, parodies of the laurel wreaths traditionally bestowed on men of greatness.[54]

The poet Kit Smart, a fellow of Pembroke College and a chronic alcoholic, periodically 'dried out' at Bethlem, courtesy of his college. Smart was addicted to 'hartshorn' (a naturally occurring stimulant also enjoyed by J. M. W. Turner and possibly the inspiration for those incredible sunsets). He was also a religious fanatic – it was said that he prayed so loudly he drove his neighbours to distraction and had to be committed for his own safety, although Samuel Johnson (1709–84) was prepared to overlook this. 'His infirmities were not noxious to society. He insisted on people praying with him; and I'd as lief pray with Kit Smart as any one else. Another charge was that he did not love clean linen; and I have no passion for it.'[55]

Johnson inspected the 'mansions of Bedlam' at least twice. On the first occasion, he was accompanied by two friends, a dramatist called Murphy and Foote, a comedian. The latter was a vicious mimic, and performed a merciless sketch about Johnson's interview with a Jacobite patient, who was hitting his straw under the delusion that he was beating the Duke of Cumberland for the atrocities he performed against the Scots after the battle of Culloden. Johnson, whose sympathies were with the Pretender, urged the man on, encouraging him to redouble his efforts and raining down blows on the straw with his own walking stick.[56] Johnson himself became something of a specialist in the field of literary madness. He noted the case of the poet William Collins (1721–59), suggesting that it was the approach of madness which drove him to the temporary relief of stimulants, the opposite of Smart, who was driven to madness *by* his drug addiction. Johnson was sympathetic to the plight of the mad because he himself was on the borderline, a melancholic and hypochondriac all his life who exhibited the common yet paradoxical combination of being sick of life and afraid of death.[57] He had suffered a nervous breakdown during a vacation from Oxford University in 1729, experiencing overwhelming sensations of irritation and despair, from which he never fully recovered. Johnson never returned to Oxford to finish his degree. But he developed coping mechanisms. His advice to other victims was that: 'It is madness to attempt to think down distressing thoughts; try and divert them.' He would read himself to sleep, and leave a light burning to frighten his demons away.

William Blake (1757–1827), the visionary poet and engraver, had the distinction of being considered mad almost from birth; when he was just six, he saw the face of God looking in at him through the window, and his mother regularly chastised him when he claimed to see angels hovering about his father's hosiery shop. When the family moved to Lambeth, he was distracted by angels hovering over Peckham Rye, and conversed with the Virgin Mary. A radical, he believed in free love and was briefly arrested for suggesting the royal family should be executed. Considered little better than a lunatic by many of his contemporaries, despite his astonishing gifts as a draughtsman, Blake's success was largely posthumous and derived from his Romantic sensibility and his astonishing imagery, such as his vision of the French Revolution as the 'Tyger! Tyger! burning bright/ In the forests of the night'. Most significantly, Blake understood that industrialised London, the city of diurnal night, inhabited by miserable natives and the rootless migrants who had left their pastoral idylls for a life of hardship, was enough to drive anyone to madness:

> I wander thro' each charter'd street,
> Near where the charter'd Thames does flow.
> And mark in every face I meet
> Marks of weakness, marks of woe.
>
> In every cry of every Man,
> In every Infant's cry of fear,
> In every voice, in every ban,
> The mind-forg'd manacles I hear
>
> How the chimney-sweepers cry
> Every blackening Church appals,
> And the hapless Soldiers sigh
> Runs in blood down Palace walls.
>
> But most thro' midnight streets I hear
> How the youthful Harlots curse
> Blasts the new-born Infants tear
> And blights with plagues the Marriage hearse.[58]

*

Witty Horace Walpole, who had witnessed the so-called London earthquake, often referred to his political rivals as potential Bedlamites. This was an apt description of Lord George Gordon, as fit a candidate for the hospital as any of the mad politicians to have graced its walls, and who was responsible for one of London's most notorious outbreaks of collective madness in 1780. Contemporaries described Gordon as a grotesque figure, stiff, lank and solemn, an eccentric, misanthropic MP who attacked all parties, sided with none and had little support among his colleagues. Gordon was obsessed with repealing the Catholic Relief Act. This Act, introduced by Sir George Savile in 1778, was in the Whig tradition of religious toler- ance and also permitted Roman Catholics to join the army, thereby boosting the ranks of troops needed to fight against America, France and Spain. Gordon's response was to incite religious hatred by rais- ing the ancient spectre of a 'Popish plot' which would overthrow the government, enslave England, and turn Smithfield Market into the headquarters of the Inquisition, torturing the populace with stakes and cauldrons.

Astonishingly, over 50,000 people were gullible enough to accept Gordon's conspiracy theories and form a Protestant alliance. Wearing their distinctive blue rosettes, Gordon's supporters cam- paigned tirelessly day and night, leafleting, pasting flyers and daubing the slogan 'No Popery' on all available surfaces, until the mania sparked off a series of riots across the country. On 2 June 1780, a mob of 50,000 marched on Westminster with a petition, deter- mined to take possession of both Houses. By two o'clock in the afternoon the crowds were so dense that it was possible for a small boy, facing the imminent threat of suffocation, to climb up on a man's shoulders and walk across the throng to the open street; a basket, tossed into the crowd, was flung from head to head, and from shoulder to shoulder, and went on spinning and whirling above them, until it was lost to view, without ever once falling among them or coming near the ground.[59]

As for the honourable members: those MPs not already in the

House had to fight their way through the mob. Carriages were stopped and smashed, wheels broken off and windows shattered; footmen and their masters dragged from their seats and rolled in the mud. Those who did struggle through to the lobby arrived with their clothes in tatters and their wigs askew, as the mob raged outside like a many-headed monster. Meanwhile, Gordon was arrested at sword point by one General Conway, and the rioters fled, informed that the Horse Guards were on their way to drive the people back with sabres.

Unrest continued into the night as wild rumours circulated, carried by desperate citizens fleeing the action: Lord Gordon had been sent to the Tower; an attempt had been made upon the life of the king; soldiers had been out shooting the insurgents. As it grew darker, the stories became more terrifying. Thirty-six separate fires were seen blazing in the metropolis. In Holborn, one onlooker witnessed a crowd of women and children fleeing as a red light flickered between the houses and a crowd approached bearing torches and the remnants of a Catholic church which they had just vandalised. With their demon heads and wild eyes, the rioters were a vision of madness, dirty, dusty, fighting, singing and smashing furniture, before flitting onwards into the night.

Quiescent for a day or two, the rioters lay low in yards and stables, flopping down exhausted in the straw. But by Sunday 4 June the mob was reinvigorated, descending on Moorfields, home to several prosperous Catholic families and Bethlem Hospital. Their target was a Roman Catholic chapel in Ropemaker's Alley. According to official sources, they were warned off and spent the night in the open. But, the following morning, in broad daylight, they pillaged and destroyed the chapel and the surrounding houses, right down to the stairs and skirting boards. They seized potential weapons: hammers, pokers, axes, saws and set upon the chapel like a working party, tearing down the altar and reducing pews to firewood. With nobody and nothing to restrain them they lit bonfires and consigned everything to the blaze: statues, vestments, holy pictures, ornaments and furniture. Like madmen on visiting day, the rioters cavorted and danced and howled as the flames lit up the windows of the hospital. The effect upon the patients can only be imagined: some dancing in ecstasy, others shrieking with horror at the prospect of the funeral pyre. That night, it was impossible to tell who were the madder – those inside Bethlem or those outside.

The riots continued the following day, with the mob targeting the home of Sir George Savile in Leicester Square. Susan, sister of the novelist Fanny Burney, witnessed the scene: 'I was terrified & shocked extremely at the rage, & licence of the Mob. In our Observatory the flames before Savile House illuminated the whole square - & my knees went knicky knocky like the Frenchman's in Harlequin's Invasion at the sight.'[60] The rioters were threatening to burn down the prisons and release the prisoners, and a rumour spread that they intended to torch Bethlem and release its desperate inhabitants, which 'suggested such dreadful images to the people's minds and was indeed an act so fraught with new and unimaginable horrors in the contemplation that it beset them more than any loss or cruelty'.[61]

Bethlem went on lockdown. The gates were barricaded, the potential kindling of straw removed from the barn and streamers of blue ribbons hung from the windows. The slogan 'NO POPERY!' was chalked on its walls. The hospital governors were, after all, accustomed to dealing with insanity, and what were these riots but a collective act of madness? Bethlem escaped burning, but the mob, which now appeared to consider themselves as superior to all authority, resolved to burn all the remaining public prisons and demolish the Bank, the Temple, Gray's Inn, Lincoln's Inn, the Mansion House, the royal palaces and the Arsenal at Woolwich. There were two attempts on the Bank of England in one single day, but both attacks were 'feebly conducted and the rioters easily repulsed', several rioters being shot dead by the military and others severely wounded.[62]

When the mob arrived at Newgate, with the intention of setting the prisoners free, they were repulsed by the gaolers, who tried to stop them breaking down the gates. The mob responded by sacking the gaolers' house and setting fire to its contents, doused with turpentine, pitch and tar. Within minutes, the fire gained control and began to spread to the prison itself, blazing high and blackening the prison wall. At first, the crowd looked on in exultation as the blaze burnt so brightly that they could read the time on the clock of St Sepulchre's Church, the hands of which had so often pointed to the hour of execution.

The heat became intense as the blaze spread to neighbouring houses; glass fell from the windows, chimneys crashed through rooftops and the London sparrows, trying to fly away, caught fire on the wing and fluttered down into the furnace. Meanwhile, the prisoners, whom the fire had been intended to free, realised they were about to be burnt alive. Locked up for the night, they had no means of escape from their cells. Their screams could be heard above the roar of the fire and the shouts of the mob. The loudest screams of all came from the four condemned men who were due to be hanged that Thursday, shouting for their lives as though they had more to look forward to than a grisly death at the end of a noose if they did survive. One young man, the son of a condemned prisoner, tried to rescue his father but was beaten back by the flames, again and again, until he skinned his knuckles beating against the blackened stone. Women looked on and shrieked, believing that their husbands would never emerge alive. They beat their hands together, covered their ears and fainted, while men broke up the pavement and hurled cobbles at the walls.

Eventually, the door gave way and many prisoners escaped, trampling down the cinders while Newgate burnt to the ground behind them. Terrified householders heard the prisoners in the street outside, rattling and dragging their chains. The following day, fifty escapees gave themselves up, preferring the predictable misery of gaol to the rioters' anarchy.

Later that same night, the mob moved on to Holborn, where a Mr

Langdale, a Catholic, had a distillery. The flames engulfed the wooden structure and spread swiftly to the surrounding properties, despite the efforts of two soldiers to pull them down. The screaming mob, the distant sound of gunfire, the terrified citizens running out of their houses and the sky itself, deadly red from soaring flames that produced a drift of smoky particles, created a vision of hell. To which was added an even more infernal dimension: the gutters blazed with burning alcohol. Flaming spirits ran through every crack and fissure, forming a deep pool into which people dropped down dead by the dozen. Scooping up the liquid in their bare hands, they drank until they died: husbands and wives, fathers and sons, mothers and daughters, women with children in their arms and babies at their breasts. Some passed out straight away; others danced, half in triumph, half in torment, until they fell into the liquor that had killed them. Burns victims, their clothing still ablaze, mistook it for water and unwittingly hurled themselves into the lake of fire, dying in agony.

The mob had the upper hand. Lacking an organised police force to impose order, the authorities lost control of London for a week. On 9 June, George III ordered the army to move in. By the time order had been restored, 285 rioters had been killed, 173 wounded and 139 arrested. Of these, only 12 were imprisoned and 25 hanged. Damage to property was estimated at £180,000, and Catholics were eventually offered a total of £28,000 compensation by the City of London and £5,200 from the government. Mr Langdale the distiller put his losses for the destruction of his premises at £100,000 but refused compensation, sagaciously asking for a tax waiver instead.[63] After this latest outrage, he realised that people were desperate for a drink. But, as they began to restore and repair their city, Londoners were not to know that the king himself was about to lose his sanity.

'OUR KING IS MAD'

Just as Queen Victoria was to define grief for a generation, the madness of George III influenced popular attitudes towards insanity. George's case history reflects the treatment options available for madness towards the close of the eighteenth century and reveals how his condition affected the popular consciousness and led to greater tolerance and sympathy. The medical historians Richard Hunter and Ida Macalpine conducted a retrospective diagnosis of George III in the 1960s, during which they meticulously examined the evidence of the king's doctors, family and servants, and came to a fascinating conclusion about the true nature of his illness. However, it is their account of his treatment which proves the most interesting, revealing contemporary practices in 'mad doctoring' and the impact of King George's madness on his family, his household and his subjects. A mad country, governed – or rather ungoverned – by mad politicians and a mad monarch, England should have been a laughing stock. But, mad or not, the nation's problems provided comic relief compared with events across the Channel.

George III's sixty crowded years upon the throne (1760–1820) saw the conquest of Canada, the exploration of Australia and New Zealand, the annexation of the West Indies and the colonisation of India. At the same time, Britain suffered the humiliating loss of the American colonies, was shaken by the French Revolution, threatened by Napoleon, and delivered by Nelson and Wellington. At home, Parliament gained ascendancy over the monarchy, a process hastened by George's own illness.

The king's first episode came in 1762, when he was twenty-four and had been on the throne for two years. He was blooded seven times and had three blisters applied. Horace Walpole attributed the disorder to the 'strange, universally epidemic cold' then prevailing, and the preliminary symptoms of later attacks usually included a feverish cold or cough, with stiffness and cramping of the whole body.[1] The first attack lasted for a month or two. Three years later, in 1765, the king was said to be indisposed once again, but a culture of secrecy had already grown up around him, and the mental derangement seems to have passed on after a month or two.

George seems to have been symptom-free for twelve years. But, in 1788, when he was fifty years old, his insanity recurred in a more acute and unmistakable form. On this, and every subsequent occasion, any form of mental stress or excitement precipitated an attack. On 12 June 1788, George snapped, going down with a chill and a 'bilious attack' (sickness and headache) apparently brought on by his failure to change out of wet stockings after getting caught in the rain. The medicines used to tackle his fever, according to one commentator, effectively drove him mad: 'the medicines which they were then obliged to use for the preservation of his life, have repelled [the fever] upon the brain'.[2] The king was attended by Sir George Baker, president of the Royal College of Physicians, but the patient showed little improvement. His condition was subsequently attributed to gout, brought on not by sybaritic living but by a diet of sauerkraut and lemonade. Notably abstemious and hard-working, George favoured a regime of vegetables, wine, and water.[3] To speed up his cure, the doctors dispatched George to Cheltenham Spa to take the waters, and recommended mutton and potatoes to build him up and rhubarb pills as a purge.

But the cure was short-lived and by October 1788 the 'bilious attacks' were back, with George complaining of skin rashes and aching legs. Suffering from poor concentration, he could not understand his dispatches and became delirious. The doctors prescribed opium, a common cure-all considered particularly favourable to the mad as it caused 'a pleasant, gay and good Humour, Courage, Bravery, Magnanimity' and took away 'Sadness, Grief, Melancholy, Fear, Depression of Spirits' and induced sleep.[4]

The official line was that the king was still suffering from gout. But Fanny Burney witnessed manic behaviour: 'He spoke, with a manner so uncommon, that a high fever alone could not account for it; a rapidity, a hoarseness of voice, a volubility, an earnestness – a vehemence, rather – it startled me inexpressibly.'[5] The following day he 'conversed upon his health near half-an-hour, still with that extreme quickness of speech and manner that belongs to fever; and he hardly sleeps, he tells me, one minute all night . . . he is all agitation, all emotion, yet all benevolence and goodness'.[6] As the king's condition grew worse, his citizens were informed that he was 'dropsical' (suffering from oedema). By 5 November, Fanny was writing to her friends that the king had become delirious at dinner, and Queen Charlotte was so upset that she fell into violent hysterics. 'All the Princesses were in misery, and the Prince of Wales burst into tears.'[7] Later, the queen commented that the king's eyes had become so deep and so dark that they were like blackcurrant jelly, and he talked so incessantly that the veins stood out in his face while the foam ran out of his mouth. To the queen's horror, George visited her room later that night, to check she was still there. As she lay in bed, with her lady in waiting at her side, the king stood staring at her for over half an hour.

Dr Baker declared himself sick, perhaps because he felt unable to offer further assistance, and Dr Richard Warren (1731–97) was called in. Warren was a society doctor. It was said of him that when he examined his own tongue in the mirror every morning he auto-matically paid himself, by transferring a guinea from one pocket to the other. Warren promptly concluded that the king's life was in danger and recommended that the Prince Regent take up the reins of power, as George was unlikely to recover his sanity even if he lived. By 9 November the diarist Grenville noted that the king was not expected to survive. It was Lord Mayor's Day, and 'the belief was universal throughout the metropolis, that his Majesty was no more, and that the awful event was with-held from publication, till the Mayor of London was sworn into office'.[8] Warren revised his own verdict on 12 November and stated that the king would survive, but never recover his sanity: *'Rex noster insanit; nulla adsunt febris signa; nulla mortis venturae indicia* – our king is mad; there are no signs of fever; no danger to life.'[9]

George's doctors were in an unenviable position. They were scared of the king, and had to account for themselves to the queen and her ministers. The future of the government hung on whatever they said. They were shadowed by the Prince of Wales and the Chancellor, harassed by public opinion and had the press breathing down their necks. They had to think of their professional reputa-tion, and above all else loomed the remorseless fact that they had no idea what was wrong with their patient.

By 20 November, King George had become completely delu-sional. He believed that London had been flooded and that he had caused it. He composed bizarre letters to foreign courts, and bestowed honours on everybody who came near him. Restraint was the only option. After an unsuccessful attempt to 'sheet' him – a technique that consisted of swaddling the patient in linen so that they could not move – it was resolved to put him in a straitjacket. George Selwyn, Surveyor-General of the Works, wrote: 'Dr Warren, in some set of fine phrases, is to tell his Majesty that he is stark mad, and must have a straitjacket. I am glad that I am not chosen to be that Rat who is to put the bell about the Cat's neck.'[10]

The king's condition was the source of such considerable alarm that the Cabinet decided he had to be placed in the care of a recognised authority on mental illness. Dr Thomas Monro, who was helping his ageing father at Bethlem, was the obvious choice, and Queen Charlotte had no objection to him, but she was reluctant to ask such a popular expert to abandon his duties at Bethlem and his lucrative private practice to devote himself to the king. George himself was reluctant to be treated by a physician so closely associated with Bethlem, and Monro was dismissed.

Eventually, Pitt, one of the few remaining supporters of the royal family, entrusted the king to Dr Francis Willis, who had made his mark on medical history by propagating the notion that insanity was curable.[11] Regarded by some as 'a physician of peculiar skill and practice in intellectual maladies' and by others as little better than a mountebank, Francis Willis (1718–1807), who had originally taken Holy Orders, qualified as a physician later in life in 1759. By 1769, he had established a reputation for treating the mad, using his own home in Dunston, Lincolnshire, as 'a House for Wrongheads'.[12] Willis eventually left Dunston, and set up a madhouse at nearby Greatford, near Stamford. This was inspired by the lunatic colony which had developed around the shrine of St Dymphna of Geel in Belgium. Under this system, the patients stayed two to a cottage, each with a keeper. At first glance, this sounds like a tolerant approach, the antithesis of the miserable private madhouses or the workhouse. Although straitjackets and blistering were regular features of treatment, as in other institutions, the patients had far more freedom. Long walks were encouraged, as it was believed fresh air and exercise were beneficial. A contemporary describes arriving in the village of 'Gretford' and being astonished to see ploughmen, threshers, gardeners and other labourers dressed in black coats, white waistcoats, black silk breeches and with carefully powdered hair. These were Willis's patients carrying out their duties, cheerfulness and neatness of dress being a feature of their treatment.[13] However, one aspect of Dr Willis's approach was anything but progressive: discipline was maintained by fear. The keeper was instructed to respond to violence with violence, and return blow for blow. If a patient escaped, the keeper's wages were stopped and he was liable for any expenses incurred in recapturing his charge.

*

One theory at the time was that separating mad people from their families increased the chance of a cure, so George was transferred to the palace at Kew, but not without a struggle. Once there, he became violent, pulled one page by the hair and attempted to kick another. Oaths and obscenities dropped from his lips – a disturbing new symptom – and he got so depressed he begged one page to kill him. Kew was most definitely not a winter palace. According to Fanny Burney, 'it was in a state of cold and discomfort passed all imagination'. There were no rugs or carpets and sandbags had to be used as draught-excluders. On 5 December Dr Willis arrived. Their first meeting was characterised by a famous exchange:

> George: Sir, Your dress & appearance bespeaks You of the Church, do You belong to it?
> Dr Willis: I did formerly, but lately I have attended chiefly to physick.
> George: I am sorry for it. You have quitted a profession I have always loved, & You have Embraced one I most heartily detest.
> Dr Willis: Sir, our Saviour himself went about healing the sick.
> George: Yes, yes, But he had not *700l* a year for it.[14]

Dr Willis was accompanied by his son and assistant Dr John Willis and three of his keepers. He also brought a straitjacket. To Grenville's horror, Willis stated that his method was to 'break in' patients, like horses in a ménage. That evening, Willis told the king that he was deranged and required management. The king became violently enraged and rushed at him, but Willis stood his ground and told his patient that he must control himself or he would put him in a straitjacket. The item was fetched from the room next door, and from that time 'recourse was frequently had to it'. Willis told Parliament that the king's condition was a result of stress and overwork and that with sufficient care he would recover.

A battle of wills commenced between doctor and patient, with Willis attempting to gain the upper hand with intimidation, coercion and restraint. Willis's regime was strict: 'for every non-compliance – refusing food when he had difficulty in swallowing, no appetite or a return of colic, resisting going to bed when he was too agitated and restless to lie down, throwing off his bed clothes during sweating attacks' – he was clapped into the straitjacket and his legs tied to the bed.

King George was subjected to the standard treatments of the day, which to modern readers appear barbaric. Blisters were applied to his legs which 'discharged well' for weeks, and he was cupped and had leeches placed on his temples for the same reason.[15] But he suffered such agony from the blistering that he had to be confined in the straitjacket and, unable to walk, pushed about in a bath-chair.

The twentieth of December was a particularly unpleasant day which saw George restrained in the straitjacket, his legs tied and his arms fastened across his breast. In 'this melancholy situation' the Willises left him until lunchtime. As he lay, George called out for his 5-year-old daughter: 'Oh Emily [his pet name for Amelia], why won't you save your Father? Why must a King lay in this Damned confined condition? I hate all Physicians but most the Willises they treat me like a Madman.'[16]

Another exquisite refinement in the king's torture was introduced in January 1789. 'The chair', a new one 'made on purpose', consisted of a 'common chair, placed upon a floor of its own, which prevents a Person from moving it, nor can it be thrown down as a common Chair might be'. When the chair was first brought into the room, the poor king was said to have eyed it with some degree of awe.[17] With irony, George dubbed it his 'Coronation Chair'.

The Prince of Wales, the Duke of York and the leaders of the opposition had been speculating about the hopelessness of George's condition, but, for the time being, Dr Willis's treatment confounded them. By February, the king was on the mend. The Willises remained in residence for another month in the event of a relapse, but, by 10 March, the Regency Bill had been shelved, 'his Majesty being, by the blessing of Providence, happily recovered from the severe indisposition with which He has been afflicted'.[18]

That night saw one of the most brilliant exhibitions of national loyalty and joy ever witnessed in England. Initiated by the people, it seemed to be a genuine tribute of their affection. London was a blaze of lights from one extremity to the other, the illuminations extending from Hampstead and Highgate to Clapham, and even as far as Tooting, while the vast distance between Greenwich and Kensington presented the same dazzling appearance, with many houses displaying brilliantly coloured lamps and ingenious stained-glass paintings. Church bells rang and cannons fired. The queen put on a firework display at Kew, depicting the King, Providence, Health and Britannia. George's beloved youngest, 'Emily', presented him with a piece written by Fanny Burney in honour of the occasion. On Saturday, 14 March, the king made a triumphant return to Windsor. Fanny Burney described the occasion as 'a joy amounting to extacy; I could not keep my eyes dry all day long'.[19] Sir Sydney Smith declared that George 'is three stone lighter than he was' while Sir Gilbert Elliot was 'much struck with the alteration in him . . . the King is quite an object of thinness, his face as sharp as a knife'.[20] The king attended a thanksgiving service for his recovery at St Paul's Cathedral on 23 April 1789 – St George's Day. Official medals were struck to commemorate the recovery of the king, and Dr Willis had some struck of his own – for advertising purposes. On one side was depicted Willis, and on the other, 'Britons Rejoice Your King's Restored 1789'.[21] Willis joined the board of governors at Bethlem and received a reward of £1,000 per year for twenty-one years, and his son, Dr John Willis (1751–1835), who had assisted him, received £650 a year for the rest of his life. The cure did much to assist Willis Senior's career: the list of patients admitted to his 'house for wrongheads' between 1801 and 1812 included a fashionable and noble clientele.[22] George sent Willis a gold watch, and in his thank-you letter Willis recommended the king to look after his health, take regular exercise including sea-bathing and sleep at least six hours a night. Another consequence of the massive publicity received from the case had Willis called to the Queen of Portugal, whose illness was characterised by the conviction that she was 'irrevocably doomed to everlasting perdition'. The treatment was unsuccessful but Willis received £20,000 for his efforts.

After a slow convalescence the king made steady progress and twelve years of good health followed, with just a couple of episodes of abdominal pain and indications that he was photosensitive, something he noticed during a visit to Weymouth. The queen's response was to have three double carriages made with cane bodies, covered in silk, which meant he could ride about the countryside at noon without being troubled by the sun.[23]

Inevitably, medical experts of the day were impelled to give their own verdicts on George's condition. Writing in 1789, Dr Robert Jones declared that the king's illness was a 'nervous fever', which should have been treated with tonics and sensible food. He confessed himself astonished to hear that the king had managed to sustain his weighty duties as a head of state while living on vegetables, wine and water, and declared the straitjacket to be 'brutal'. Dr Jones was also frankly appalled by the use of the term 'insanity' with regard to the king as the label was enough to destroy 'a man's credit and happiness for ever'. Worse still, for a monarch, such an imputation 'not only affects the credit and importance of the nation he governs, but must fall upon his offspring: and the more especially, as this disease is supposed, without any ground for such a supposition, to be hereditary'. Dr Jones also argued that George's treatment was completely inappropriate, and that he should have been allowed to see his wife and family whenever he wanted, and offered 'animal food', i.e. meat and dairy, a 'proper quantity of wine' as well as being allowed to listen to music and read his favourite books.[24] In brief, say Hunter and

Macalpine, 'Dr Jones advised the physicians to invigorate the body, and to afford every consolation to the mind of their royal patient – no bad precept for psychiatrists of any age.'[25]

By contrast, Mr Andrew Harper, an obscure army surgeon from the Bahamas and author of *A Treatise on the Real Cause and Cure of Insanity* (1789), argued that George had not actually been mad at all. Harper, who had no formal medical education or experience in treating the mad, was scarcely out to make a name for himself as a society doctor, or publicise a private asylum. In fact, he condemned the 'ignorance and absurdity' of consigning 'the unfortunate victims of Insanity to the cells of Bedlam, or the dreary mansions of some private confinement'.[26] He did not put forward any treatment options for George, but, as a soldier and royalist, clearly saw it as his mission to free the king from the imputation that he was mad, claiming that it was ridiculous to think the king had been driven to distraction 'by abstemious living, severe exercise and want of sleep. These causes produce general debility, and . . . predispose to melancholy; but that they should occasion Insanity is utterly impossible.' Harper also criticised Willis's severe treatment of the king: 'A state of coercion is a state of torture from which the mad under any circumstances, revolts.'[27]

The king's illness later featured discreetly in medical texts. For instance, Dr William Pargeter's *Observations on Maniacal Disorders* published in 1792. Pargeter regarded the king's illness as an outbreak of mania and argued that: '*management did much more than medicine* in the cure of Madness . . . Some few years ago, a case in medicine occurred, which agitated this kingdom, and engaged the attention of all *Europe.* This case was universally, I believe, thought to have been maniacal.'[28] Finally, the Reverend Joseph Townsend, a former medical student at Edinburgh turned Wiltshire vicar, diagnosed the 'case in which the whole nation felt deeply interested' as '*mania melancholia*' or that 'species of mania which is commonly preceded by and alternates with *melancholia*'. Townsend argued that this condition was brought on by 'anxiety and grief, intemperance, deep study, violent passions and emotions, with disappointed love and wounded pride', all of which led to a 'vehement and impetuous circulation of dense and melancholic blood through the weakened and flaccid vessels of the brain'. Two centuries later, all these causes were to re-emerge as classic factors in the development of manic-depressive psychosis.[29]

In 1801 George III suffered another attack, with similar symptoms but of such severity that his life was despaired of. This time, it appeared that the king had suffered organic impairment to the brain. He cried at almost anything, and attempts at paperwork proved disastrous, with George becoming so perplexed that he grew catastrophically angry, and such a fidget that he rolled up handkerchiefs at the rate of fifty a day. The nation was threatened with chaos: at one point over 800 documents went unsigned. Dr John Willis had to oversee the signature of these documents, which gave him an extraordinary amount of power: his duties even extended to being given Cabinet minutes regarding a proposition of peace with France. The presence of the Prince Regent, who wanted to gain power himself, complicated matters, the Prime Minister, Addington, was considered 'weak' and poor Queen Charlotte, herself suffering from ill health, was caught between solicitude for her husband, keeping Willis on and her own anxieties. In his debilitated state the king was almost totally isolated, being surrounded by frightened relatives, impotent politicians and useless doctors.[30] When it was becoming obvious that the king had not recovered, a cruel scheme was devised whereby the doctors kidnapped him and took him back to Kew. On this occasion, Willis's approach was to inspire fear. He believed he could terrify a patient into obedience by staring at him, although George maintained that physical violence had been involved, and that on more than one occasion he had been knocked down, 'flat as a flounder'.[31]

Another attack came in 1804, complicated by failing sight due to cataracts. Dr Samuel Foart Simmons, physician of St Luke's, was called in and George seemed to respond well to the treatment, cheerfully submitting to the straitjacket and other indignities. By 1810, George should have been celebrating fifty years on the throne. Instead, seventy-two years old and virtually blind, he succumbed to his final, and most severe, bout of madness. The attack seems to have been triggered by the death of Emily (Amelia), his favourite daughter, and was characterised by acute mania and severe delusions. Much to the queen's disgust, he became sexually obsessed with the Duchess of Pembroke and was convinced they were conducting an affair. He talked incessantly for hours, telling endless anecdotes about people who had long since died, discussing his own illness and reciting the mad scenes from *King Lear* or the blindness of Milton's *Samson Agonistes*. Sometimes, he conversed with angels, speaking with infinite pity of his loved ones who were still trapped in the mortal sphere. At other times he was lucid: on one occasion Queen Charlotte entered the room to find him playing the harpsichord and singing a hymn, at the end of which he knelt down and prayed to God to free him from his terrible affliction. Then he burst into tears, and succumbed to another episode of madness. The Regency Bill received the Royal Assent in 1811, and George spent the last ten years of his life confined to Windsor Castle, dying insane, just as his ancestor Henry VI had done before him.

While previous authorities had suggested that George's condition was a form of manic-depressive psychosis, Hunter and Macalpine came to a different conclusion, controversial by the standards of the 1960s, when they published their results. After scrupulous examination of George's case history, Hunter and Macalpine deduced that, in the concern about his mental fitness to govern, vital symptoms were missed, and that he was actually suffering from porphyria, a rare genetic disorder. Symptoms of this condition include skin complaints, photosensitivity, coloured urine, hallucinations, paranoia – and excessive hair. In folklore, porphyria gave rise to the myth of the vampire (frightened of sunlight) and the werewolf. The disease itself has blighted northern European royalty for generations.

*

Whatever its cause, the impact of the madness of King George upon the history of psychiatry cannot be overstated. Although his actual periods of insanity added up to less than six months over an eighty-three-year lifespan, his affliction was so public, and so tested practitioners to find a cause and cure, that 'the mad-business', already emerging as a fashionable specialism, was dragged into the limelight. Once mad doctoring had been seen to be beneficial in the treatment of a great personage, it would inevitably become a respectable branch of medicine. After the king's crisis of 1788–9, doctors could never again haughtily disdain acquaintance with the subject. Class also played its part. The aristocracy and the upper classes were the first to accept madness as indicative of a refined and sensitive temperament.

George's encounters with the Willis family may have been barbaric, but there were other therapies which the king was fortunate to avoid, including a primitive form of electric shock treatment, brought about by the invention of the frictional electric machine, similar to a Van de Graaff Generator, which operated by creating static electricity. A craze for electricity galvanised the country, with travelling showmen shocking men, women and children out of their senses for sixpence a time in 1747. In the same decade, the Leyden jar for accumulating electricity was developed, and medical men were swift to spot the therapeutic possibilities of the new agent. First used for local pain relief, it was soon applied to the treatment of paralysis, once doctors realised that an electric shock produced muscle contractions. It was inevitable that nervous disorders would be the next target. By 1756 Richard Lovett, lay clerk of Worcester Cathedral, published *The Subtil Medium Prov'd*, an account of electricity's 'various Uses in the animal Oeconomy, particularly when apply'd to Maladies and Disorders incident to the human Body',[32] which attracted the attention of John Wesley, the founder of Methodism. A humane man, Wesley had already protested against James Monro's brutal regime at Bethlem, and argued the case for 'electricity made plain and useful'.

Electricity soon became an accepted form of treatment, and electrical machines and departments were established in the London hospitals. In 1793 the first 'electrical dispensary' was founded in London, 'with a view to afford a new benefit to the lower orders of mankind'. In its first year, 3,274 patients were treated; 1,401 were pronounced cured and 1,232 were 'relieved'. Benjamin Franklin received two severe electric shocks during his own experiments with electricity. He was knocked unconscious and suffered from temporary amnesia. Enthusiastically, he suggested 'trying the practice on mad people!' His recommendation was taken up by John Birch, surgeon to St Thomas's Hospital, and George Adams, whose family of instrument makers supplied the machines. Birch subsequently wrote up his experimental treatment of a patient suffering from 'melancholy' by treating him with electrical currents applied direct to the head and passed through the brain.

A porter from one of the East India warehouses was sent to Birch in November 1787, in a state of melancholy induced by the death of his child and a previous breakdown. The patient had been afflicted for two weeks by the time Birch examined him. He allowed his wife to lead him about the house, but never spoke to her. He showed little interest in his surroundings, and sighed frequently. His appetite and sleep were moderate, and his pulse was slow.

Birch covered the patient's head with a flannel, and rubbed the electric sparks all over his cranium; he seemed to find this 'disagreeable' but said nothing. On his second visit, 'finding no inconvenience had ensued', Birch passed six small sparks through the brain in different directions. The moment the patient went into the next room and saw his wife, he spoke to her, and by the evening he was cheerful and talking about going back to work. Birch repeated the treatment in the same manner on the third and fourth day, after which the patient returned to work. Birch followed him up for three months, and then discharged him, asking him to return if he had a relapse.

Another of Birch's cases was a popular singer, who became

extremely melancholy from a variety of distressing causes. His disease had gained ground upon him so severely that he was unable to work, although his physical condition was sound, his appetite moderate and his body regular. Birch treated him in the same manner as his previous patient, with a series of six shocks passed through the head. Within a fortnight, the singer was asking Birch if he should accept a booking for a summer season at one of the theatres. Birch told the singer that he should go ahead if he felt equal to the engagement. Birch continued to treat him for the next fortnight, at the end of which the singer made a confession. Before the consultation, he told Birch, he had been determined to put an end to his life, and had pensively walked along the banks of the Serpentine in Hyde Park, 'when a thought of religion impressed him with the horror of the design'. Another time, he had taken up his razor, only to be prevented by the footsteps of a friend approaching. The same day, he sought out Birch, a matter, he believed, attributable to divine intervention. He said that the shock treatment had led to a refreshing sleep, and that subsequently he had woken up every day feeling like a new man, and was full of admiration for the remarkable change that the powers of electricity had wrought in his mind. After this conversation, Birch discharged the singer, 'and he fulfilled his engagement that summer with his usual applause'.[33]

According to Hunter and Macalpine, shock treatment derived and gained clinical support from three different sets of clinical observations: the first was that systemic diseases, especially the febrile variety, often were terminated favourably by a 'crisis'; the second was that the insane appeared to improve following illness or injury, and the third that some patients with hydrophobia, the consequence of rabies, appear to have been cured by the shock of 'having been several times cast into Water', as Goulart wrote in 1607. As a result, from the classical period onwards, doctors attempted to reproduce natural crises artificially in the insane by any means possible – purges like hellebore, which induced vomiting and diarrhoea, bleedings, narcotics, all designed to induce a 'revulsion of the system' severe enough to alter the patients' minds. These methods acted either by interfering directly with the brain and the metabolism (as in the case of opium, for example) or causing apathy and forgetfulness of depressive, delusional or hallucinatory ideas and feelings.

One particularly horrific method was that of producing shock *usque ad deliquum* – 'to the brink of death'. Similar to the ducking treatment used to test witches, it worked on the principle of suffocating mad ideas, and was introduced by the Dutch physician and philosopher J. B. van Helmont in 1692. The basis of his theory was the supposed antagonism between water and hydrophobia and hence insanity. Helmont believed that in both conditions the 'too violent and exorbitant Operation of fiery Life' required extinction with water. Patients were rendered unconscious by being suspended head first under water until 'their upper Parts were drowned' after which they were revived – if possible. Thomas Willis in 1683 wrote up treating a 'furious maid' by ordering that she be carried out of doors by women in the middle of the night, 'and put into a Boat, and her Cloths being pull'd off, and she tyed fast with a Cord, should be drenched in the depths of the River' – with strict instructions 'that she might not be stifled in the Water'.[34]

Helmont's second, more sympathetic cure for melancholy was based on the principle that since our thoughts and ideas are formed out of water, weeping was the best treatment, permitting the watery humour 'to run away in tears', a precursor of the therapeutic axiom of having a good cry – and he noted that 'persons over-taken with some great grief or affliction, when they cannot discharge their Sorrow by weeping, do often fall into some Distemper or Sickness, because the Idea of the cause of their Sorrow, by this means encreaseth, and continues still present with them'.[35]

King George III's own sympathy towards the mad was demonstrated by his compassionate treatment of Margaret Nicholson, who

*Margaret Nicholson, who attempted to kill King George III
with a cake knife.*

attempted to stab him in 1786, after his first attack of madness but
before he endured the second, florid bout. Originally from
Yorkshire, Margaret Nicholson (1745–1828) had been a high-
ranking servant, employed by the aristocracy. In her youth, she had
become the mistress of a Guards officer, and even moved into his
marital home, only to become destitute when he died. She took a
number of jobs in service, but, desperate to keep up appearances,
fell into a life of genteel poverty, skipping meals to buy clothes and
even having to share a bed with a maidservant (she could only
afford to pay half her keep). It is scarcely surprising to learn that by
this stage, Margaret was regarded as mad, and often talked to herself. Matters were not improved by a fling with a Swiss valet which
resulted in the loss of her job. Hoping for marriage as a solution,
Margaret was doubly devastated when he abandoned her. By 1786,
at the age of forty-one, she was living in reduced circumstances at
the home of Mr Fiske, a stationer, in Wigmore Street, Marylebone,
and struggling to survive as a seamstress, the only option for women

no longer considered 'respectable' enough for domestic service. Mr
Fiske later admitted that Margaret was 'very odd at times'[36] and
suffered from delusions of grandeur. Margaret had become
obsessed with the royal family, and seemed desperate to obtain a
post in the royal household, although she went a strange way about
it, maintaining that George III was not entitled to be king. In 1786,
she sent a George a petition on the theme of tyrants, usurpers and
pretenders. According to *Sketches in Bedlam* (1823), this is what happened next:

> On the 2nd of August 1786, as the King (George III) was alight-
> ing from his chariot at the garden entrance to St James's [Palace],
> a woman, very decently dressed, in the act of presenting a peti-
> tion, which His Majesty was receiving with great condescension,
> struck a concealed knife at his breast; which happily he avoided
> by drawing back. As she was making a second thrust, one of the
> yeomen caught her arm, and, at the same instant, one of the
> King's footmen wrenched the knife from her hand. The King,
> with great temper and fortitude, exclaimed, 'I am not hurt: take
> care of the poor woman; do not hurt her, for she is mad.'[37]

Margaret was easily overpowered and arrested, and spent hours in
custody without saying a word. She was even strip-searched, to
ensure that she was not actually a man disguised as a woman to
achieve his evil purpose. When she finally spoke, Margaret broke
down and claimed that it had all been a mistake: she had been
reaching for the petition, but pulled out an ivory-handled dessert
knife instead, which strikes one as a bizarre defence: how many
people go equipped to eat pudding? And this defence was soon
undermined by the discovery of Margaret's petition among the
king's papers, and her extraordinary claim that the crown belonged
to her and if she did not receive it, 'England would drown in blood
for a thousand generations.'[38] Margaret's landlord, Mr Fiske, was
dragged out of bed in the middle of the night and interrogated

separately as the authorities suspected the pair were involved in a conspiracy. He was seized with such violence that his wife, seven months pregnant, was taken ill.

The authorities, suspecting that Margaret was counterfeiting madness to escape Bridewell, sent for the Monros to ascertain her mental state. But when she appeared before the privy court Margaret behaved in such 'a very wild and extravagant manner' that it left nobody in any doubt. Interviewing her, Dr John Monro and his son Thomas had both agreed that 'having paid every proper attention to the culprit, and particularly having visited her that morning, she was insane'.[39] John Monro added that she was the worst case he had ever seen: 'in her conversation yesterday she burst out without any apparent cause into a fit of Laughter so violent as to make it necessary for her to support herself against the back of a chair', and that she must have been in this state for at least ten years. The Monros' testimony as expert witnesses, together with the discovery of further letters attesting to Margaret's right to the throne, was enough to send her straight to Bethlem without facing trial. As Mr Fiske commented, Margaret had finally got what she wanted: a job for life at His Majesty's pleasure.

Arriving at Bethlem, she was greeted by Dr Monro and treated kindly by the steward, Henry Weston, who invited her to dine with his household. Margaret conducted herself very well at dinner, apart from remarking that she expected a visit from the king. At four o'clock, she was taken to her cell, where she was chained to the floor by one leg. She appeared perfectly composed, asking only if she could have a pen and paper. Margaret spent the following six months in solitary confinement. Eventually, King George sent word saying that he wished Margaret to receive sympathetic treatment and care from the hospital. As a result, Margaret spent the rest of her life as an 'incurable' in the criminal wing. It was four years before Margaret was permitted to leave her cell, but she was granted certain privileges: she did not have to mix with the other criminal lunatics and was permitted tea, gingerbread and tobacco snuff, which she took in large quantities. A model patient, Margaret lived out her days in Bethlem, and died in 1828 at the age of eighty-three.

*

As the potential assassin of George III, Margaret became an object of fascination. Another would-be regicide emerged as equally notorious in the form of James Hadfield (c. 1771–1841). A soldier in the 15th Dragoons, Hadfield was injured at the battle of Incelles, having his arm broken by a musket ball and receiving several sabre wounds to the head. The head injury caused brain damage, leading to a complete change in his personality. Discharged from the army on medical grounds, he became deluded, telling anyone who would listen that the end of the world was nigh. From 1796, Hadfield found work as a silversmith in London. Just as he seemed to be reconciling himself to his mental illness and life in Civvy Street, Hadfield encountered Bannister Truelock, a religious fanatic who convinced him that the Messiah himself was about to issue out of Truelock's mouth, and the only thing which lay between them and the Second Coming was George III himself. Truelock persuaded Hadfield that if he killed the king, all the obstacles to the progress of their religion would be removed. Hadfield, he claimed, had been chosen to accomplish this task. Hadfield's condition was deteriorating: on 14 May 1800, he attempted to kill his baby son, 'for the benefit of mankind'.

Filled with remorse, Hadfield felt that he should die, too, but, reluctant to commit suicide, he imagined that an assassination attempt would result in his own death at the hands of others. Two days later, on 16 May 1800, Hadfield arrived at the Drury Lane Theatre, armed with a pistol, and an array of lead shot, slugs and bullets. When the doors of the theatre pit were opened, and the crowd surged forward, a young woman declared: 'Oh, sir! The handle of your umbrella is running into my breast!' That was no umbrella: it was the butt of Hadfield's pistol. James Smyth, author of *Sketches in Bedlam*, takes up the story:

His Majesty had scarcely entered his box, when in the act of bowing with his usual condescension to the audience, a pistol was fired by Hadfield, who sat in the pit on the second row from the orchestra. The ball struck the roof of the royal box, just at the moment when the Queen and princesses were entering. His Majesty with great presence of mind, waved his hand as a signal to dissuade the royal party from making their immediate appearance, and instantly standing erect, raised his right hand to his breast, and continued bowing for some minutes to his loyal subjects . . . After the first moments of astonishment had subsided, some musicians from the orchestra seized Hadfield, and dragged him over the pallisadoes into the music room.[40]

Hadfield went on trial for treason, but it soon became evident that he was insane, and medical evidence was given in his defence:

Mr Cline, the surgeon, said that he examined the wounds of the prisoner yesterday. He had no doubt that the sabre cuts in his head had injured the brain, nor any difficulty in assigning this as the probable cause of his present madness. A man under such circumstances might sometimes wear the appearance of sanity if there was no exciting cause to provoke his delirium. Dr Creighton said that he had no doubt but that the prisoner was insane. He could converse coolly on common topics, but when he spoke to him of religion, or of the crime for which he now stood arraigned, he immediately betrayed symptoms of derangement. He was not a maniac; his insanity was of a particular kind. When he asked him respecting this attempt on the King's life, his answer was, that he knew he was ordained to die a sacrifice like Jesus Christ.[41]

Hadfield's defence counsel, Erskine, pointed out that it is 'most difficult to draw up a line between a perfect and a partial insanity, and that such cases should be well weighted, lest there should be an injustice on the one side, or too much indulgence on the other'. Erskine would not say that an 'idle and frantic humour' constituted an excuse for committing every offence, only that the man's state of mind at the time of committing it should be taken into consideration. He successfully convinced the jury that Hadfield's mind was 'most dreadfully deranged' and hence that 'by the laws of England he cannot be found guilty'.[42] Hadfield was found not guilty by reason of insanity and he was sent to Bethlem, where Truelock also became a patient. Two years later, Hadfield assaulted another patient, Benjamin Swain, by punching him in the head. Swain tripped over a bench and fell to the ground, dead. It was alleged that Hadfield had murdered Swain, but the hospital authorities maintained that the death was a tragic accident. Soon afterwards, Hadfield escaped, getting as far as Dover before he was arrested and sent to Newgate for fourteen years, after which he returned to Bethlem. Smyth describes him in 1823 as a grumpy old man, but not without his distractions: 'Though his manners and language are those of a vulgar, low-bred fellow, he is cleanly in his person and regular in his habits and ingenious in his amusements. He makes handsome straw baskets, which he is permitted to sell to visitors, and for which he obtains from 3s. 6d. to 7s. 6d. each. He receives a pension from the government of 6d. per day in consideration of his former military services.'[43] Surrounded by pet birds and cats, Hadfield wrote poetry which he sold to visitors, and he had other interests, too: in 1826 he applied to the authorities for 'liberty to hold communication with a Female through the Railings'; just what sort of communication is explained by the fact that permission was refused 'on account of the great indecency of his conduct on former occasions'.[44] The hospital paid for a wig to cover Hadfield's head-wound in 1833. After his death, in 1841, a post-mortem confirmed that this wound had indeed caused the brain damage which gave rise to his severe mental disorder.

*

Margaret Nicholson and James Hadfield were held under the provision of George III's Criminal Lunatics Act, confined indefinitely at Bethlem rather than facing the gallows for treason. This was a typically sympathetic piece of enlightened Georgian legislation, showing a growing awareness of the plight of the mad. It was a similar spirit of concern which drove the Quaker philanthropist Edward Wakefield to visit Bethlem in 1814. Wakefield, who had drawn up plans to create a new asylum in London, was not made welcome. While the hospital was desperate for government funding, the last thing the governors wanted was adverse publicity. As Wakefield was to discover, Bethlem had deteriorated behind its beautiful façade. When Wakefield arrived with a hospital governor, Alderman Cox, on 25 April 1814, the steward, Peter Alavoine, tried to prevent them from gaining entry. Undeterred, Wakefield returned on 2 May, with another governor and Charles Weston, an MP. Wakefield's account of the visit, given before the parliamentary select committee on madhouses the following year, makes grim reading.

In the women's galleries, Wakefield found that one sick room contained about ten patients, each chained by one arm or leg to the wall, the chain allowing them merely to stand up by the bench or form fixed to the wall, or to sit down on it. The nakedness of each was covered by a blanket-gown only. Even the feet were naked. In another room he encountered a former governess, half-naked and chained to the wall. Wakefield and his colleagues were particularly outraged by this treatment of a lucid, young, middle-class woman, surrounded by 'wretched beings'.[45] Conditions were no better for the men, with six patients chained to a wall, five handcuffed, and one particularly noisy case manacled by his right arm and leg. Another witness testified to seeing patients fastened to benches and tables, stark naked and freezing cold. Apart from putting them in isolation, there was no way of separating 'mild and frantic patients', which inevitably led to violent assaults, including one Polish soldier brutally attacked by another. Wakefield, clearly a man with an agenda, may have been provocative and sensational in his reports, but intervention was clearly essential. One of the most poignant observations was that the patients, both men and women, welcomed visitors and missed life outside. Their window, overlooking Fore Street, had become the chief source of entertainment, their window on the world.

Wakefield singled out two patients as exceptional examples of poor treatment. The first was James Tilley Matthews, former tea-broker in Leadenhall Street and self-confessed spy. Matthews, considered dangerous to king and country, had been charged with spying after travelling to France as an unofficial peace envoy during the Napoleonic wars. As an English citizen of French descent, he had apparently offered his services to Lord Liverpool as a double-agent. Receiving no reply from Liverpool, Matthews had denounced the lord from the public gallery of the House of Commons as a diabolical traitor and been committed to Bethlem as a result. Matthews was admitted in 1797 and placed on the incurable list the following year. A well-educated, cultured man, he suffered from elaborate hallucinations, but he was not violent, and there were several attempts to have him released. Matthews was allowed a special room, with many privileges, where he could draw and write. Intrigued by this patient, John Haslam, the apothecary, produced a book entitled *Illustrations of Madness* (1810), containing first-person accounts of Matthews's feelings and sensations. It constitutes one of the first psychiatric case histories. If, as we have seen, Matthews was deemed eccentric but harmless, his detention in Bethlem seems unjustified. Wakefield certainly thought so, stating that Matthews was 'a very unfit person for confinement in Bethlem'.

Matthews's incarceration becomes more understandable given the climate of the times. Not only was England at war with France, but on the domestic front, the Luddite movement threatened to sweep away the monarchy. The authorities had just cause to be nervous: on Monday, 11 May 1812, the Prime Minister, Spencer

Perceval, was assassinated by John Bellingham, who was hanged within days. Bellingham was described as 'an alleged lunatic' but all his claims to insanity were dismissed before witnesses could be called. While Margaret Nicholson and James Hadfield had been spared and sentenced to life at Bethlem, successful assassins were not to be given a second chance. There was an ambivalent reaction to Bellingham's execution, with a cheering crowd accompanying him to the scaffold, not because he was a murderer, but because Perceval had been viewed as a draconian authority figure, totally bent on the destruction of their liberties. The assassination was to have a permanent impact on two of Perceval's sons. The oldest, Spencer Perceval Junior, became an MP and a lunacy commissioner. A religious enthusiast, he apparently went mad in the House of Commons in 1832. The younger brother, John Thomas, had a breakdown in 1831 and, after writing an influential book on his experiences in Ticehurst Asylum, helped found 'the Alleged Lunatics Friendly Society' in 1845.

*

James Tilley Matthews was diagnosed by Dr Thomas Monro and Haslam as suffering from 'political delusions', confirmed by Matthews's descriptions and immaculate technical drawings of the 'Air Loom'. Matthews believed that a criminal gang, profoundly skilled in pneumatic chemistry, lived near Moorfields and tormented him with this diabolical machine emitting rays which possessed his mind and created an appalling stench. These 'thought waves' could even be ratcheted up to different speeds, including the ominous 'Lobster-cracking' and 'Brain Saying' which produced thoughts in Matthews's head against his will. The 'Air Loom Gang' were a Jacobite gang intent on forcing England into war with France, and included 'Bill the King' (the ringleader of the tormentors), 'Jack the Schoolmaster', the innocent young Charlotte, who apparently spent most of her time chained up naked, 'Sir Archy', a woman who dressed as a man and swore constantly, and the sinister 'Glove Lady' who actually operated the machine. This crew inflicted the most excruciating tortures on their victim. With the turn of a lever or the flick of a switch they infected his blood, or induced agony in his nerves and muscles. Matthews also maintained that his 'Air Loom Gang' was but one of many all over London, influencing the minds of politicians and public figures, including the Prime Minister, William Pitt, over whom they had a particularly firm grasp. He even maintained that one gang had inspired his fellow patient, Hadfield, to assassinate George III.

Diagnosed as suffering from persecution mania, or paranoid schizophrenia in modern terminology, Matthews died in 1814 in Fox's London House Asylum in Hackney, to which he had been moved for a change of air. But there is another dimension to Matthews's sad case: leaving aside his mental deterioration, the possibility exists that he really was a spy, a theme explored in more detail by Greg Hollingshead in his excellent historical novel *Bedlam*.

*

Wakefield's most sensational investigation concerned the fate of James Norris, an American marine who had been harnessed and chained up for fourteen years. A sketch of Norris in chains by an artist called Arnold was engraved by George Cruikshank and widely circulated in the press. Editors seized on this outrage with relish and characteristic inaccuracy, printing 'William [sic] Norris" portrait and telling the world that 'this unfortunate Man was confined about Twelve Years, in the Manner represented in this Engraving, in Bethlem Hospital. Of which Hospital Dr MUNRO [sic] is the Physician, and Mr JOHN HASLAM the Apothecary'.

Norris had been admitted to Bethlem in 1800 through the Office for Sick and Wounded Seamen, and transferred to the incurable wing a year later. Wakefield was told he was fifty-five years old, and had been confined for around fourteen years. When Wakefield went to visit he found Norris confined in an extraordinary contraption designed to prevent him from movement. He was fastened to a long chain which went through the partition into the cell next door and enabled his keeper to drag him close to the wall whenever the keeper wished. Norris tried to stop this by wrapping the chain in straw, to stop it going through the wall, but his attempts were hopeless, as he had a stout iron ring fastened round his neck, connected to an upright iron bar which was 6 feet high. Another iron bar, about 2 inches wide, was riveted around his upper body, and another device pinioned his arms close to his sides to stop him lashing out at his keepers. He was also secured at the waist by further bars and chains.[46]

The harness, which had been in place since June 1804, showed that Norris could scarcely move, as the chains were only 12 inches long. The publicity surrounding Norris's case caused uproar, and gave Wakefield the evidence he needed to promote reform. But when he returned to Bethlem on a subsequent visit, accompanied by a group of MPs, Wakefield discovered that Norris's harness had been modified, and the chains lengthened.

Again seeing the opportunity for a cause célèbre, Wakefield did not mention the rationale behind Norris's draconian restraint. Diagnosed as a 'dangerous and incurable lunatic' on 14 February 1801, Norris was extremely violent. In 1803 he stabbed one of the keepers, who had gone into his cell to quieten him down. According to one eyewitness, the keeper struck Norris, who retaliated, 'and the consequence was, Norris being a very powerful man, he got him down, and would have murdered him perhaps with a shovel, but that one of the patients went to the assistance of the keeper, and that Norris stabbed him with a knife; I believe he stabbed both the keeper and the patient, and that was the reason of Norris being solitarily confined. The keeper was in a state of intoxication.'[47]

According to a subsequent investigation by the governors, Norris's violence increased and 'his bodily strength being considerable, and his cunning and dexterity greater than those of any other patient, he became a terror to every person whose duty or inclination brought them into the Hospital'. By 1804 he had bitten another patient's finger off and urgently needed stronger restraints, hence the manufacture of the apparatus in which Wakefield found him. The governors concluded that the apparatus was a good method of restraining a dangerous patient, and caused him no pain, as it incorporated 'an open worked frame encircling the body with apertures for the arms', enabling the patient to 'feed himself, to keep himself clean, and to assist himself in the ordinary evacuations of nature'.[48] Norris's restraint appears barbaric, but is understandable as a means of protecting the staff and other patients in the days before the 'chemical cosh'. Bethlem's governors maintained that Norris's treatment was humane and that the patient was furnished with books and papers, and spent the time playing with his pet cat, which also performed the role of controlling vermin.

*

Wakefield's investigation of Bethlem was just one of a number of inquiries being conducted up and down the country. Intended as refuges of solace for the poor and the demented, asylums had developed a reputation as massive and gloomy mansions, little better than prisons, with unglazed windows guarded with strong iron bars, narrow corridors, dark cells and desolate courts, where no tree, nor shrub, nor flower, nor blade of grass grew, presided over by terrible attendants, armed with whips, accompanied by savage dogs and free to impose manacles, chains and straps, at their own brutal will. It was scarcely surprising that people viewed these buildings with horror, and walked the long way round after sunset, to avoid hearing the cries and yells which made night hideous.[49]

Godfrey Higgins, a local magistrate, investigated one such asylum, at York, after allegations of cruelty from a former plaintiff. He had committed an offender to the asylum in good physical health, only to hear from the man's wife months later that he had been so badly treated he was unfit for work. Higgins investigated and exposed appalling abuse, including records forged to conceal deaths among the patients, widespread use of chains, embezzlement, 'conditions of utter filth and neglect', rape and murder.[50] A building designed for fifty-four patients held 103; one cell 8 feet square contained thirteen women and he discovered hidden cells the sight of which made him vomit. The *York Herald* campaigned for further inquiries after exposing the case of Hannah Mills, a melancholy girl from Leeds who had died in the asylum and whose parents had never received a satisfactory explanation. But before any inquiry could proceed, York Asylum burnt to the ground in a mysterious fire in December 1813, killing four patients and destroying all records.

A select committee on lunacy was convened in 1815 as a response to the public outcry. Led by the reformers Sir George Rose and Lord Ashley, this powerful committee included William Tuke, whose own madhouse, the Retreat at York, was a bastion of enlightened or 'moral' treatment, and important parliamentarians such as Peel the Younger, Lord Robert Seymour and Sir William Curtis. Under scrutiny were Bethlem, York, St Luke's, Nottingham County Asylum and Tuke's own Retreat, as well as the conditions of pauper lunatics in workhouses. While the latter came under the jurisdiction of the Poor Law (an early form of social welfare), hospitals such as Bethlem were privately run and unaffected by legislation. The select committee exposed enormous discrepancies in treatment and conditions between the different establishments.

In addition to Wakefield's evidence, employees at Bethlem were cross-examined about the state of the hospital. One George Wallet, who had taken over as steward after Alavoine was sacked, provided some disturbing details of conditions: two male and two female keepers struggled to supervise sixty-eight female patients and fifty-two male. Patients' 'cribs' or beds were lined with straw which was changed once a week, conditions regarded as unacceptable in the average stable. The weekly diet was divided into four 'meagre days' consisting of porridge, bread, cheese and beer, and three 'meat days' (seven ounces of meat, potatoes and more beer).

Wallet's evidence became more alarming as he revealed that, while the keepers struggled to contain their unruly, undernourished patients, the physician of Bethlem was notable by his absence. When asked how often Dr Thomas Monro attended, Wallet replied: 'I hear he has not been round the house but once these three months.'[51] Haslam, by contrast, attended regularly, but only for half an hour a day, visiting only specific patients. By this stage, another event cast a shadow over Bethlem, leading Monro and Haslam to panic and blame each other: James Norris had died on 26 February 1815.

The official cause of death was tuberculosis, but Wakefield stated that extreme confinement and lack of exercise had taken its toll. Wallet admitted that Norris had died of 'constipated bowels', a post-mortem confirming that, as a consequence of the long state of constipation, Norris's intestines had burst.

Monro held Haslam responsible for Norris's death. Haslam then attacked the reputation of Dr Bryan Crowther, the former surgeon to Bethlem and Bridewell, who had died in April 1815. Haslam claimed Crowther had been an alcoholic, and so insane for the last decade of his life 'that his hand was not obedient to his will' and he regularly required a straitjacket. (The psychiatric historians Hunter and Macalpine subsequently believed, after studying Crowther's handwriting, that he had suffered from Parkinson's disease.)

Monro, an eloquent orator, accustomed to soothing the nerves of his wealthy clientele, defended his regime, telling the committee that he used the same treatments as his late father, Dr John Monro, and saw no reason to change them. He admitted that his private practice at Brook House took up the majority of his time. As a fashionable society doctor, Monro was not unusual in concentrating on his private practice. But then Monro admitted that he never kept records and further condemned himself by stating that there was one treatment for the rich, and another for the poor, declaring that chains were fit only for pauper lunatics: if a gentleman were put in irons, he would not like it. More damning still, he argued that there was no cure for madness and that the patients were not given medicine during the winter months as the hospital was so cold that it was thought inappropriate.

Further evidence of the appalling conditions at Bethlem came in 1818, with the publication of a pamphlet by a former patient who rejoiced in the name of Urbane Metcalf. The author, a hawker who sold ribbons and garters door to door, had spent periods in Bethlem between 1805 and 1817, under the delusion that he had a claim to the throne of Denmark. Metcalf was 'a neat little man, of peculiar aspect: his face curiously formed, small and sallow, with a stiff black beard; his eyes diminutive, black and piercing, like those of a water rat'.[52] Although the authorities dismissed him as a troublemaker, it appears that 'his innuendoes against two or three of the officials were not wholly symptoms of diseased and irritable nerves'.[53] Mattresses, for instance, were never entirely dry: they were taken to an upper room, deloused and washed, but never dried out. 'I myself had a damp bed given me which I laid on for some time, and fear I shall feel the effects of it through my future life,' he wrote, 'as I have for some months past been subject to a pain in my loins, which I never had before.'[54] Incontinent patients were kept in the cellars, where they slept naked on loose straw that caused outbreaks of scabies. Down there, out of earshot of Dr Monro and the governors, they became the tortured playthings of sadistic keepers.

Although he had nothing but praise for 'Mr Wallet, whose kindness never sleeps',[55] Metcalf claimed that the entire hospital was run for the benefit of the staff, many of whom were cruel and drunk, and who enforced order by instructing stronger inmates to bully the weak. The ringleaders were 'three villains', a despicable trio named Blackburn, Rodbird and Allen, 'wretches whose least crime is an abuse of humanity'.[56] Metcalf's catalogue of abuse included the case of poor Popplestone, whose leg rotted off as he was chained up for such a lengthy period that the metal cut into his flesh, and an incident during which a Mr Baccus, eighty-six, collapsed in the green yard. When a fellow patient trod on him, Blackburn encouraged the patient to go on stamping; 'Baccus,' we are told, 'is since dead'.[57]

In 1816, the report of the select committee was sent to the

governors of Bethlem, who promptly refused to re-elect Monro and Haslam. Cast as the scapegoat for conditions at Bethlem, Haslam found himself unemployed and without a pension at the age of fifty-two. He was so poor that he was compelled to sell his library, a lifetime collection of 1,000 medical books. But, four years later, Haslam retrained as a physician and ended his days as a fellow of Pembroke College, Cambridge. The Monro dynasty was not finished yet: although Dr George Tuthill became the new physician of Bethlem, Edward Thomas Monro, son of Thomas Monro, was made second physician. Haslam was replaced as apothecary by Edward Wright, who had trained at Edinburgh and had a keen interest in phrenology.

Wakefield's investigation and the subsequent select committee

Chained up for twelve years – the American marine William Norris,
whose treatment caused a scandal.

eventually led to the 1828 Madhouses Act designed to 'regulate the Care and Treatment of Insane Persons'. This legislation was slow to develop, held back in more than one instance by members of the House of Lords who had a vested financial interest in private mad-houses and who feared they would lose revenue in the event of reform.

Bethlem's chaotic management and institutionalised failure was reflected in its physical structure: since 1800, the 'palace beautiful' had been in a state of collapse. Sir William Bolton, complaining about the state of the cement during its construction, had been vin-dicated, and, once again, the hospital was on the move.

SCANDAL!

After less than 125 years, the palace beautiful, where Swift and Cowper had glimpsed their future in the faces of raving patients, was fit only for demolition. John Howard, founder of the League for Penal Reform, had commented on the structural problems, the lack of water supply to the upper floors and the failure to segregate violent patients from passive. The roof leaked, the cellars were unwholesome and the hospital had not been painted for fifteen years. The surveyor James Lewis presented an alarming report stating that the entire structure was dangerously insecure because of subsidence. Not one floor was level, or one wall upright. The walls, staggering under a heavy roof, had not been tied together throughout the whole of the buildings, as they should have been; and the brick piers in the basement, designed to carry the weight of the superstructure, had been whittled away to provide extra storage.[1] The foundations had not been laid on piles but instead rested precariously on the soft soil of the old London moat. Fissures and settlements were visible everywhere, summoning up an alarming vision of the entire hospital collapsing into a vast hole in the ground. Repairs would cost £8,000 and take five years to complete.

And Bethlem's locale had changed. Once open and airy, Moor-fields had become crowded and noisy. Finsbury Pavement encroached on the west of the hospital, and on the north and east stood ranks of sheds, occupied by old-clothes sellers and second-hand furniture dealers with stalls full of cracked mirrors and broken-down beds. The governors had no choice: Bethlem must be rebuilt once more, elsewhere.

The new Bethlem was among a number of dedicated lunatic asy-lums being built at the time. By 1792, hospitals for the insane founded by voluntary subscription included Liverpool Royal Lunatic Hospital, Manchester Royal Lunatic Hospital, York Lunatic Hospital and Bethel Hospital, Norwich. The 1808 County Asylums Act allowed counties to levy a rate to build asylums. Its main purpose was to remove lunatics from jails and workhouses to buildings where they would be easier to manage, rather than cure. These new county asylums included Nottingham, 1811, Bedford, 1812, Norfolk, 1814, Lancaster, 1816, Lincoln and Cornwall, 1820, Edinburgh, 1813, and Glasgow, 1814. The Glasgow asylum was constructed in the shape of a star, based on the 'Panopticon' design devised by the philosopher and social reformer Jeremy Bentham. The 'Panopticon' or 'all-seeing eye' was intended for 'any sort of establishment where persons of any description are to be kept under inspection' and ensured that all patients, or prisoners, remained per-petually under surveillance: the cells were constructed in such a way that there could be no place to hide.

The opportunity to rebuild the hospital promised a fresh start for Bethlem. However, progress was slow. With bureaucratic torpor, the governors deliberated between a rebuild in Moorfields and the acquisition of new land. The Drapers' Company offered the gov-ernors seven acres in breezy Islington, near the workhouse. By 1805, the committee had agreed to erect a new building on this land but the plan had to be abandoned when it was discovered that the land was in trust, and could not be sold. After making an unsuccessful bid for a site behind the foundling hospital at Ball's Pond,

Clerkenwell, the committee eventually decided, in 1807, that St George's Fields would be the ideal location. A further two years passed before the authorities agreed to exchange the two and a half acres in Moorfields for eleven acres in St George's Fields, a marshy area of southeast London occupied by pleasure-gardens and a spa. Moorfields was prime development land, and therefore more valuable than the new site. A preliminary agreement for an 865-year lease was drawn up on 29 September 1809.

St George's Fields took its name from the church of St George the Martyr, Southwark. Nearby was the causeway that the Romans had built across the marshes from London Bridge to Newington. Fanatical crowds, from Gordon's mob to the Chartists, had poured through on their way to Westminster. In 1642, Parliamentarians built a fort to defend London from the king, which later became the site of the infamous Dog and Duck tavern. In the 1730s, one enterprising proprietor hit upon the notion of advertising the local waters as a cure for the most obstinate diseases, claiming that St George's was a spa to rival Epsom or Tunbridge Wells. By 1754, the tavern's attractions included a coffee house, a bowling green, and even a swimming pool with gardens and discreet alcoves for customers of a retiring disposition. Alas, the tavern's reputation declined over the years and by 1775 Garrick was referring to the 'frowsty bowers' of the Dog and Duck as peopled with half-drunk fauns and 'dryads breaking lamps'. Popularly referred to as 'the Surrey college of crime', the tavern became a den of thieves and finally lost its licence in 1787. Part of the land became the home of the School for the Indigent Blind, with a magdalen hospital and a home for female orphans nearby. As for the medicinal powers of the Dog and Duck waters: they were analysed in 1856, and found to contain many impurities, but local residents claimed that, by drinking the spa waters, they were protected from the cholera epidemics which ravaged neighbouring boroughs.[2]

The new Bethlem required an architect, and to this end an advertisement appeared in *The Times* on 3 July 1810, offering a reward of £200, £100 and £50 for the best three designs. One competitor, the award-winning architect James Gandon (1743–1823), was so keen to produce an ideal hospital that he had consulted John Howard at every stage of his drawings. However, developing a new Bethlem was an unhappy experience and his research was the stuff of nightmares. 'The design I made for that hospital very nearly terminated my existence,' he told his biographer. 'It was necessary that I should visit every apartment in the original structure. In these visits I encountered the most deplorable cases. At last I experienced sleepless nights, and when I did at last procure any rest, I was troubled with horrible dreams of the affecting scenes I had witnessed. I was at last attacked by brain fever, and my medical attendants had no hope of my recovery. But through the affectionate care of my wife, aided by a strong and vigorous constitution, I gradually recovered.'[3] Gandon's experience became the source of another Bedlam myth, that of the mad architect who designed the new hospital but ended his days there. In years to come, a famous architect *did* indeed end up in Bethlem. Poor Augustus Pugin, driven to a breakdown by kidney disease, brandy and overwork, was committed in 1852 and only removed after a public outcry.

Gandon's plans earned him third place but contributed to a nervous breakdown, while the winner was E. John Gandy, of King's Cross. His scheme resembled a combination of St Luke's Hospital and the existing Moorfields building, in the same stern, imposing classical revival style as University College, London and the British Museum. Three storeys high, it consisted of a central block and wings extending from either side, which were later expanded to house further patients. The front entrance boasted six plain Doric columns supporting a central pediment that bore a memorial to Henry VIII, erroneously assumed to be the founder: HEN. VIII. REGE. FUNDATVM CIVIUM LARGITAS PERFECIT. The governors recommended the design to the surveyor, James Lewis. The foundation stone was laid on 18 April 1812, but the pumpkin-shaped dome, which gives the building its distinctive appearance, did not appear until 1842, when Sydney Smirke (best known for the circular reading room at the British Museum) enlarged the chapel to accommodate 220 worshippers, reflecting the fact that the hospital's population had more than doubled.

The original design of the porch featured a cupola. In 1812, during the Napoleonic war, the Admiralty complained that the new hospital would interrupt telegraph transmissions between the Admiralty and West Square, and proposed putting a semaphore on the roof. The request was repeatedly refused by the governors, on the grounds that 'with weird, waving arms a semaphore would, undoubtedly, have called up in many a morbid mind the vision of a dread unearthly genie, mocking and flouting the victim in its clutches, or spelling out to the doomed soul messages of unutterable horror and woe'.[4]

Cibber's 'brainless brothers' were placed in the entrance hall, where they were hidden behind curtains that could be whisked aside on committee days. The front entrance, which abutted on to Lambeth Road, was surrounded by a short wall and massive iron railings revealing landscaped grounds. Like other asylums built at the time, Bethlem was intended to be a self-sufficient community, equipped with everything necessary for the functions of a large institution. There was a laundry, to be staffed by patients under strict supervision, and the kitchen occupied the basement. Exercise yards were placed at the back of the hospital, alongside apartments for the superintendent and the steward, a pond, the original source of the miraculous 'Dog and Duck' water, and a pigsty. There were also workshops, although these were not completed until 1844. These had originally been designed to provide employment for the male patients. As early as 1822, Lord Robert Seymour, chairing a parliamentary select committee on madhouses, had stated that employment was the best medicine for certain forms of mental illness, and that the manufacture of mats, paper bags and slippers might be highly therapeutic and raise funds for the hospital.

On Thursday, 24 August 1815, 122 patients were conveyed in hackney carriages, without accident or incident, to their new home, at a cost of some £18. However, their first winter must have been an uncomfortable one. The steam-based central heating system only operated in the basement and the windows in the top storey were not glazed, so that the sleeping cells were either exposed to the full blast of cold air or were completely darkened.[5] The windows were too high for the patients to see out, although the governors claimed that this prevented outsiders from looking in, and that the unglazed windows permitted the ventilation of 'the disagreeable effluvias peculiar to all madhouses'.[6] The windows were glazed in 1816.

*

As the Bethlemites settled into their new home in Lambeth, another asylum was rising in north London, at Colney Hatch (now better known as Friern Barnet). Middlesex County Pauper Lunatic Asylum had originally opened at Hanwell in 1831. By 1846, 800 patients were jostling for space in a building originally designed for 600, and it was clear than another asylum was required. The second one opened at Colney Hatch in 1851, designed to rescue pauper lunatics from 'the neglect and inattention of the workhouse, or the cupidity, ignorance, and cruelty, too often practised by those who farmed them in private asylums'. Hunter and Macalpine have described it as offering asylum 'for society's impossibles, victims of the double misfortune of lunacy and pauperism'.[7]

There was an ever growing population of such unfortunates in north London, suffering from little understood, then untreatable conditions such as vitamin deficiencies, diabetes, lead poisoning, encephalitis, brain tumours, syphilis, tuberculosis, brain, heart and kidney diseases and birth trauma. There were always hundreds more patients awaiting admission than there were beds available.

Colney Hatch was built on a site originally called Lowen's Farm and Hollick Wood, which had belonged to Sir William Curtis, former Lord Mayor of London, investment banker and Tory MP. Consisting of 119 acres at Bet's Stile, near Colney Hatch, between

Finchley Common and Southgate, the site was chosen because the Great Northern Railway was being constructed to pass alongside it and because of its proximity to the Grand Junction Canal, which would make it easy to deliver bulk supplies. Colney Hatch derives from the Latin *colonia* and hatch, or gateway, indicating that it was once on a Roman gateway into London.

Designed by S. W. Daukes, the massive new asylum offered accommodation for up to 1,000 patients – ten years later this figure had doubled, with the female department one-third greater than that of the males. As well as the asylum itself, there was a chapel for 400 people, apartments for two residential medical officers, a residential medical superintendent and a matron, committee rooms, reception rooms, a surgery, infirmaries, baths, storehouses, brewhouses, bakehouses, laundries, workshops and farm buildings and a porter's lodge. There was an artesian well, 350 feet deep, for the supply of water and a ballroom, 112 feet long, for the amusement of the unfortunate occupants of the asylum. The asylum had its own cemetery and even its own gasworks. Apart from access to the railway siding, there was only one entrance, so that every single person or object which entered or left the asylum had to pass the eagle eye of the porter.

The asylum building, as described in *The Pictorial Handbook of London* (1854), was 'in the Italian style of architecture', with stone groins and dressings, and an extreme length of 1881 feet 8 inches and a depth of 670 feet 6 inches. The total number of rooms, including the common offices, chapel and infirmaries, was 987 and there were more than six miles of corridors and wards. All angles, throughout the building, had circular bricks to prevent patients injuring themselves, the open fires had locked fireguards and the hospital also offered 'improved Padded Rooms, that all important aid to the Modern System of humane treatment practised at this Asylum' to safeguard patients during violent episodes without the need for physical or chemical restraint.[8]

The corridors and central colonnade were paved with a substance referred to as 'the patent metallic lava of Messrs Orsi and Armani'. This material was asphalt, the limitations of which soon became obvious: not only did asphalt create a dark and gloomy impression, but it retained moisture and 'urinous smells'.

The foundation stone was laid on 8 May 1849 by Prince Albert, accompanied by 'an august assemblage of noblemen and gentlemen'. Benjamin Rotch and Henry Pownall, of the Middlesex magistrates, dedicated the asylum to non-restraint and promised that no hand or foot would be bound here, while a writer in the *Journal of Psychological Medicine and Mental Pathology* hoped that the interior of the asylum

> would not be permitted to remain so dead and prison-like as those we find at present in our public asylums. We would fain hope that those gloomy days have passed away, and that the new county asylum at Colney Hatch will be essentially a *curative* institution ... now that the progress of mental and cerebral pathology has clearly demonstrated that insanity is, in its early stages, as curable as any other disease incident to humanity, we anticipate that, with the advantages which this asylum can command, it will soon acquire an European reputation.[9]

On 1 July 1851, the chapel was dedicated and the cemetery consecrated. On 17 July, the first patients arrived, from workhouses and private madhouses. One hundred and thirty-five patients were admitted in the first week, which was not without anxiety for the authorities, as some of the wards and buildings 'were not, perhaps, in that state of completeness necessary for the accommodation of their expected inmates'.[10] This was aggravated by the general inexperience of the attendants. But the new hospital was considered to be such an achievement that *A Guide through Colney Hatch Lunatic Asylum* was issued for visitors to the Great Exhibition at Crystal Palace in 1851, 'among whom were many men of high standing in the ranks of philanthropy, art, science, medicine and architecture'.

Unfortunately, the only thing Colney Hatch gained a reputation for was its colossal size. Within five years of opening, it was being condemned as out of date, with dark, tunnel-like wards, inadequate ventilation and poor lavatory facilities. The Gothic windows, which only opened an inch or two to stop the patients escaping, were merely 'panes of thick opaque glass imbedded in the walls'.[11] It took another forty years to get them replaced with sash windows, although air bricks provided some ventilation. There was also another problem. According to Hunter and Macalpine, the 1,500 inhabitants of the asylum produced gallons of sewage which went directly into Pym's Brook, a stream flowing through the grounds that later became the North Circular Road. From there, the sewage was carried down to Southgate, leading to complaints from the residents. When an inspector from the General Board of Health investigated he discovered 'a filthy open cesspool, calculated to poison the whole neighbourhood' at Bound's Green. Under public pressure, a sewage works, complete with filterbeds, was added to the Colney Hatch site.[12]

In some respects, Colney Hatch operated more like a prison than a hospital. Patients were admitted after they had been declared insane by their parish doctor and an order had been signed by a magistrate. Unlike the routine at Bethlem, patients were not interviewed at the hospital itself but at an office in Upper Street, Islington. If they recovered, patients were 'released' for a trial period of one month, and if this proved successful they were then formally discharged. If not, they were 'retained' for a further period.[13]

Patients were divided into 'curable' and 'incurable' according to the duration of illness and 'complications' such as paralysis, epilepsy and dementia including 'structural' or irrecoverable brain disease. One- to two-thirds of uncomplicated cases of mania, melancholia and monomania were found to recover, especially if they received early treatment. But many severely disabled patients were sent to the asylum permanently, leading to inevitable overcrowding.

Chronic patients with mental and physical disabilities took up the majority of beds, and there was also the complication of cross-infections such as tuberculosis, typhoid and dysentery. Sheer weight of numbers made individual treatment difficult.

The asylum doctors worked in far more demanding conditions than other specialists. They had no control over admissions and did not even see their patients before they came in. They had limited nursing staff, could not call upon experts from other hospitals, and had to deal with all medical and surgical contingencies, including performing operations, delivering babies and carrying out post-mortems. Much of their time was taken up with paperwork, keeping registers and casebooks and a daily medical journal as well as weekly, monthly and biannual reports for the commissioners in lunacy. The committee attempted to justify this on the grounds that the number of patients the doctors had to care for was 'exceedingly small', with about thirty male patients a year 'taking physic' (out of a total of 515) and fifty women a year out of 770. 'We are a hospital only in occasional instances, an asylum always.'[14] And an asylum that lingered in the public imagination as a particularly grim destination, at best the butt of music hall jokes, at worst, a place of high walls, long grey buildings and mysterious suffering.

Its most famous patients included Dorothy Lawrence (1896–1964), a young reporter who disguised herself as Private Dennis Smith of the 1st Leicestershire in order to fight in World War One. Betrayed and unmasked, Dorothy was sent back to England and forbidden to write about her experiences. Taken in by an Islington cleric, Dorothy was committed to Colney Hatch in 1925 after claiming that he had raped her. Nobody believed Dorothy, and she spent her remaining nearly forty years in the asylum. Also listed among the patients was one Aaron Kosminski (1865–1919), a Polish Jew committed in 1891, and believed by some to have been 'Jack the Ripper'.

With the move to Lambeth, it seemed as though Bethlem was finally on the mend, ready to let go of the past and establish itself as

'The New Bethlem of St George's Fields', now the Imperial War Museum.

an efficient modern hospital. Visiting in 1817, the Duke and Duchess of York and the Duke of Gloucester expressed the highest satisfaction in the accommodation and treatment of the patients,[15] while an inspector in 1836 commented that Bethlem was 'scrupulously clean', with the galleries and cells swept every morning, and scoured out once a week, and the entire hospital whitewashed throughout once a year.[16]

But, sadly, once again this outward appearance proved deceptive. Despite a change of address and attempts at reform, Bethlem was still beset by the old, familiar problems. In 1835, it was discovered that large sums of money had disappeared and the treasurer, Thomas Coles, fled to Calais, leaving Bridewell and Bethlem with a net loss of £12,000.[17] Another familiar scenario emerged with an investigation into the conduct of medical superintendent and apothecary Edward Wright (c. 1788–1859), who had been dismissed in 1831 on the grounds of gross misconduct: he was accused of being drunk on duty, sexually assaulting a female attendant[18] and being found at night with female patients, his clothes 'dishevelled'.

Wright defended himself by claiming that the matron and keepers were unreliable and the latter were never in the galleries when needed, and that food and medicine were poorly administered. He also denied being a 'sot and a drunk', stating that as a gentleman he was incapable of any impropriety. Experts have suggested that Wright was, in fact, victimised, on the grounds of his interest in phrenology, the allegation being that he preferred dissecting skulls to treating his patients. The science of phrenology, which had been gaining credibility in medical circles, operated on the principle that mental function was dictated by the anatomical structure of the brain and skull; the heads of musicians, for instance, possessed certain readily identifiable features; so did the heads of 'idiots' – and lunatics, particularly criminal lunatics, a theme taken up by Mary Shelley in *Frankenstein* (1818). Phrenologists also believed that an individual's environment should be adapted to their mental capacities, a view which had important implications for the medical treatment of congenital lunatics. However, to the uninitiated, such experiments were taboo: one keeper described Wright's activities in the 'dead house' or mortuary in horrified tones. He painted a ghoulish portrait of Wright as a psychiatric Frankenstein, taking off the heads of the dead patients and placing them in pickling pans until the flesh was removed. Given the contemporary fear of body-snatching and dissection, this reaction from a layman was understandable. Nevertheless, Wright received support from Dr Monro, the apothecary Dr William Wood and other pioneers who had been present during his dissections.

While the governors might just have been prepared to overlook Wright's anatomical experiments, alcoholism and sexual misconduct, it was his failure to keep accurate patient records that constituted his real downfall, and he was condemned as 'a degraded character' whose conduct had been so infamous that no gentleman could lend him his support.[19] Wright went to Syria, where his alcoholism escalated to the extent that he could scarcely practise medicine. Returning to London in 1834, he left for Australia soon afterwards and became a successful doctor in Adelaide, until a prescription error proved his downfall. Wright maintained that he had only prescribed the appropriate amount of morphia for his patient to take after dinner, but when the said patient died of an apparent overdose, Wright withdrew from public life. He was later vindicated, but never practised again.

One person who did have a good word to say about Wright was the author of *Sketches in Bedlam* (1823), a collection of case histories attributed to James Smyth, 'an attendant', in which Wright is described as a man who 'performs all the duties of his situation, arduous as they are, with diligence and regularity'. This glowing tribute has led to the suspicion that Wright himself was the author.

Although legislation requiring the regular inspection of asylums and private madhouses had been introduced by 1828, Bethlem was exempt. With nineteen governors of Bethlem in the House of Commons and thirteen in the Lords, anything threatening their interests had been struck out. Bethlem remained exempt in 1845, when the Lunacy Act was passed. This became the benchmark for mental health legislation until 1890 and changed the status of lunatics from prisoners to patients. Following this Act, the Lunacy Commission was set up to inspect conditions in public and private asylums and hospitals and scrutinise the provision of care for pauper lunatics in workhouses. The commission consisted of eleven Lunacy Commissioners, six of whom (three medical, three legal) were employed full-time on £1,500 a year, and was responsible for the county asylums and licensed madhouses. Following mounting evidence of abuse, the Lunacy Commissioners attempted to inspect Bethlem in 1848, but had their application rejected. Further attempts were thwarted, despite notorious incidents such as the case of Hannah Hyson. Hannah's father, T. J. Hyson, wrote to the president of Bethlem, Sir Peter Laurie, on 21 April 1851:

I now, Sir, bring to your Notice a case of either cruelty or wanton neglect, in which my Poor Girl (our only Child) has fallen a sacrifice, caused by or through the neglect of one of the Female Nurses or Keepers belonging to Bethlem Hospital. Now, Sir, for the facts, which can be verified by any respectable Witnesses.

On Friday, April 4, my Daughter was admitted a Patient into Bethlem Hospital: on leaving her I was informed I might call in 8 or 9 days and enquire how she was; I called on April 12, which was 8 days. I saw both the Doctor and the Nurse, and was told she was somewhat better, that she took her food better; I went away satisfied. On the following Thursday I could not rest, something seemed to haunt my mind my Daughter was worse, I consequently wrote a Note to Dr Wood stating my fears, and begging of him if any bad symptoms appeared to let me know, that her Mother might be with her; Dr Wood was kind enough to forward me a Note in return to mine, informing me no bad symptoms had appeared, and that my Poor Girl was discharged; Me and her Mother immediately went to the Hospital, saw Dr Wood, who rung for my Daughter – she was brought up to us. What our feelings were I hardly can tell, my Poor Girl could not stand, and was a complete Idiot. But, Sir, what was my horror when called upstairs by her Mother and others, when they had undressed her to put her to bed, her body, her legs, and her arms had above 20 wounds and lacerations on them, 2 also on her face; her bones ready to start through the skin, how caused or inflicted no one who has seen her but wish and desire to know. Her Medical Attendant can speak as to her condition both before her admission and since her return. And if, Sir Peter, you would condescend to pay my humble abode a visit, you would then see I have not made the case one iota worse than it really is; in fact my pen but feebly tells the sad tale. I have no doubt ere these lines reach you my Poor Girl will be in her Coffin, but that shall not prevent your satisfying yourself as to the truth of my statement.[20]

Hannah Hyson died hours after that letter was written. Four days later, the consultant of Bethlem, Alexander Morison, and the surgeon, William Lawrence, carried out a post-mortem. Morison's statement read: 'I found several superficial bruises on different parts of her body, and redness and tendency to excoriation about the nates, none of them at all connected with the cause of her death, which was occasioned by General Paralysis. The bruises I consider to be accidental, and in no way to be attributed to want of care and kindness.'[21] The post-mortem also stated that Hannah had been violently disturbed for two or three weeks before her death, and that the authorities had been told about the scratches on her face which were probably self-inflicted, as Hannah was in the habit of crawling about the institution on her hands and knees.[22] But Hannah's grieving father refused to accept that her death was due to natural causes. He demanded an inquiry, which was finally granted, but he was unfortunately too ill to attend. By this time, the matter had passed into the public domain, in the wake of an even more sensational case, that of Ann Morley.

*

Ann had been admitted to Bethlem on 6 October 1850, and was discharged on 27 December. Soon after, she was admitted to Northampton Lunatic Asylum, where Dr Nesbitt, the medical superintendent, described her state on admission as 'most deplorable'. Ann had become skeletally thin, and so weak that she could not even sit up. She had a prolapsed uterus and anus, with massive mucous discharges, was paralysed and oedematous from the waist down and her entire body was covered with abrasions and flea bites. She was also 'quite unconscious of the calls of nature, and her urine and faeces passed under her'. Nesbitt's treatment consisted of, first of all, a comfortable bed with frequent changes of linen, morphine, to sedate her, a tincture of oak bark, to soothe her skin problems, and a generous diet. Under this regime, Ann was on her feet again within three weeks and made a progressive improvement.

Always a quiet patient, and grateful for attention, she was entirely cured within a month. As Ann began to recover, she complained about her treatment at Bethlem. She claimed that she had been given a black eye by a nurse, the bad-tempered 'Black Sall', within days of her arrival, and forced to sleep on straw in the basement; this had caused the abrasions on her skin. On one occasion, Ann's quilt had been removed and she had been forced to sleep naked; on another, she was hosed down with cold water, despite being ill.[23] Nesbitt took Ann's complaints seriously, and they formed the basis of the Lunacy Commission's investigation of Bethlem. Other voices soon joined the litany of complaints: the story emerged of a Mr Hawes, a strong, muscular man reduced to a skeleton within weeks of admission, and restrained with a stocking during attempts to force-feed him. He died soon after discharge.[24] The Lunacy Commission issued a damning report. Once again, Bethlem stood accused of cruelty, abuse and indifference. The visiting physicians performed their duties in a superficial and imperfect manner: they never inspected the hospital or made night visits, and the treatment of their patients was left to Dr Wood, the resident apothecary, keeping him so busy that he had no time to attend to his own duties.

When asked to explain Ann Morley's appalling treatment, the governors argued that her case was not unusual, and that 'difficult' female patients routinely slept naked in straw and were hosed down with cold water, and that these conditions were common through-out England and France. Edward Monro, Morison and the matron, Henrietta Hunter (daughter of John Haslam), all professed ignor-ance of this abuse,[25] suggesting that they had no idea of what went on in their own hospital. The commission also attacked the govern-ors on the grounds that they 'cherry-picked' middle-class patients, who were easier to discipline and more likely to recover, instead of fulfilling their charitable purpose by taking on pauper lunatics. Middle-class patients, argued the commission, should be treated in a private asylum; Bethlem, due to its charitable status, should take on more patients who 'earned their livelihood by manual or daily labour'.[26]

In their defence, the governors claimed that Hannah Hyson had died of 'a disease of the brain' (possibly syphilis) and that Ann Morley's injuries were because of the long journey from London to Northampton. Other witnesses were dismissed as disgruntled former employees with a grudge. Dr Wood admitted that there had been a clash of personalities between himself and the matron since 1847, when she had taken responsibility for the female wing and prevented him from initiating the reforms he thought necessary, and added that he had not received any support from the governors. Another scapegoat, Wood was cast out into the wilderness, but not before he had said this: 'I have had to contend with difficulties which have never been appreciated. I have been oppressed with an amount of labour, and ceaseless anxiety, and overwhelming responsibility to the very verge of human endurance. With a limited authority and no assistance I have struggled to promote the welfare of those committed to my charge.'[27]

The most damning indictment of conditions at Bethlem came from Monro himself. After thirty-six years of unremitting attendance at the hospital, Monro asserted that he was deeply attached to it, but he blamed the governors for its lax management. Doctors were busy men, and his obligations to his private practice did not permit him to spend as much time at Bethlem as he would wish. Medicine seemed to have changed, too, since the days of his father and grandfather. The idea that a doctor should take an interest in public health or the social background of his patients was lost on him: it had never occurred to him that his duties extended to knowing the case history of every patient, or examining the condition of the hospital. He professed himself quite shocked that modern physicians were expected to have such extensive duties. This was a shocking enough admission, but Monro's most revealing words were reserved for the case of Ann Morley. Stating that her evidence was appalling, and, 'if it were really true, then reform was necessary', he admitted that he knew nothing of the basement cells where she had been held: this department was 'clearly as distinct from my sphere as that of the architect or the cook'.[28]

This provoked a tart response from the hospital's governors to the effect that they were sorry to learn of Dr Monro's view of his duties[29] and *The Lancet* condemned Monro's 'lofty opinions' as obsolete and accused both 'quasi-physicians' of neglect, while the *Journal of Psychological Medicine* went further and condemned Bethlem's regime of 'systematic cruelties, violence and neglect'. Bethlem was a model asylum – the model of what an asylum was like half a century ago, set up as a warning 'to remind us of what a good institution should be, by the hideous exhibition of evil'.[30] Nothing seemed to have changed, apart from the Christian name of Dr Monro.

Despite his incompetence, Dr Edward Monro hung on tenaciously at Bethlem until 1855, under the new title of 'consulting physician'. Morison resigned in 1853 with an annual pension of £150. And Bethlem at last found its redeemer, in the form of the new resident medical superintendent, William Charles Hood, just twenty-eight years old and fresh from Colney Hatch. Under Hood, Bethlem was to become a haven for two particular types of patient: the middle classes and the criminal lunatics.

9

UNDER THE DOME

Westminster, 1843: a shot rang out and the Home Secretary lay dead on the steps of the Treasury. 'He shall not break my peace of mind any longer!' shrieked Daniel McNaughton, content in the knowledge that he had completed his mission to assassinate the hated Tory Sir Robert Peel. That is until the arresting officers informed him that the dead man was not Sir Robert Peel at all. In a case of mistaken identity, McNaughton had killed Peel's private secretary, Sir Edward Drummond.

That shot rang round the United Kingdom. It inspired a national panic that resulted in the Lunacy Act of 1845 and inspired 'the McNaughton rules', an index determining criminal insanity. McNaughton's shooting of Drummond was the latest in a series of attacks on public figures, inflaming the fear of revolution. As we have already learned, Bellingham had murdered the Prime Minister, Spencer Perceval, in 1812. In 1818, David Davis had shot at the Secretary of War, Lord Palmerston, lacerating his side with the ball. Davis believed that Palmerston was personally responsible for Davis losing his rank of lieutenant in the 62nd Regiment of Foot. In 1840, Edward Oxford, a house-painter, had attempted to shoot the young Queen Victoria in her carriage, while in 1842, stage carpenter John Francis took a shot at the queen while her carriage drove along the Mall. These perpetrators suffered very different fates, reflecting changing attitudes to criminal insanity. While Bellingham was hanged within days, McNaughton and Oxford survived to become some of the most famous patients in Bethlem's criminal lunatic department, and Francis too escaped the gallows.

Daniel McNaughton, a wood turner from Glasgow, was tried at the Central Criminal Court, Old Bailey, in March 1843. It soon became obvious that McNaughton was suffering from paranoia. He believed that he was being hounded by Glaswegian Tories who had compelled him to shoot the Home Secretary as punishment for interfering in politics. 'They persecute me wherever I go,' he protested. 'I cannot sleep at night, they have driven me into a consumption, they wish to murder me!'[1]

McNaughton was examined by nine doctors, including Edward Thomas Monro of Bethlem and Alexander John Sutherland of St Luke's. When asked if the prisoner was delusional, Monro replied: 'Most certainly. The act, coupled with the history of his past life, left not the remotest doubt of the presence of insanity sufficient to deprive the prisoner of all self-control.' This was despite the fact that McNaughton seemed capable of managing 'all the ordinary affairs of life' and had maintained a moral perception of right and wrong. Monro's colleagues concurred, and stated that 'the deed of murder flowed immediately from the delusions'. The Crown had called in no expert witnesses, since its own physicians had come to the same conclusion, and the case was halted. The jury found McNaughton 'not guilty on the ground of insanity'.

The verdict caused outrage. McNaughton was seen as having gone unpunished for his crime, which created doubt in the public mind about the reliability of criminal law, and fear as to how often the ordinary citizen was at risk from madmen. One MP tried to introduce a Bill outlawing the plea for insanity in cases of murder, but nobody would second it. Even the legal authorities were uneasy:

the ruling had, after all, been very different when Bellingham shot Spencer Perceval. Bellingham's defence was not permitted enough time to provide evidence of his insanity, and as a result Bellingham was found guilty and hanged within a week of the offence.[2] In the House of Lords, Lord Brougham announced his intention to clarify the law relating to crimes committed by offenders alleged to be partially insane, and complained that the legal definition of knowing right from wrong, knowing one sinned against the law of God and nature, knowing the act to be forbidden by the law of one's country, was vague and indefinite. The true test was: had McNaughton been capable of distinguishing between right and wrong, that is to say, 'right' as in 'according to the law' and 'wrong' as in 'an act condemned and punishable by the law'. If the perpetrator knew what he was doing, if he knew at the time of committing the desperate act that it was forbidden by the law, that was his test of insanity; the only real sound and consistent test.

Lord Cottenham cautioned that the Lords could not listen to any doctrine which proposed to punish the deluded. 'Was the mind diseased sensible of the disease under which it laboured?' He thought not. If it were, there could be no complete delusion. Lord Lyndhurst's view was that the theory of delusion, directed to one or more persons and confined to one or two points merely, while the unhappy patient might on all other topics and with reference to all other members of the community be very intelligent and acute, was yet too imperfectly understood to pass fresh legislation – a view which still troubles juries a century and a half later, as they struggle to determine whether a murderer is a sane criminal or a killer who has acted while the balance of his or her mind is disturbed. In the face of all these uncertainties and differences of opinion among the Law Lords, the Lord Chancellor submitted a list of five questions to a panel of judges for their clarification. Their answers constitute what is known as 'The McNaughton Rules' and these still govern criminal law with respect to insanity to this day.

Edward Oxford, the house-painter who had shot at Queen

Victoria, was convicted of high treason on 18 July 1840. A newspaper columnist asserted that Oxford's crime resulted from 'excessive vanity and a desire to become notorious if he could not be celebrated', but he turned out to be one of Bethlem's success stories in the end. After spending his years in confinement knitting and playing the violin, Oxford was deemed to have made a good recovery and, in 1863, was offered a choice between Broadmoor and a one-way ticket to Australia. Oxford chose the latter course, changed his name to 'Freeman' and disappeared into a new life in the southern hemisphere.[3] John Francis, meanwhile, faced the statutory penalty for high treason: to be hanged, drawn and quartered, although his pistol might not even have been loaded. Prince Albert was so appalled by this draconian sentence that he intervened and the sentence was commuted to transportation for life, with hard labour. As Francis began his journey to Van Diemen's Land, Prince Albert received a letter of gratitude from the boy's father, thanking him for sparing the son's life.[4]

David Davis, sadly, was not so fortunate. Committed to Bethlem on 19 May 1818 for shooting at Lord Palmerston, his case notes record that he amputated his own penis and sent it to the Secretary of War in a parcel. He eked out his days at Bethlem, supported by a small pension from the army, almost all of which was spent on pastry.

*

The criminally insane have always formed part of the population of the mad. In previous centuries, numbers of insane people, whose homicidal or destructive mania had not been detected, tramped up and down the country, committing mysterious murders, setting hayricks or houses on fire and maiming cattle. Such people often escaped detection, for they showed – often they had – no consciousness of crime, and they moved rapidly from place to place.[5] As a rule, the fate of these disturbed individuals was execution or gaol. If they were fortunate, they were sent to Bethlem, which had always taken a proportion of murderers, usually acute cases deemed to be a substantial risk to the community. John Gozna, the resident medical officer, noted that during the period 1772–87, twenty out of the 2,000 patients had committed murder. Other cases had included Margaret Nicholson and James Hadfield, held under the Criminal Lunatics Act rushed through in 1800 after Hadfield's attempt on the life of George III, and which was intended to provide for the safe custody of the insane who had committed treason or were guilty of ordinary criminal offences.[6]

Unfortunately, although this Act protected the public from the criminal lunatic by removing such individuals from society, it did nothing to protect the lunatics from themselves by providing better treatment. In 1806, the reformer Sir George Onesiphorus Paul wrote to the Home Secretary to point out that many so-called criminal lunatics were languishing in jail, serving terms far in excess of their offences, either disrupting their fellow inmates, or, if held in solitary, suffering rapid mental deterioration.

Prompted by increasing concern over the fate of 'criminal lunatics', the government had pledged £10,000 towards the new Bethlem in 1807, contingent upon providing two wings for sixty criminal lunatics, whose fees would be paid by the state but who would be managed by the hospital. These quarters opened in 1816, and were enlarged in 1838 when the hospital was expanded to make space for 364 patients and remained in use until 1863 when criminal lunatics were moved to the newly built Broadmoor.

When the young William Hood was elected resident medical superintendent in 1853, he took responsibility for more than 100 of the country's 436 criminal lunatics.[7] Conditions in the criminal wings were particularly grim. Two forbidding blocks in the back gardens of the hospital, they consisted of dismal arched corridors, feebly lit at either end by a single window in double irons, and divided in the middle by gratings, 'more like those which enclose the fiercer carnivora at the Zoological Gardens than anything we have elsewhere seen employed for the detention of afflicted humanity'.[8] Overcrowding was so extreme that it was almost impossible to

provide employment or diversion for the inmates, and the only pas-
times readily available were fives and running in the exercise yard,
and knitting and reading in the 'crepuscular galleries'.[9]

Hood, with his reforming zeal, attempted to improve conditions
for the criminal lunatics. His rationale was that homicidal, suicidal,
noisy and dirty patients should be segregated from their less offensive peers.[10] Hood divided his male criminal patients into three
types, those who were insane but refined, those who were little educated but harmless – and the third class, regarded as 'debased',
violent and highly dangerous, and who pretended to be mad in
order to escape prison. Hood solved the problem of overcrowding
in the criminal wings by moving forty of the more orderly and
refined male criminal lunatics into the refurbished wards of the
main hospital itself without any detrimental results. The non-
criminal patients were relocated elsewhere. Conditions were
preferable to prisons such as Millbank or transportation. In fact, the
life of a criminal lunatic at Bethlem was perceived as such a soft
option that the hospital was referred to as 'the Golden Bank' in
prison slang.

Notorious patients included Captain Johnson, who killed the
entire crew of his ship, *The Tory*, and Patrick Walsh, 'a ferocious
maniac, more like a tiger than a human being', who led a mutiny on
HMS *Hermione* in 1797 and murdered a fellow patient, Dennis
Leonard, in 1820.[11] Others, immortalised in *Sketches in Bedlam*
(1823), included George Barnett, a lawyer's clerk who abandoned
the technicalities of drawing up wills in favour of writing love letters and poems to an actress, Frances Kelly. When Miss Kelly failed
to reciprocate, Barnett arrived at her theatre in Drury Lane on 16
February 1816 and shot at her while she was on stage. Charles and
Mary Lamb were in the audience, since Charles was also infatuated
with Miss Kelly and her 'divine plain face', and some of the bullets
fell into Mary's lap. Mercifully, Miss Kelly 'escaped his desperate
purpose'.[12] It seems unlikely that Miss Kelly would have responded
to Barnett's advances, even if his poetry had been of any merit. The

author of *Sketches in Bedlam* describes him as 'a foolish, frivolous simpleton of mean and pitiful appearance, and by no means calculated to inspire the tender passion'.[13]

With its vivid descriptions and tabloid sensationalism, *Sketches in Bedlam* offered a virtual tour of the hospital, replacing the visiting days of the previous centuries. Once again, the public could gasp in horror or sympathy for its wretched inmates, and meet many of the familiar stereotypes, such as mad lawyers, doctors and soldiers, even a mad hatter, one Joseph Redfern. Among the female patients, recognisable figures emerged, including women driven mad by love or suffering delusions of grandeur. The unfortunate Caroline De Guth, for instance, managed to combine both conditions, being 'disappointed in love [and] thinks she is Queen of Bedlam'.[14]

It is in the casebooks, however, that one finds the sad, forgotten stories of less illustrious patients, such as Hester Watson, forty, of York Castle, single, no children, who was found insane after she 'destroyed her mother by beating her head against a Brick Floor'.[15]

Ann Clark, forty, was committed on 7 December 1839, sent on from Hoxton Asylum. Ann had married a rich old man, and, when he died, married again, this time a man who 'cared more for her money than for her'. Giving birth to a child, she 'cut its head off, it being 12 months old'. Ann received a royal pardon, but had no family or friends to care for her, and was sent to the Hoxton poorhouse.[16]

Ann Byrom, thirty-six, was also committed for infanticide in February 1839. Her death sentence was commuted to five years. 'She has destroyed 3 illegitimate children successively soon after their birth by placing them under a basket in a drain and sitting on the basket. Such revolting conduct escaped detection until the last deed when she was convicted – not the slightest evidence of contrition exists. Were the same circumstances to occur again, she would not for a moment scruple to adopt a similar course.'[17]

Another mother, Hannah Smith, committed on 27 November 1837 at the age of forty-two, was sent to Bethlem after the 'wilful murder of her son, Samuel Smith'. Seen to be making good progress at the hospital, she was not told immediately of the death of her daughter, following a botched abortion. When the keepers eventually broke the news, two years after the event, Hannah was inconsolable.[18]

There are accounts of unremitting despair, such as Lucy Dancer, thirty-three, committed on 12 June 1823, for 'the murder of her infant'. Lucy 'endeavoured to cut her [own] throat with a steel spring and more recently secreted a pair of scissors from the ward and when they were discovered tried to strangle herself at night with her garter'.[19]

One vivid description is that of Philippa May, committed on 9 August 1820 for 'the murder of the woman who slept in the same room with her'. Philippa was described as appearing 'much older than stated in the care paper' with 'short white hair and a particularly short wrinkled face. Always on the ground in a corner with her knees all but touching her chin. She is rather a remarkable object when a stranger enters the room. She has a habit of pointing her skinny finger at the person she addresses, in a way only seen in descriptions of a witch addressing a victim.'[20]

Patients were not always safe from their fellow inmates. On 31 May 1844, Joseph Hull, who had been committed to Bethlem for sodomy, had a portion of his left ear bitten off by another patient, James Connell.[21] Extreme self-harm was common: Charles Burton, thirty-two, was admitted on 3 September 1841 because he had killed his sister, 'on believing rumours circulated that he was in the habit of having connection with her'. Like the unfortunate David Davis before him, Charles amputated his penis, 'that it might not again get him with disgrace'. '[T]he reports that were in circulation and are believed to be correct' on investigation were subsequently proved to be true.[22]

Richard Dadd (1817–86) was one of Bethlem's most notorious patients, although early indications suggested that artistic merit, rather than homicide, would constitute his claim to fame. Born in Kent, Dadd's artistic skills led to a place at the Royal Academy,

Richard Dadd: one of Bethlem's notorious criminal lunatics,
he was a gifted artist who murdered his father.

where he was described by the painter William Frith as 'a man of genius'.[23] During a spell travelling in the Middle East, Dadd began to experience mental problems and became convinced that his father was the devil. Dadd invited his father to travel to Cobham, Kent, where, after supper at an inn, they went for a walk in Cobham Park. The following day, his father's body was recovered from the park. He had been stabbed to death. Dadd escaped to France, with the expressed intention of killing the Emperor of Austria, and attacked another traveller on board ship. Dadd was captured and sent to Bethlem, where Hood described him as 'a violent and dangerous patient, for he would jump up and strike a violent blow without any aggravation and then beg pardon for the deed'. There was no remission for Dadd's delusional symptoms and he continued to believe that his murderous behaviour resulted from being possessed by evil spirits. Although his behaviour was disgusting: 'a thorough animal, he will gorge himself with food till he actually vomits and then again return to the meal', Hood admitted that Dadd could be 'a very sensible and agreeable companion, and shew in conversation a mind once well educated and thoroughly informed in all the particulars of his profession in which he still shines'.[24]

But, like James Tilley Matthews, Dadd received humane treatment: as an educated, refined criminal lunatic, Dadd was given a large airy room and art materials so that he could continue painting, completing two of his best-known works at Bethlem: *Contradiction: Oberon and Titania* (1854–8) and *The Fairy Feller's Master-stroke* (1855–64). These visions of the spirit world are technically superb but vaguely disturbing, swimming with hallucinatory detail. Transferred to Broadmoor in 1863, he died of tuberculosis in 1886.

*

Reforming the criminal department was only one of Hood's actions when he took over as the first resident physician. Aged just twenty-eight years, enthusiastic and ambitious, Hood had seen 'moral treatment' put into successful practice at Colney Hatch. Eager for reform, Hood reminded the governors that Bethlem possessed a unique role as one of the oldest charitable institutions for the insane in Europe.[25] To this end, he introduced administrative changes that would benefit the moral and physical welfare of his patients, and research and teaching facilities for medical students. In his first report to the governors, Hood declared his ambition to: 'secure the services of the best class of attendants, both male and female, and with this view your Committee will liberally consent to give any amount of wages necessary to engage persons, who are undoubtedly respectable, as well as humane and intelligent'.[26] A head nurse was appointed to the female side of the hospital, and another to the male, and the matron was given extra responsibilities, including more visits to the female wards, day and night.

Hood's vision for Bethlem took three forms: he believed in moral treatment and the abolition of restraint, moved the criminal department to Broadmoor (the world's first establishment for the criminally insane opened in 1863, in a then remote part of Berkshire thirty-two miles from London) and threw Bethlem open to the educated middle class with limited resources. Hood's rationale was that an entire class of mentally distressed gentlefolk had been created for whom there were no available options: the shabby genteel, driven to madness by financial pressures: 'the greatest social pressure, the fiercest struggle for existence, and the keenest competition for employment, is to be found among the middle classes, it surely cannot be a matter of surprise that amongst such there should be a larger and continually increasing number of insane'.[27] 'It is on the middle classes of society that the calamities incidental to madness fall the most severely; they depend for existence on the continued power of being industrious; if the mind fails, that power is lost, and all the evils of poverty gradually surround them'.[28]

Clerics, doctors, authors, artists, mechanics and governesses were all liable to insanity, but they were not poor enough to go 'on the parish' (an early form of welfare) and not rich enough to afford private madhouses. Hood owed this view to his mentor, John Conolly (1794–1866), who had argued that there was no class that stood so much in need of asylums as the middle class. Conolly related the case of one of his patients at Hanwell Asylum. This was a clergyman, 'an intellectual man', who spent his time in good works in his large parish, until he was driven to insanity by overexertion. The clergyman was cared for at home by two attendants, who spruced him up whenever his doctors were expected to call, but the moment they were gone, they strapped him to his bed and went off drinking. As a result, the clergyman became even more agitated, and required more violent restraint, and was eventually admitted to Hanwell. He had been fastened down for so long that he had lost the use of his legs, but made a full recovery. And although he was grateful for the interventions at Hanwell, he was also appalled that he had to be treated as a pauper lunatic to get cured. Conolly could mention other cases: another cleric who paid a large proportion of his income to support his insane uncle whom he never saw, but who was incarcerated in a private madhouse where his treatment was dubious in the extreme.[29]

One class of patients suffered from Hood's reforming zeal: Bethlem no longer offered refuge to pauper lunatics; instead, they were banished to the newly opened county asylums.

However, in keeping with his views on moral treatment, Hood transformed the appearance of Bethlem. Like Tuke at the ground-breaking Retreat in York, Hood's mission was to create a hospitable, rather than a hospital environment, the appearance of a loving home where patients were cared for with compassion and dignity. One of Hood's first tasks was to

abolish *all* those *gloomy* appendages which characterised of old the external appearance of the madhouse, and which diffused *gloom* and despondence through the interior of the building. The massive iron bars, which now darken and disfigure the bedroom windows of this Hospital will be removed and replaced by windows of a lighter and more cheerful appearance, similar in construction to those recently introduced in the front windows of the ground floor.[30]

To his contemporaries, Hood's achievements appeared magical: wooden bedsteads replaced straw in the non-acute wards; pictures materialised on the walls, carpets rolled down freshly painted corridors; birds sang in their cages while books and magazines fluttered in the newly opened library. Every Sunday, patients sang their hearts out in the chapel, beneath Smirke's gleaming glass dome. The moral treatment also included a good diet, wine with dinner and a nightly dose of morphine, making this a humane and progressive regime. Outside, a new airing ground was developed, with gravel walks, grass, flower-beds and a bowling green. Patients able to labour were kept occupied in the workshops and laundry, while their leisure time was also designed to help them develop social skills, a vital aspect of moral treatment. For the more learned residents, an in-house magazine, entitled *Under the Dome*, carried stories and articles submitted by patients and staff, from reports of cricket matches (doctors were selected as much for their prowess on the field as their expertise in psychiatric medicine) to the history of the hospital, a labour of love on the part of the chaplain, the Reverend Geoffrey O'Donoghue, which would eventually be published as *The Story of Bethlehem Hospital*. Compliant patients were even permitted to leave the hospital on escorted excursions to Kew Gardens, the National Gallery or the Smithfield cattle show. Skittles, bowls, prayer meetings and even dances were on offer, with music held to be therapeutic. A ballroom was included in the plans for Colney Hatch Asylum; St Luke's Hospital had an annual Christmas dance, as did Bethlem, where there had been a ballroom since 1838.

On 24 December 1859, the *Illustrated Times* carried an account of a ball at Bethlem, introducing the piece with the sentiment that a ball at Bedlam seemed as much of an anomaly as a fair at Pentonville or a flower show at Charing Cross Hospital. A retrospective glance, however, at the modern treatment of lunacy and the gentle and soothing remedies available would soon convince the reader that a 'soirée dansante' in the great civic hospital for lunatics was a perfectly rational and desirable addition to the treatment introduced by benevolent and learned men who have 'made mental maladies their study' and devoted time and energy to the painful and laborious task of the care of the insane.

Despite the fact that comfort, kindness and relaxation were now the rule in all well-conducted asylums, in place of the horrible old regime of whips, gags, manacles, straitjackets, chains, straw beds, dark cells, revolving chairs and violent shower-baths, and although the padded cells were disappearing for all but the most suicidal and hysterical, the writer believed that such hospitals still had a somewhat gloomy aspect. Decorate the place with pictures and busts as you may, furnish the wards with books and journals, with chess and draught boards, with embroidery frames and artists' materials, it is impossible to banish that pervading melancholy, that lonely distress, that indefinable sense of deprivation and bereavement. Amusements of a sedentary nature, however consoling, are not sufficient to vanquish desolation and ennui. Torpid minds and flagging spirits require more active recreation, they require a spur, a 'fillip', an increase of vitality, and to meet these ends there cannot be any more desirable solution than the ones offered by the governors of Bedlam – namely, a billiard room for the men, and a ballroom for patients of either sex.

The ballroom is described as 'a spacious apartment', lit by large louvre windows and prettily decorated on festal occasions. The events themselves, supervised by Dr Hood and the other medical officers, are distinguished by the organisers' regard for etiquette and urbanity: nothing that could be regarded as wildness or extravagance is perceptible in the patients' demeanour or attire as they join in the quadrilles and polkas. 'There is nothing to remind us of the "Bedlam" of Hogarth, with its poor drivelling maniacs, with latten swords, rushen crowns, and paper tiaras,' comments the journalist. And neither does it remind him of the famous engraving of the old Moorfields building (see p. 90) where a madman has let a wooden sword and fool's cap down by a string from his grated window into the ditch below. On the other hand, he admits, you can tell that the patients have really made an effort on this occasion, and made an attempt to dress up in honour of the event.

Watching these 'crazy people', many of them young and attractive, all of them peaceful and orderly, the writer begins to wonder if they are actually mad, and whether it would not be appropriate to unlock the gates of Bedlam and let them loose on the world again. Alas, no. All we are seeing is the sunny side of a wretched picture of humanity: these patients are the only ones deemed fit enough to attend. Tomorrow, some of them might be howling and flinging themselves about in dreadful convulsions. Others take no part in the dance, but merely sit placid and quiescent on the surrounding benches, their hands folded, their gazes a thousand miles away, utterly indifferent to what is passing around them. 'You feel in the midst of the merriment that *there is something wanting*, that the wine is corked, that the cake has a leaven of madness in it, that there is only elevenpence-halfpenny out of the shilling in the pockets of the dancers, that there is a tile off the roof of the ballroom.'[31]

*

This was a flippant conclusion, but the author does at least concede the therapeutic value of the ball. Charles Dickens attended a similar event at St Luke's Hospital, and provided a vivid account of the proceedings in 'A Curious Dance Round a Curious Tree' for *Household Words* in January 1852.[32] Dickens approaches the topic with similar misgivings: 'Even now, an outside view of St Luke's Hospital is gloomy enough; and, when on that cold, misty, cheerless afternoon which followed Christmas Day, I looked up at the high walls and saw, grimly peering over them, its upper storeys and dismal little iron-bound windows, I did not ring the porter's bell

Transformation: a female ward in Bethlem c. 1860. Note the carpets, birdcages and floral displays.

(albeit I was only a visitor, and free to go, if I would, without ring-
ing it at all) in the most cheerful frame of mind.'[33]

Compared with Bethlem, St Luke's presents a grim prospect.
Hackney cabriolets are parked by the wall, some of the drivers
asleep inside their vehicles with their legs poking out, suggesting
that their 'Christmas Box' had come in an alcoholic form. All
human life is there, outside the hospital: flaming gas-lights, oranges,
oysters, paper lanterns, butchers and grocers, bakers and public-
houses, omnibuses rattling by. Ballad-singers, street cries, street
passengers, street beggars, and street music; there were cheap theatres within call and wretched little chapels, too. There were homes,
great and small, by the hundred thousand, east, west, north and
south; all the busy ripple of sane life (or of life, as sane as it ever is)
came murmuring on from far away, and broke against the blank
walls of the Madhouse, like a sea upon a desert shore.

As he arrives, Dickens recalls an anecdote about a woman of
great strength and energy, who had been driven mad by an infuriated ox in the streets. Animals frequently escaped from Smithfield
Market, but on this occasion the woman seized the creature literally
by the horns, and so, 'as long as limb and life were in peril, vigorously held him; but, the danger over, she lost her senses, and became
one of the most ungovernable of the inmates in the asylum'. She was
later released uncured.[34]

Admission is through a stone courtyard and a hall, adorned with
wreaths of holly, and Dickens wonders how it looked to patients
when they were first received, and whether they distorted it to their
own wild fancies, or left it a matter of fact. Entering a long, long
gallery, he sees, on one side, a few windows; on the other, a great
many doors leading to sleeping cells. Outside the iron cage enclos-
ing the fireplace between two of the windows stands a motionless
woman. The fire casts a red glare upon the walls, upon the ceiling,
and upon the floor, polished by the daily friction of many feet. At
the end of the gallery, in the common sitting room, are several
women: all silent, except one, who sews a mad sort of a seam and

seems to be scolding some imaginary person. Dickens notes the tac-
iturnity of mental patients: 'there is no solitude more complete', an
observation that will be familiar to any visitor to a psychiatric hospital to this day.

Dickens then visits a workroom, featuring coloured prints, a
china shepherdess on the mantelshelf, carpets, stuffed chairs and an
open fire. The occupants, less listless and sad, work earnestly at
some unspecified task. At one end of a cheerless gallery, he spots a
piano, 'with a few ragged music-leaves upon the desk. Of course,
the music was turned upside down.' He tells us there are several
similar galleries on 'the female side', and one set apart for incurable
'boarders' whose families or friends pay a weekly sum. 'The experience of this asylum did not differ, I found, from that of similar
establishments, in proving that insanity is more prevalent among
women than among men.' Of the 18,759 inmates Saint Luke's
Hospital has received in the century of its existence, 11,162 have
been women and 7,587 men. Female servants are, as is well known,
more frequently afflicted with lunacy than any other class of persons. The table, published in the Directors' Report, of the condition
in life of the 107 female inmates admitted in 1850 sets forth that
while, under the vague description of 'wife of labourer', there were
only nine admissions, and under the equally indefinite term 'house-
keeper', no more than six, there were of women servants,
twenty-four.

On the male side Dickens presents: three men engaged in a game
of bagatelle; another patient kneeling against the wall apparently
deep in prayer; two walking rapidly up and down the long gallery
arm-in-arm, but, as usual, without speaking together; a handsome
young man deriving intense gratification from the motion of his
fingers as he plays with them in the air; two men standing like pil-
lars before the fire-cage; one man, with a newspaper under his arm,
walking with great rapidity from one end of the corridor to the
other, as if engaged in some important mission which admitted of
not a moment's delay.

Once again, Dickens notes 'the same listless vacuity here', and suggests that if the patients were kept occupied (as they were at Bethlem), 'the proportion of cures would be much greater'. He also observes that the patients are in the grip of an obesity crisis. Inactivity occasions a rapid accumulation of flesh. Of thirty patients, who had been residents for around eleven weeks, twenty-nine had gained weight at the average rate of more than a pound per week each.

The ball itself took place in another gallery, a brown sombre place, dimly illuminated by a light at either end, adorned with holly. The staircase was curtained off, and near it the musicians were cheerfully engaged in getting all the vivacity that could be got out of their two instruments. At one end were a number of mad men, at the other, a number of mad women, seated on forms. Two or three sets of quadrille dancers were arranged down the centre, and the ball was proceeding with great spirit, but also great decorum.

Dickens encounters a number of lunatic stereotypes, the patients usually to be found in all such asylums, among the dancers. These included 'the brisk, vain, pippin-faced little old lady, in a fantastic cap – proud of her foot and ankle; the vacantly-laughing girl, requiring now and then a warning finger to admonish her; and the quiet young woman, almost well, and soon going out'. And then there is 'the old-young woman, with the dishevelled long light hair, spare figure, and weird gentility'. She wears a frock of faded black satin, and languishes through the dance with a lovelorn affability and an air of resignation to her circumstances. We recognise this lady, of course, as one of the standard madwomen: genteel, beautiful, obsessed with her appearance, a more benevolent Margaret Nicholson, perhaps, a younger Miss Havisham, an Ophelia. (A Victorian doctor noted that every asylum had its 'Ophelia', a faded beauty crossed in love and rendered sexually promiscuous by mental illness.)

For partners, there were the sturdy bull-necked thick-set little fellow who had tried to get away last week; the wry-faced tailor, formerly suicidal, but much improved; the suspicious patient with a countenance of gloom, wandering round and round strangers, furtively eyeing them behind from head to foot, and not indisposed to resent their intrusion. There was the man of happy silliness, pleased with everything.

Just as in Bethlem, not everybody danced. The watchers huddled together without communicating. Some watched the dancing with lacklustre eyes, others rested weary heads on hands and moped; others had the air of eternally expecting some miraculous visitor who never came, and looking out for some deliverance that would never happen. The attendants joined in and the dancing became so enthusiastic that the quaint pictures of the founders, hanging in the adjacent committee-chamber, must have trembled in their frames. There were also sundry bright young ladies who had helped to dec-orate the Christmas tree and a few members of the resident-officer's family; and, shining above them all, and shining everywhere, his wife, Charlotte Eliza Walker, the resident matron, who evidently had 'no Christmas wish beyond this place, but to look upon it as her home, and on its inmates as her afflicted children'.

And then it was time for the patients to be admitted in a line to pass round and admire the Christmas tree. For Dickens, this was a bizarre sight. The tree stood in the centre of the room, growing out of the floor, a blaze of light and glitter. To someone who had just stepped into the hospital, from everyday life, it was a very sad and touching spectacle. 'I could not but remember with what happy, hopefully-flushed faces, the brilliant toy was associated in my usual knowledge of it, and compare them with the worn cheek, the list-less stare, the dull eye raised for a moment and then confusedly dropped, the restless eagerness, the moody surprise, so different from the sweet expectancy and astonishment of children, that came in melancholy array before me.' When the sorrowful procession is closed by 'Tommy', the favourite of the house, a harmless old man, with a giggle and a chuckle and a nod for everyone, Dickens finds the event such a travesty that 'I think I would have rather that

Tommy had charged at the tree like a Bull, than that Tommy had been, at once so childish and so dreadfully un-childlike.'

But Dickens's final words, on the treatment of the insane, testified to the value of the work being carried out at St Luke's. It was an imperfect hospital, in an imperfect world, but the staff were doing their best, and Dickens honoured those who devoted themselves to the task of lifting the affliction of insanity by all human means, and who substituted humanity for brutality, kindness for maltreatment and love for hatred. In many ways, this description resembled Hood's mission statement at Bethlem, particularly his treatment of women.

10

MAD WOMEN

During his trip to St Luke's, Charles Dickens noted that insanity was more prevalent among women than among men. As we have seen, the author provided pen portraits of archetypal mad women in his account of the Christmas dance. More significantly, Dickens was responsible for creating one of the most notorious mad women in the character of 'Miss Havisham' from *Great Expectations*, a lady who takes her place alongside Charlotte Brontë's pyromaniac Bertha Mason as one of the most memorable female lunatics in nineteenth-century fiction.

The mad woman, real or imaginary, has always been an intriguing cultural construct, and no more so than in Victorian England. The feminist critic Elaine Showalter has observed that during this period, the stereotype of madness shifted from male to female, with Caius Cibber's 'brainless brothers' yielding to the genteel maiden, such as the seductive young woman in George Dyer's sonnet 'Written in Bedlam: On Seeing a Beautiful Young Female Maniac' where the poet describes seeing 'a sweet maid with an angel face and gentle bosom'.[1] Unlike Cibber's naked maniac, this lunatic is unthreatening, pathetic and quite possibly uninhibited enough by 'erotomania' to be sexually available.

In this chapter, we shall look at the lives and treatment of three famous Victorian 'mad women' – at least one of whom was not 'mad' at all – and then examine the fate of their fictional counterparts, 'Bertha Mason', the first Mrs Rochester and 'Miss Havisham', the jilted recluse.

*

By 1861, Bethlem seems to have had a good record for its treatment of women. When the Lunacy Commissioners visited Bethlem in this year, they found the patients tranquil and in a satisfactory condition, the wards and rooms in good order, and the patients of both sexes expressing themselves in terms of gratitude for their kind treatment.[2] One particular example of Hood's kind treatment was the case of a young mother admitted on 7 July 1856. The patient was suicidal. The father of her two children neglected her, and she was convinced that she had no bowels, a delusion intensified by acute constipation. It emerged that she was suffering from a tumour, and when this was removed, her condition improved. Hood regarded this case as significant on three counts: the patient's physical state had affected her mental well-being; once the cause was removed, she recovered her sanity; and the tumour was excised with advanced surgical techniques resulting in little loss of blood. The patient made a full mental and physical recovery.[3]

Hood's patient was fortunate compared with women in other institutions. Although advances in basic physiology indicated that the womb did not actually move about the body and cause hysteria, the pathology of female mental illness had scarcely evolved beyond the mediaeval period. The medical establishment took the view that merely to be in possession of a cervix predisposed one to insanity, and women were considered cripplingly vulnerable to their emotional state.[4] The two standard diagnoses for women's madness consisted of hysteria and melancholia, both thought to originate from overwrought sensibilities, gynaecological problems or 'erotomania', which could mean anything from making eyes at the curate to healthy sexual desire. (Hannah Smith, one of Bethlem's criminal lunatics, was observed to have 'an insatiable Venereal appetite'.) [5] 'Hysteria' remained the archetypal female functional nervous disorder, the symptoms of which included shortness of breath, pains in the chest, fainting and seizures, as well as mental derangement. The father of modern medicine, Hippocrates, isolating the condition in his *Diseases of Women*, maintained that the illness was found primarily in virgins, spinsters and widows and that the cure, inevitably, was sexual intercourse.

Those women not blighted by hysteria were considered equally at risk from melancholia, a more subdued form of mental distress characterised by lethargy, tearfulness, starvation and suicide, often the result of romantic disappointment. Dr Alexander Morison, a consultant at Bethlem, noted in his *Outlines of Lectures on Mental Diseases* (1826) that of the 562 cases treated at the hospital, twenty-five were the result of 'disappointed love' and twenty of these patients were female, leading him to conclude that 'the passion of love makes girls mad; jealousy, women mad; and pride, men mad'.[6]

As we have seen from the example of Ophelia, driven to distraction by her unrequited love for Hamlet, and by countless despairing maidens scrawling their names on the cell walls, heartbreak was a guaranteed route to madness for many a maid of Bedlam. There can be no better illustration than one of Bethlem's most poignant anecdotes of lovesickness, the tale of poor Rebecca Griffiths. This sad love story began in 1780, when a young merchant from the East India Company arrived in London to stay with his uncle on Fish Street Hill. The young man, whose name was Dupree, was waited on by the servant of the house, a country girl named Rebecca Griffiths. Rebecca was chiefly remarkable for the plainness of her person, and her quiet, retiring manner. After a pleasant trip to London, young Dupree began to grow homesick, and prepared for his departure; the coach arrived at the door, and the inevitable shaking of hands, tender salutations, adieus and farewells followed in the usual abundance. Rebecca, who had seemed extraordinarily depressed for some days previously, helped to pack the luggage. The leave-taking of friends and relations was finally complete, and Dupree squeezed a guinea into Rebecca's palm with a brief 'God bless you, Rebecca!' before springing into the coach. The driver cracked his whip, and the vehicle was rolling rapidly out of sight, when Rebecca, who had stood vacantly gazing on what had passed, suddenly emitted a piercing shriek. The family, who had been going back into the house, turned round in alarm to see Rebecca rushing wildly after the coach, running fast as lightning along the middle of the road, her hair streaming in the wind, and her whole appearance that of a desperate maniac! The men of the family, accompanied by members of the Watch, ran after her, but did not catch up with her until she arrived in The Borough. They took her, in a state of incurable madness, to Bethlem, where she died some years later. As for Dupree's guinea, her richest treasure, her only wealth, Rebecca never let it leave her hand. She grasped it still more firmly in her dying moments, and at her request, in the last gleam of returning reason, just before her death, requested that the guinea be buried with her. But legend has it that it was prised from her cold and dying fingers by a heartless keeper, and that her ghost might be seen every night gliding through the dreary cells of that melancholy building, in search of Dupree's gift, mournfully asking the glaring maniacs for her lost guinea. The saddest aspect of the tale is that Dupree confirmed, after Rebecca's death, that he had never taken advantage of her or indulged in the most trifling of liberties. But she had loved him, hopelessly, and paid for it with her sanity and with her life.

The belief that women were at the mercy of their bodies, from puberty to the menopause, resulted in some desperate remedies. Dr Edward Tilt, for instance, regarded menstruation as so dangerous that it should be retarded for as long as possible, with the aid of cold showers, meat-free diets and the wearing of drawers. He maintained that feather beds and novels, on the other hand, could only

hasten sexual maturity.[7] Tilt regarded menopausal women as pitiful creatures, and the idea of their partaking in sexual intercourse
ridiculous and absurd. Husbands of menopausal women were
advised to withhold their conjugal rights, and he recommended
that any stirrings of desire should be treated with ice-cold douches,
ice enemas and the application of leeches to the labia. Tilt observed
with relish that: 'the suddenness with which leeches applied to this
part fill themselves, considerably increases the good effects of their
application, and for some hours after their removal there is an
oozing of blood from the leechbites'.[8]

The most extreme treatment was that of Dr Isaac Baker Brown,
who introduced the practice of clitoridectomy as a cure for female
insanity.[9] A member of the Obstetrical Society of London, Brown
was convinced that madness was caused by masturbation and that
by removing the clitoris he was saving women from a life of hysteria, spinal irritation, idiocy, mania and death. Masturbation
started at puberty, and the symptoms included depression, loss of
appetite, quivering eyelids and the inability to look people in the
eye. Even more disturbing, these girls demonstrated a desire to
leave home and train as nurses or become nuns.

As a woman, it is impossible to write objectively about Brown's
practice of female genital mutilation. Between 1859 and 1866 he carried out his 'sexual surgery' at a private clinic in London. In the
1860s, he moved on from clitoridectomy to the removal of the labia.
He operated on patients as young as ten, on idiots, epileptics, para-
lytics, even on women with eye problems. His patients also included
women who wanted to take advantage of the Matrimonial Causes
Act of 1857, an early form of divorce law. In each case, Brown's
patients returned to their husbands. Brown was also convinced that
his surgery represented a cure for nymphomania, as he had never
seen a recurrence of the case once he had operated on a woman.

There can be no doubt that these operations were an extreme
form of social control, conducted by a man whose own claim to
sanity was questionable. Brown's patients included such perceived

mavericks as 'Miss E. R.', who, aged thirty-four, had never received a proposal of marriage. Miss E. R. was rude to visitors, took long walks on her own, was regarded as 'forward' towards gentlemen and said that people's faces were masks. She called her mother Mrs Devil and her father 'God'. After the operation, Miss E. R. was sedated with opium before entering high society, where she became 'universally admired'. Another young patient was brought before Brown on the grounds that she was assertive, disobedient to her mother, sent visiting cards to men she fancied and, worst of all, spent most of her time in 'serious reading'. Mutilated by Brown, she was married with a baby within two years, and pregnant with her second.

Brown was expelled from the Obstetrical Society in 1867, after patients complained about being coerced into treatment. Leading psychiatrists including Forbes Winslow and Henry Maudsley testified that female masturbation was not a cause of insanity. One surgeon, so appalled by Brown's approach, ridiculed it by suggesting that the clitoris was not the problem, it was the arms and hands, so should these be cut off instead? Failing that, how about restraining patients by tying their arms behind their back? It was left to the pioneering Dr Seymour Haden to point out that the procedure represented an abuse of male authority and that to practise it was to cheat and victimise women, an observation which gives an indication of the sexual power relationships in Victorian medicine.

Women were also considered to be at risk from the taint of hereditary madness. In the 1850s, rumours circulated that Queen Victoria was succumbing to the madness which had claimed her grandfather, George III. Matthew Sweet, Wilkie Collins's editor, tells us that when Prince Albert was sent a copy of *The Woman in White* he admitted that he was 'completely cowed, living in perpetual dread of bringing on the Queen's "hereditary malady"'.[10]

Deviance of any sort from the sexual stereotype was enough to get a woman certified insane. *Sketches in Bedlam* includes the portrait of Charlotte Dully, a 45-year-old mother from Putney. 'This poor woman has contracted a most singular persuasion,' we are told. 'She fancies herself to be a man, and sometimes styles herself a boy; and, when spoken to, she bows, scrapes, and puts her hand to her head in every respect like a footman. She is particularly attached to the matron, whom she calls her beauty, and is quite uneasy every day until she sees her.'[11] As if lesbian tendencies or transsexual leanings were not enough to get a woman locked up, being a full-blown eccentric also guaranteed internment. Elizabeth James, forty-eight at the time of her admission in 1821, was a larger-than-life character who took to parading outside her house wearing a turban and carrying a staff, like a soldier on sentry duty. She was also famous for carrying a brass ladle in her muff; no explanation was given for this, although it may have been for the purposes of self-defence. A famous figure throughout London, she was seen round the capital in various extraordinary outfits including a leopard skin apron, odd-looking furs, tippets and cloaks, and always followed by a big crowd. Fond of a drink, which may have been the cause of her loud behaviour, Elizabeth was described as 'Amazonian, of huge size, with masculine features and the voice of a stentor'.[12] It seems clear to us in the twenty-first century that Charlotte and Elizabeth were harmless eccentrics who certainly did not belong in a mental hospital, or even in custody. And it is almost impossible to believe that they represented such a threat to society that they needed to be locked away.

*

There were, of course, exceptions, women who were regarded as a genuine danger to themselves and others. One such, driven beyond endurance by domestic responsibilities, financial pressures and intellectual frustration, was Mary Lamb (1764–1847), for ever referred to as the sister of Charles Lamb. (It seems indicative of her second-class status that the chief details of Mary's life appear under her brother's entry in Harvey's *Oxford Companion to English Literature*.) The Lamb family had always been educated, but poor. Mary and Charles's father, John Lamb, was a lawyer's clerk. As children, they lived near the Temple, which Charles remembered affectionately for its church, its halls, its garden, its fountain and its river. Mary had little formal education but early on in life, by accident or design, she fell into the habit of reading whatever she could lay her hands on, browsing at will without much selection or prohibition, dreaming that perhaps she too would one day be a writer.

But Mary's adult life was less idyllic, as the younger Lambs desperately tried to support their ageing parents. Mrs Lamb was an invalid, and John Lamb had developed dementia. Despite his literary ambitions, Charles became a clerk in the East India Company, while Mary contrived to make a living by her needle, working as a seamstress and caring for her elderly mother. In 1792, the family moved to Little Queen Street, Holborn, where there was plenty of work for Mary, sewing silk gowns for the garment industry. Mary even took on an apprentice, a young girl, to help with the sewing. But old Mr Lamb grew distracted and confused, and Mrs Lamb became increasingly demanding. Charles himself experienced a period of insanity and went into Hoxton madhouse, with the subsequent loss of earnings, although he returned to the East India Company once he had recovered. As time went by, the harassed Mary experienced a series of breakdowns. One afternoon, on 22 September 1796, Mary's condition was so alarming that Charles went off to fetch her doctor, but unfortunately did not find him at home. Later that day, while the family were preparing for dinner, Mary seized a knife from the table and rushed at her little apprentice, chasing her round the room 'with fearful menaces'. Mrs Lamb called upon Mary to desist, with eager and terrified calls, and then tried to intervene. Mary turned upon her mother with wild shrieks, and stabbed her through the heart, before hurling the knives and forks round the room, one of which struck her helpless old father on the forehead. The apprentice's screams and Mary's own shrieks brought the landlord running upstairs, but it was too late; he was confronted with the horrific sight of the old woman lifeless in her chair, her daughter standing over her with the knife still in her hand, her father bleeding from a head wound and weeping beside his murdered wife and the young girl cowering in the corner as Charles was prising the weapon from his sister's fingers.

An inquest was held the next day, but Mr Lamb senior was too demented to appear as a witness. Mary and Charles were present at the inquest, and the jury unhesitatingly returned a verdict of lunacy. Mary was fortunate to escape the gallows. Instead, Charles had her confined to a private madhouse, in Islington, where she received sympathetic and compassionate treatment. According to one historian, this ghastly incident completely changed the direction of Charles Lamb's career. He had recently fallen in love, for the only time in his life; however, he realised that his sister demanded all his care and, at twenty-one, put aside all thoughts of marriage in order to take responsibility for Mary. He was also sensitive enough to recognise the appalling pressure which resulted in Mary's outburst. In a letter to his old school friend the poet Samuel Taylor Coleridge, Charles commented:

Poor Mary, my mother indeed never understood her right. She loved her, as she loved us all with a mother's love, but in opinion, in feeling, and sentiment, and disposition, bore so distant a resemblance to her daughter, that she never understood her right. Never could believe how much she loved her – but met her caresses, her protestations of filial affection, too frequently with coldness and repulse. Still she was a good mother, God forbid I should think of her but most respectfully, most affectionately. Yet she would always love my brother above Mary, who was not worthy of one tenth of that affection, which Mary had a right to claim. But it is my sister's gratifying recollection, that every act of duty and of love she could pay, every kindness (and I speak true, when I saw to the hurting of her health, and most probably in great part to the derangement of her senses) through a long course of infirmities and sickness, she could show her, she ever did.

Charles visited Mary frequently at the madhouse, where she appears to have been treated well. 'The people of the house are vastly indulgent to her,' he told Coleridge. 'She is likely to be as comfortably situated in all respects as those who pay twice or thrice the sum. They love her, and she loves them, and makes herself very useful to them.' Charles paid around £50 per annum for Mary's care at Islington, and she was subsequently looked after at home, recovering sufficiently to fulfil her dreams of becoming a writer, collaborating with Charles on *Tales from Shakespeare* (1807) (Mary wrote the comedy section) and publishing a book of essays, *Mrs Leicester's School* (1808). But Mary always faced the threat of a relapse: the Lambs never left home without a straitjacket.[13]

*

Mary Lamb's story was tragic, but she did at least receive sympathetic and humane treatment, in a private madhouse and then at home. By contrast, the tradition of imprisoning difficult, subversive or merely unwanted women by sending them to madhouses was still in full swing. Threats of wrongful incarceration, that very social evil that had moved Defoe to call for a change in the law, were still very much alive and featured regularly in Victorian fact and fiction, leading to a popular conviction that doctors were colluding with families to put away difficult relatives who were not, in fact, mad at all.

One of the most famous cases was that of Rosina Bulwer-Lytton (1802–82), the estranged wife of Edward Bulwer-Lytton, later 1st Baron Lytton, a Liberal MP and popular novelist known in the press as 'The Knebworth Apollo' – a reference to his stately home.[14] A spirited Irishwoman, angered beyond endurance by her husband's infidelities, Rosina had become estranged from her husband in 1836, and he took custody of their two children, alleging abuse and neglect. Lytton was particularly keen to raise his son, the future heir to Knebworth. Rosina retaliated with her own novel, *Cheveley, or the Man of Honour* (1839), which documented Bulwer-Lytton's abuse and parsimony (her allowance was only £400 a year), and endless public and private letters, many delivered to her husband's club scrawled with obscenities. Matters deteriorated further in 1848, when the death was announced of their daughter, Emily. Lytton claimed that the 19-year-old had died at Knebworth, her father by her side. In fact, he had abandoned her, leaving her to die of typhoid in a London lodging house. Rosina had not even been informed that she was ill.

Bulwer-Lytton's literary and political career went from strength to strength: he was a Cabinet minister, Rector of Glasgow University and in receipt of a £20,000 book deal, the biggest in literary history.[15] Rosina was boycotted by publishers who feared her husband and his influential friends, including Dickens and Wilkie Collins.

On 16 May 1851, Rosina threatened to assault Queen Victoria and Prince Albert when they attended the opening night of Bulwer-Lytton's play *Not So Bad As We Seem* which featured Wilkie Collins and Charles Dickens. In response, Bulwer-Lytton had Rosina abducted and committed to Wyke House Lunatic Asylum in Brentford, where she was certified insane by no lesser authorities than John Conolly and Forbes Winslow. Bulwer-Lytton made every effort to suppress the story, banning his friend Mark Lemon, the editor of *Punch*, and the editor of *The Times* from mentioning the story. However, the *Daily Telegraph* was not so reticent, and the scandal which followed was so enormous that Conolly and Winslow were forced to reassess their patient, finding her perfectly sane after all. Rosina was released after less than a month.

Rosina's most outrageous attack came in June 1858, when Bulwer-Lytton stood for reselection before a crowd of voters in his Hertford constituency. Rosina leapt on to the platform and launched a bitter tirade against Bulwer-Lytton. 'Steadily fixing my eyes on the cold, pale, fiendish, lack-lustre eyes of the electioneering baronet, I said, "Sir Edward Earle Bulwer Lytton, after turning me and my children out of our house to run an unexampled career of vice, you have spent years in promulgating every lie of me, and hunting me through the world with every species of outrage . . ."'[16]

Bulwer-Lytton's jaw dropped and he fled from the hustings as the mob began cheering for 'her ladyship!' None of this was reported in *The Times*, of course, as Bulwer-Lytton was close to the editor. Most surprising of all, his constituents were quite happy to reselect Lytton for another term.

When Collins wanted to create a suspense novel about an ageing, bad-tempered baronet who incarcerates his wife in a lunatic asylum, Rosina wrote to him saying that she could give him plenty of material if he wanted to create 'the most dastardly villain in literary history'. 'The man is alive, and is constantly under my gaze,' she told him. 'In fact, he is my husband.' [17]

*

Rosina Bulwer-Lytton was more fortunate than another literary wife, Isabella Thackeray (1816–93), who married the novelist at the age of eighteen. After bearing Thackeray three daughters in three years – the second of whom died during babyhood – Isabella succumbed to acute post-natal depression, compounded by the Thackerays' financial woes as the young author struggled to live by the pen. A change of scene was advised, and Thackeray took his wife home to Ireland – but during the crossing Isabella threw herself out through a porthole and floated in the sea for twenty minutes before being rescued. By the time they got to Ireland, she was 'quite demented'.[18]

Despite Thackeray's financial problems, he sent Isabella to expensive clinics in France and Germany, and even attempted, disastrously, to care for her at home. Private madhouses were inspected, but the author recoiled in horror. Eventually, he hit upon the solution. In 1845, Thackeray set up a separate establishment, a house in unfashionable Camberwell, the other end of London from his Kensington home, where Isabella was put in the charge of Mrs Bakewell, effectively a private nurse, for £2 a week. Thackeray visited at first, but as he became more successful, and Isabella grew more erratic, the visits ceased and, as Professor John Sutherland has commented, the children grew up with an idealised vision of their absent mother, who was living less than five miles away.[19] Isabella lived on in Camberwell, until 1893.

*

The diverse fates of Mary Lamb, Rosina Bulwer-Lytton and Isabella Thackeray reflect the treatment of mad, or supposedly mad, women in Victorian England. While they struggled against genuine mental illness, incarceration and neglect, their fictional counterparts were being identified as templates for female insanity. Charles Dickens created one of the abiding images of demented femininity in the character of Miss Havisham, 'the strangest lady I have ever seen', chatelaine of Satis House (roughly translated, Latin for 'I have had enough!'), a shuttered, dusty mansion which she has not left in years. When Pip, the narrator, first meets Miss Havisham, she is dressed all in white, in satins, lace and silks, her shoes are white, and she has a long, white bridal veil, half-fastened as though she has been interrupted in the act of dressing. Gloves, jewels and a prayer book are to hand, as if she is preparing for her wedding. And then Pip, the young narrator, realises that the 'bride's' hair is white, and that the white clothes are not white at all, but faded and yellow, that the bride herself has withered like her dress, designed for a young, rounded woman, and now hanging on her gaunt and angular frame. She reminds him of nothing so much as a skeleton he had once seen that had been disinterred in the ashes in an old dress from a vault in an old church; or a waxwork at the fair.[20]

Time has stopped for ever for Miss Havisham, who has not looked on daylight for years, ever since the moment she learned, at twenty minutes to nine on the morning of her wedding day, that her bridegroom had jilted her.

Miss Havisham's only pleasure in life is to take revenge upon mankind: she manipulates the delicate mind of her young ward, Estella, and trains her to be a heartbreaker. A lonely spinster with a twisted mind, Miss Havisham exemplifies the fate of a woman without a man; she is little more than a ghost, a living corpse. And by the end of the novel, Miss Havisham is not just eccentric; she is dangerously self-destructive. Overcome with remorse after ruining the potential romance between Pip and Estella, she becomes hysterical. Pip relates: 'I looked into the room where I had left her, and I saw her seated in the ragged chair upon the hearth close to the fire, with her back towards me. In the moment when I was withdrawing my head to go quietly away, I saw a great flaming light spring up. In the same moment I saw her running at me, shrieking, with a whirl of fire blazing all about her, and soaring at least as many feet above her head as she was high.'

Pip attempts to smother the flames with his greatcoat, and the couple struggle on the ground like desperate enemies, fighting to the death, as Miss Havisham's shrieks fill the air. Disturbed by the fire, generations of beetles and spiders race across the floor, while patches of tinder float in the smoky air and fall to the ground in a black shower – the ashes of Miss Havisham's wedding dress.[21]

Miss Havisham eventually dies of her injuries, but with her tragic demise comes sanity, of a kind: the implication is that, overwhelmed with remorse for her treatment of Pip and Estella, she had deliberately cast herself into the fire.

*

In the case of our second literary mad woman, Bertha Mason, there can be no remorse. Charlotte Brontë's Bertha Mason is a maenad, a destructive and elemental force of nature, a victim of hereditary insanity who has no more self-control or consciousness than a wild animal, whose mother, a Creole, was 'both a mad woman and a drunkard!'[22] Brontë has been criticised in some quarters for this portrayal of the archetypal madwoman in the attic; it seems strange that a writer with such progressive, liberal credentials could have created such a negative, racist stereotype of female madness. In fictional terms, Bertha is the shadow side of Brontë's governess heroine, Jane Eyre. While Jane is prim and stoical, Bertha is the embodiment of dark, dangerous sexuality, implied by her French-Caribbean ancestry. Jane, self-sufficient, stoical, and not particularly physically attractive, nevertheless wins the heart of Byronic Mr

Rochester, master of Thornfield Hall, through sheer force of personality. It is only half-way through their wedding ceremony that Jane learns that the mysterious lady lunatic who lives in a remote part of Thornfield has a prior claim on Mr Rochester: 'In the deep shade, at the further end of the room, a figure ran backwards and forwards. What it was, whether beast or human being, one could not, at first sight, tell: it grovelled, seemingly, on all fours; it snatched and growled like some strange wild animal; but it was covered with clothing; and a quantity of dark, grizzled hair, wild as a mane, hid its head and face.'[23] This creature, variously described as a hyena, a maniac, a lunatic, attacks Mr Rochester and bites him, though he retains his composure sufficiently to make introductions: 'That is *my wife*,' he tells Jane.[24] Bertha is depicted in terms which we recognise from previous descriptions of the mad: bestial and dangerous. There is no sympathy here.

Devastated, all trust in Mr Rochester lost, Jane makes her escape and almost sets off for India with a missionary, only to receive a telepathic summons from Mr Rochester. When she eventually returns to Thornfield, it is greatly changed: instead of a stately home, she finds a blackened ruin. The façade is a shell perforated with paneless windows; the roof, the battlements, the chimneys have all crashed in. The damage is not recent: walking around the ruins, Jane realises that winter snows have drifted through the empty archways, winter rain has beaten through the casements, spring has cherished vegetation so that grass and weeds wave between the fallen rafters. Investigating, Jane eventually gets an account of the disaster from the retired family butler. The house had burnt down months ago, at harvest time: 'A dreadful calamity! Such an immense quantity of valuable property destroyed: hardly any of the furniture could be saved. The fire broke out at dead of night, and before the engines arrived from Millcote, the building was one mass of flame. It was a terrible spectacle: I witnessed it myself.'

Unaware of her identity, the butler tells Jane that the blaze was caused by the 'lady lunatic', Bertha Rochester, who had escaped after her nurse got drunk on gin, a regular occurrence. Roaming about the house, Bertha had set fire to Jane's bedroom. The moment Mr Rochester discovered the fire he had got all the servants out of their beds and helped them outside, before going back into the house to rescue his mad wife – but then the servants called out to him that she was on the roof!

> '. . . she was standing, waving her arms, above the battlements, and shouting out till they could hear her a mile off: I saw her and heard her with my own eyes. She was a big woman, and had long black hair: we could see it streaming against the flames as she stood. I witnessed, and several more witnessed Mr Rochester ascend through the skylight on to the roof: we heard him call "Bertha!" We saw him approach her; and then, ma'am, she yelled, and gave a spring, and the next minute she lay smashed on the pavement.'
>
> 'Dead?'
>
> 'Dead? Aye, dead as the stones on which her brains and blood were scattered.'[25]

Bertha Mason and Miss Havisham are terrifying, destructive figures. They are also, as Professor John Sutherland has argued, examples of the consequences of 'moral treatment'. These lunatics exemplify the damage that can be done by lack of restraint: tragedy strikes when Bertha escapes from her drunken keeper; Miss Havisham's fate is to become a human torch. At the time *Jane Eyre* was published (1847), the issue of mechanical restraint had become the subject of passionate debate: while Hood maintained that the majority of his patients did not require it, his successor at Bethlem would put restraint back on the agenda again – with dreadful consequences.

11

TRANSFORMATION

By the time Dr Hood left Bethlem in 1862, after nine years as medical superintendent, something of a 'halo effect' had developed around the man who was acclaimed as 'this kind and wise labourer in the field of mercy' by the *Illustrated London News*.[1] In his final report, Hood concluded that 'We have been mercifully spared from any accident or act of violence. No epidemic has raged, nor has suicide surprised or shocked us. A great amount of harmony has prevailed among the inmates, and each ward has independently represented much of the sociability of a large family.'[2]

Sadly, Hood's legacy did not last. From 1868, seclusion or solitary confinement was reintroduced, along with padded cells for the most violent patients.[3] In 1871, mechanical restraint was brought back; and the period during which Dr George Savage became medical superintendent (1878–88) saw Bethlem notorious in the press once again.

Patients complained of force-feeding and brutality and questions were asked in *The Times* when a death rate of 14.4 per cent in 1887 raised issues about patients' safety and the suicide rate appeared to be three per year (in 1873 and 1887). This issue was also noted in

1879, when it was announced that Bethlem received suicidal patients from private asylums, where they had been kept on suicide watch, but who were not supervised so closely at Bethlem. The hospital's policy that 'the irritation of suspicion is removed and many such cases get well'[4] appears potentially lethal.

One of the most famous specialists in madness, Dr George Henry Savage (1842–1921) was president of the Medico-Psychological Association of Great Britain and held teaching roles at Guy's and the University of London, as well as running a flourishing private practice. A celebrated amateur sportsman, excelling at mountaineering, angling and fencing, Savage took a pragmatic view of the 'mad-doctoring' trade. As far as he was concerned, insanity was a hereditary disease of the brain. These opinions were based upon his own observations: 'I have seen two cases, born of parents who were in Bethlem while they were pregnant, so that the children were saturated with insanity while still in the womb. The mothers told me that these infants seemed to be perfect little devils from birth.'[5] Savage maintained that the physician's role consisted of being 'the responsible guardian of the lunatic'.[6] The only appropriate method for this was through restraint:

Treatment of the insane at present comprises treatment by drugs, and the treatment by seclusion, i.e. by the removal from home and home associations. Before proceeding to my special points I must briefly refer to these. I believe that drugs in a few cases are very useful in breaking down habits of sleeplessness, restlessness, violence, or the like, but that they should be used with a sparing hand, and certainly not continuously. I believe that every patient of unsound mind who is being kept quiet and controlled by chloral, bromide, opium, or any other sedative or hypnotic is being badly treated. I would rather tie a patient down constantly than keep him always under the influence of a powerful drug.[7]

He claimed this was effective after seeing:

a patient violent, destructive, and maniacal who, having assaulted his fellow-patients and destroyed property and threatened suicide, when he found himself completely controlled in a prolonged warm bath for three hours became convinced of the inutility of his violence and from that time became more amenable to more congenial treatment, and I have known a chronic case of insanity benefited materially by a few hours in the padded room or even an hour's restraint, so that habits of destructiveness, such as tearing paper from the walls, or jumping on chairs, have been checked, and the patient has been thereby less likely to injure himself and is rendered altogether a more hopeful case than before restraint.[8]

But concern was growing over Savage's harsh regime. In September and October 1888 a number of letters appeared in *The Times*, from Savage's colleagues and from laymen, attacking his treatment of patients at Bethlem, particularly with respect to drugs and mechanical restraint. On 26 September, Sir James Clark Lawrence, president of Bridewell and Bethlem Royal Hospitals, wrote to *The Times* defending Savage, and stating that Bethlem had been inspected by the Lunacy Commissioners in August and nothing untoward had been reported. On 2 October, Sir James Charles Bucknill alleged that Lawrence had spent little time at either institution and that far from the last inspection being satisfactory, Lawrence had failed to mention one glaring irregularity: this was the fact that out of 264 patients resident at Bethlem in 1887, thirty-eight had died that year in the hospital – 14.4 per cent of the hospital's population. This compared unfavourably with the national average mortality rate of 7.28 per cent in similar institutions. The report also revealed that during the first twenty-six days of June 1887, 18 out of 264 patients had been mechanically restrained, compared with only 25 cases of restraint recorded during the same period in all the institutions in the United Kingdom *combined*.

The Lancet sprang to Savage's defence, declaring that laymen were not entitled to comment on medical issues, and it appeared that Savage felt impervious to criticism from the press, although *The Times* had a good reputation, and did not stoop to publish unsubstantiated and potentially libellous attacks on innocent victims. Savage seemed set to weather the crisis, and even published an explanation and justification of the methods of mechanical restraint in use at Bethlem. These included:

(*a*) 'Soft gloves' of which each hand is separate and padded to the thickness of about an inch, and which are fastened by a strap round the wrist with a screw button. (*b*) 'Strong dresses', made of stout linen or woollen material, and lined throughout with flannel. The limbs are free to move, but the hands are enclosed in the extremities of the dress, which are padded. (*c*) 'Side-arm dresses', made of the same stuffs as the last, but in these there are two attached pockets to the side of the body of the dress, into which the hands of the patient are placed. By this means, though the patient can walk about his room, such dresses being used at night, he cannot make use of his hands to injure or destroy. (*d*) I employ the wet and also the dry pack. The former is so commonly used that I need not describe it; but as the dry pack is seldom used with the insane, I therefore wish to point out that in this mode of treatment I have the patient wrapped in a sheet or a blanket, and if very restless a second may be used. The patient is then placed on a mattress, and retained there either by means of an attendant, or else by applying a sheet over the patient, which is fastened under the bed. In a few instances, in which there was exhaustion, with some bodily ailment as well, such as swelling of the feet, I have placed the patient in a side-arm dress, and then lightly packed him, so as to ensure the recumbent position, and in one similar case I had tapes applied to the side-arm dress and fixed to the bed. The result was the saving of the patient's life. I have used a belt once with attachment of the elbows to it, so that the patient, who was given to injuring himself by nicking and rubbing, was thus prevented from so doing. I maintain that every physician with experience has a right to private judgement on the treatment of his cases, and that is practically what I claim and for which I suffer abuse.[9]

Savage maintained that his severe treatment was appropriate, even acceptable, as a method of bullying patients into submission. He also practised blistering, and towards the end of his life, recommended that purging 'may be essential and necessary'. In his last recorded statement he even reflected that 'I am inclined to think that the scourging of the lunatic in times past might have occasionally been a help to recovery.'[10]

Most disturbing of all, Savage also approved of other doctors who employed similar methods, such as Dr Yellowlees of Glasgow, who: 'Makes a point of attracting the feelings and the sentiments in cases of masturbation, for he transfixes the prepuce in a slow, almost solemn way, at the same time that he preaches a very stirring sermon on the weaknesses of the vice and the probable results if the habit continued.' The *OED* defines 'transfix' as a transitive verb meaning to 'pierce with a lance, etc.', which suggests that some form of scalpel was used on the offending member.[11] Savage's endorsement of such a barbaric, not to say *perverse* form of aversion therapy suggests that he did indeed live up to his name.

Savage seemed impervious to the correspondence in *The Times*. But then his colleague, Dr George Thompson, wrote to *The Lancet* accusing Savage of careless and excessive use of medication to sedate his patients. Savage responded with a one-paragraph plea of innocence on 3 November, but by this point he was merely going through the motions: the night before, on 2 November 1888, he had enjoyed a testimonial dinner at the Café Royal in honour of his retirement.

*

While it is tempting to see the reintroduction of restraint as evidence of one man's individual barbarity, Dr Savage's approach reflected a change in attitude towards the end of the nineteenth century. The period of therapeutic optimism – the belief that patients could recover through moral treatment – had been replaced by therapeutic pessimism, derived from the Darwinian concepts of natural selection and the 'survival of the fittest'. According to Henry Maudsley, the gloomy genius of late Victorian psychiatry, 'lunatics and criminals are as much manufactured articles as are steam-engines and calico-printing machines'.[12] They were not accidental or anomalous, and science could discover why they came about. Madness was no longer the result of industrialisation, rainy Sundays and too much gin: it was the product of a 'hereditary organic taint'. Influenced by the theories of the forensic psychologist Cesare Lombroso (1835–1909), Darwinian psychiatrists believed that physical characteristics, detectable by the trained eye, indicated a predisposition to madness and criminality. These included: 'An irregular and unsymmetrical conformation of the head, a want of regularity and harmony of the features, malformations of the external ear, tics, grimaces, stammering and defects of pronunciation, peculiarities of the eyes and even a predilection for puns.'[13] To illustrate the fact that this was all abject nonsense one only has to look at the example of the writer Virginia Woolf, a great beauty in her youth, who was nevertheless diagnosed as hopelessly insane by five eminent psychiatrists, Henry Savage among them.

Therapeutic pessimism meant that women in particular were scrutinised for signs of mental degeneracy, for fear lest they pass on their taint to the next generation. Criminal tendencies were indicated by badly shaped heads, flat foreheads and big ears.[14] According to one authority, potential victims could also be identified by their looks. The feminist critic Elaine Showalter tells us of the extraordinary views of Furneaux Jordan, a Birmingham surgeon, who claimed that a certain type of woman was almost guaranteed to become a casualty of domestic violence. If a woman possessed the unfortunate combination of delicate skin, thin eyebrows, a curving spine and a 'sharp tongue', it would be almost impossible for a man to refrain from beating her. Jordan claimed that he had witnessed this phenomenon across the class divide, from domestic servants to landed gentry, when they were admitted to hospital covered in bruises or critically injured.[15]

An even more sinister development of therapeutic pessimism was that of eugenics, or selective breeding, a concept later seized on with enthusiasm by British intellectuals, and subsequently the Nazis. Savage was just one of many psychiatrists who maintained that hereditary insanity would ultimately lead to the extinction of the human race and his successors argued that clamping down on reproduction and immigration was the only means to prevent this. One Dr F. W. Mott claimed that children born to 'the pauper, to the alien Jew, to the Irish Roman Catholic, to the thriftless casual labourers, to the criminals' all carried a 'neuropathic taint', a comment echoed by another doctor who claimed that unregulated immigration made Great Britain a dumping ground for the unfit and that England had become the asylum of the world.[16]

Despite the dreary climate of therapeutic pessimism, certain advances were being made in the field of psychiatric medicine. Among these was a recognition that certain categories of mental or physiological disorder were not, in fact, evidence of 'madness' but specific conditions, such as epilepsy and 'idiocy', although all too often pauper victims of these conditions were swept up into the great asylums for the simple reason that the authorities had nowhere else to put them.

A notable exception was Park House Asylum, in Highgate, opened by the pioneering Dr Conolly and paid for by public subscription, for the benefit of 'the English idiot, a shambling knock-kneed man who was never a child, with an eager utterance of discordant sounds which he seemed to keep in his protruding forehead, a tongue too large for his mouth, and a dreadful pair of hands that wanted to ramble over everything – our own face included' who would otherwise have been left to rot in a work-house, 'wallowing in the lowest depths of degradation and neglect: a miserable monster, whom nobody may put to death, but whom every one must wish dead, and be distressed to see alive'.[17]

Dickens visited Park House in 1853, and spotted various conditions which now sound suspiciously like autism or even dyslexia, including so-called 'idiots' who could assemble watches and work out complicated mechanical designs, but scarcely string two words together. Park House was a fine detached house, beautifully situated at a considerable elevation above the metropolis, looking down over the spot where Richard Whittington heard the bells summon him back to his destiny as Lord Mayor of London. The altitude was significant, as it was believed that 'cretins' or idiots did better at a higher elevation. Dickens found the male schoolroom as quiet and orderly as any he had ever seen, and also inspected a basket-weaving session, with 'some little fellows busily plaiting straw of various colours'.

> In another room, the whole male body had turned out on parade, and were being drilled by an old soldier; going through their exercise with such precision, that onlookers were disposed to suggest the addition of an Idiot Corps to the Militia. Then came a work-room full of girls, sewing, and making little fancy ornaments with beads and parti-coloured strips, and rooms full of children of all ages, in the keeping of female attendants whose pleasant and patient countenances were a strong assurance of their being well selected, except in only one instance where we certainly derived a less agreeable impression ... everybody seemed devoted heart and soul to the good work in hand.[18]

Dickens himself was at a loss to explain the origins of idiocy, reviewing the popular theories of the day, including the idea that if a mother was sufficiently frightened her child would be born an idiot, and even the notion that idiocy was a result of poor dentition, a bizarre concept which held currency among fringe practitioners until the early twentieth century and led to some unfortunate mental patients having all their teeth extracted.

*

As the classification of mental illness developed, anecdotal explanations and old wives' tales jostled alongside the developing medical model. For instance, William Mosley maintained that madness was the result of external causes. In his list of events destined to drive you crazy, he includes all the usual suspects such as 'Hard, intense and *long-continued studies*', onanism and disappointed love, as well as some more unusual triggers:

11thly. Domestic disturbances and quarrels have made more husbands, wives, and daughters nervous, than the sword has slain; and ought, on this ground, to be most religiously guarded against . . .

14thly. The excessive desire of children.

15thly. Extreme hunger, continued some days.

18thly. Great fear.

21stly. Blows on the head.

22ndly. Mal-formation of the *cranium*.

23rdly. Lightning.

24thly. Gambling.

25thly. Jealousy.

26thly. The sudden death of persons in our presence.

27thly. The horrors of a storm at sea.

28thly. The fearful associations of being awoke from sound sleep while the house is on fire.

29thly. The sight of a public execution.

31stly. And INFLUENZA – are but a few of the exciting causes of nervous disease that have come under our notice.[19]

Another cause, according to one Princess Lieven, was seafood. In a letter to Prince Metternich on 27 January 1821, she relates the sad fate of a gentleman friend:

It is less than three weeks since he came to call on me. I was alone with him. He told me that he was sometimes seized by fits of madness, during which he was not responsible for his actions. At this alarming information, I went up to the bell-cord and stood sentinel until the Duke of York came in and rescued me from our *tête-à-tête*. Afterward, I told my husband that I thought Hardenbrot was talking very incoherently. He made enquiries and was told that he was in excellent health and had never shown any sign of madness. Two days later, he went off his head. He was put in charge of two doctors from Bedlam and died yesterday in a violent fit of madness . . . Don't ever think of eating lobster after dinner: this is what the poor lunatic used to do![20]

In 1844, the Metropolitan Lunacy Commissioners devised a more specific classification. This consisted of:

I. Mania, which is thus divided:
    1. Acute Mania, or Raving Madness.
    2. Ordinary Mania, or Chronic Madness of a less acute form.
    3. Periodical, or Remittent Mania, with comparatively lucid intervals.
II. Dementia, or decay and obliteration of the intellectual faculties
III. Melancholia
IV. Monomania
V. Moral Insanity.
The three last mentioned forms are sometimes comprehended under the term Partial Insanity.
VI. Congenital Idiocy
VII. Congenital Imbecility
VIII. General Paralysis of the Insane.
IX. Epilepsy
To these heads may perhaps be added 'Delirium Tremens', since

it is mentioned, as a form of Insanity, in the Reports of some lunatic asylums.[21]

*

It was not until the close of the nineteenth century that classifications of mental illness as we would recognise them began to emerge. One major cause, now mercifully rare, was identified, while two sets of diagnostic criteria evolved which are with us to this day. The first of these was a condition with distinctive physical characteristics referred to as 'GPI' or 'Paralytic Dementia'. GPI was a form of progressive dementia characterised by delusions of grandeur, failing memory, facial tics, slurred speech and unsteady gait.[22] It was an incurable disease, resulting in utter helplessness and death within three years of onset and its victims were predominantly male. Asylum doctors regarded it as a complication of insanity, while the physicians at the National Hospital for Nervous Diseases argued that it was not a neurological disorder but a consequence of hereditary madness, alcoholism, sexual excess, overwork, domestic problems, disappointed love, reversals of fortune and even smoking. GPI was commonly believed to have been recognised as a disease in its own right in French asylums in the 1820s, although Bethlem's John Haslam gives us a recognisable case study in his *Illustrations of Madness* (1810). This describes a 42-year-old man admitted in June 1795, suffering from delusions of grandeur, ostensibly caused by heat exhaustion. A gardener by trade, he had travelled all over Europe in his younger days. His mind began to run on what he had seen there, and he fancied himself fluent in all languages, living and dead, and that he was actually the King of France, or the King of Denmark. At other times, he claimed to be an aristocrat whose family had come over with William the Conqueror. He was irritable and contentious, but after ten months or so was regarded as fit enough for discharge. But the following year he relapsed and was readmitted with a 'paralytic affection: his speech was inarticulate, and his mouth drawn aside. He shortly became stupid, his legs swelled and afterwards ulcerated: at length his appetite failed him; he became emaciated, and died December 27th of the same year.' When his brain was opened, Haslam noted evidence of brain damage, including great quantities of water between the membranes, a deep brown 'blotch' on the right hemisphere and 'turgid' veins in the ventricles.[23] Haslam was convinced that this indicated a physiological cause for the patient's symptoms but he failed to make the connection and recognise that this cause was syphilis and it was to be another century before the mystery was solved.

By 1844, the Lunacy Commission had classified GPI as 'incurable and hopeless' and caused by organic disease in the brain, and noted that the condition 'seldom occurs in females, but mostly in men, and is the result almost uniformly of a debauched and intemperate life'. During its third and final stage, the patient lost

> not only the power of locomotion, but can neither feed himself nor answer the calls of nature. He becomes more and more weak and emaciated, but generally perishes under some secondary disease, such as gangrene, sloughing of the surface of the body, or diarrhoea, unless he be cut off at an earlier period by an apoplectic or epileptic attack, to which these patients are very liable. The disorder of the mind is peculiar in this affection. It is generally a species of monomania, in which the individual affected fancies himself possessed of vast riches, and power.[24]

The German psychiatrist Richard von Krafft-Ebing (1840–1902) had his own theories about the origins of GPI. As befitted a doctor whose own field of research was human sexuality, Krafft-Ebing believed that the disease had a physiological cause. Rather than being the by-product of a 'debauched and intemperate life', GPI was actually the result of a sexually transmitted disease: syphilis.

The earliest recorded references to syphilis come from 1495, when it was suggested that the disease was introduced into Europe from the New World (although the counter-argument is that the

Europeans took it with them to the Americas). In 1495, an attack broke out among Italian troops, and spread across Europe, reaching England and Holland the following year. It reached India in 1498. In 1500 there was a syphilis epidemic in Europe and in 1505 it reached China.[25]

Syphilis is caused by an organism called *Treponema pallidum*, which is a type of bacterium called a spirochete, and is characterised by three stages: primary syphilis, secondary syphilis and tertiary syphilis. Syphilitics often experience a period of latency, in which no symptoms are visible. Syphilis is usually transmitted through sexual intercourse but can also be transmitted from mother to child *in utero*, a condition known as congenital syphilis.

In cases of primary syphilis, a lesion or 'chancre' is visible on the genitals or other parts of the body, and often goes unnoticed, healing without treatment. At this stage, the condition lasts between ten and fifty days. While the chancre is healing, the second stage begins, indicated by a rash which appears between six weeks and six months of infection. This rash was the reason for the little black spots sported by society beauties and courtesans in the sixteenth and seventeenth centuries: they were designed to hide the symptoms of venereal disease. The rash resembles chicken pox or dermatitis, and can be accompanied by aching joints, fever and palpitations and infectious weeping sores, teeming with spirochetes. At this stage, if the patient recovers, there is a latent period, when the symptoms disappear. A patient can remain in this state of latency for between three weeks and thirty years.

The third and final stage is tertiary syphilis, or 'late syphilis', when characteristics occur such as gummy or rubbery tumours resulting from the concentration of spirochetes in the body's tissues with the destruction of vital structures. At this stage, syphilis attacks the cardiovascular and central nervous systems, causing heart valve damage, or even aneurisms, and softening of the brain tissues, leading to progressive paralysis and insanity.

The earliest remedy for syphilis was mercury, which was applied to the lesions and remained the only treatment option between the fifteenth and nineteenth centuries, although an undesirable side effect was death from mercury poisoning. By the Victorian era, entrepreneurs such as William Earl were advertising fantastic remedies which would effect 'a complete and radical cure' without recourse to mercury. It was possible to get away with these fraudulent claims in a society where the causes and cures of venereal disease were scarcely a matter for public debate. One remedy which did have some validity was the development and use of potassium iodide. This represented an important advancement in the treatment of syphilis as it was effective even in the late stages of the disease (while mercury was not) and because it paved the way for the discovery of an even more potent and effective treatment, although it would not be until 1928, when Alexander Fleming discovered penicillin, that a satisfactory cure would be found and not until 1945 that penicillin became widely available and accepted as the treatment of choice for syphilis.[26]

In 1897, Krafft-Ebing injected syphilis into nine GPI patients. None of the patients said that they had ever had symptoms of syphilis, but none of them developed the symptoms of syphilis after the injection, suggesting that they had already been exposed to the disease and contracted it in the past. In 1905, the Wasserman test for syphilis was developed, and in 1912 doctors at Colney Hatch followed up Krafft-Ebing's research. Forty patients diagnosed with GPI underwent a Wasserman test and out of these forty patients, thirty-eight gave a positive reaction for syphilis. A year later, the hospital tried lumbar puncture as a test, but this was a new procedure and only revealed eleven cases. To the practised eye, the symptoms of congenital syphilis were indeed visible. The disease had its own 'stigmata' as a photograph from the Colney Hatch archives shows. This is the image of a young boy with keratitis (inflammation of the cornea), rhages (retinal haemorrhages) and notched incisors, also known as 'Hutchinson's Teeth'. Recognisable to the doctors of the time, congenital syphilis is now so rare that it could easily be missed.

Another important form of classification emerged in 1896 with Emil Kraepelin's model of 'dementia praecox', first used by Morel in 1860 and described as 'irrecoverable cortical brain disease producing a particular kind of mental enfeeblement in the young'. Many patients recovered, nonetheless, but were then reclassified as suffering from manic depression, the other major division of Kraepelin's system, and which differed from dementia praecox as it occurred in attacks. Kraepelin was convinced that dementia praecox had an organic origin, and tasked his assistant to find lesions in the brain. The assistant failed, but, instead, in 1907, he discovered neuropathological changes characteristic of a form of presenile dementia which now bears his name – Alzheimer.[27]

In 1908, Eugen Bleuler developed his own theory of dementia praecox by claiming that the disease had psychological, not neurological, origins, and that the disorder was caused by inner conflicts, emotionally charged complexes and sexual fantasies which were so unbearable that the patient developed a fragmentation of their personality as they struggled to cope, leading to a complete withdrawal from painful reality. His name for the disease? 'I call it "schizophrenia",' he wrote, 'because the "splitting" of the different psychic functions is one of its important characteristics.'[28]

*

Classifications of this sort, although they might have been blunt diagnostic instruments, did at least mean that at last the concept of 'madness' was being recognised as a genuine physical and mental entity rather than the result of demonic possession or an excess of black bile. But the majority of the mad, untreatable and unvalued, remained incarcerated in the great asylums, which were little more than prisons designed as hospitals. Bethlem, meanwhile, had undergone nothing less than a fairytale transformation. By the time the Reverend Geoffrey O'Donoghue was putting the finishing touches to his popular history of the institution, he compared the change to the final scene of a pantomime. With O'Donoghue's genial guidance, let us imagine what it might have been like to visit the hospital one rainy afternoon in October. Slipping through the gateway, away from the clamour of Lambeth Road, with its omnibuses, carriages and lively Cockney voices, you note with admiration the lush circular lawns and rose bushes, before glancing up to admire the distinctive pumpkin dome and noble portico. Passing through the entrance hall, you are not subjected to the disturbing sight of Cibber's 'brainless brothers'. These statues have been banished to the Victoria and Albert Museum on the grounds that such dread reminders of mental agony and the mind in ruins cause distress to visitors and patients alike.

In front of you stands the steward's office; to the left, the dispensary, and in front of that 'the physician's parlour' where the resident physician was 'at home' to bewildered visitors who wanted some explanation for their loved one's condition. To the left of this, an administrative office, reassuringly full of the bureaucratic impedimenta of desks, pigeon-holes and dusty ledgers. Electric lighting has been installed, and a primitive telephone system connects every part of the hospital.

The female wards on the east side of the building could be mistaken for the drawing room of a ladies' club. There are flowers and pictures everywhere, and you feel as if you could sit down on one of the sofas and order afternoon tea from a maid as you flick through a novel or an illustrated magazine. This analogy holds good for the male wards on the western side, which resemble a Pall Mall club, with their smoking rooms, billiard tables and cavernous armchairs which, in O'Donoghue's vivid phrase, 'would transform Spartans into dreamy lotus-eaters'. You might not be able to call for coffee or liqueurs, but someone can always find you a cigarette, 'or some forgotten grains of loose tobacco, for we are all devotees of the mystic weed' as O'Donoghue confesses. (This is one aspect of life in a psychiatric hospital which never changes.) The only giveaway to the institution's purpose is those tiny windows, too small for you to wriggle through if you suddenly found yourself unavoidably detained, whatever your protestations of sanity.

O'Donoghue described this evolution as 'grub into butterfly' and in certain, practical ways, Bethlem by 1914 did seem transformed. Nurses had been recruited at a good salary, commensurate with that offered by London County Council, and the hospital boasted a 50 per cent recovery rate,[29] assisted by the fact that only patients who were 'considered curable' were accepted. Bethlem appeared to be an exemplary institution, although not every patient was satisfied with their treatment.

*

The novelist Antonia White (1899–1980) was a patient at Bethlem for ten months in 1922, and recounted the experience in her auto-biographical novel *Beyond the Glass* (1954). White's was one of the first authentic voices of the mad (as opposed to those who were declared mad, like poor Nathaniel Lee, or claimed to be sane, like Alexander Cruden). White had no doubt that she had lost her mind during this stage of her life, and subsequently referred to her madness as 'the beast'. But conditions at Bethlem, or 'Nazareth Royal Hospital', as she names it, are austere to the point of brutality.

After a violent fit of hysteria, the main protagonist, Clara, wakes to find herself lying on a mattress on the floor in a dirty, white-washed cell. There are no sheets, just blankets, and she is bitterly cold.[30] Then come violent hallucinations, caused either by illness or medication: given straw to lie on, Clara becomes convinced she is a horse, 'ridden almost to death, beaten till she fell'; after the horse dies, a child sows turquoises around the outline of her body in the ground and she rises again, a 'horse of magic with a golden mane, galloping across the sky'.[31] Clara is also a stag, and a salmon, suffocating in a dry stone cell, desperate to reach the waterfall beyond the bars, wriggling and gasping, scraping its scales on the stone floor. Interspersed with these frightening delusions come accounts of Clara's treatment. She is given a coarse brown dressing gown and dragged off for a series of baths, first boiling hot, then freezing cold, topped off with a bucket of ice-cold water. During one of her attacks, Clara is taken off to 'pads', a room lined with bulging grey rubber, with a small window, shaped like an eye, through which a red face watches her – and laughs.[32] On another occasion, Clara is wrapped in a stiff canvas sheet, like 'sailcloth' and confined to a 'manger', a wooden bed lined with straw. Further torment comes in the form of two nurses and a young man with a basin and a length of tubing who force-feed Clara to save her from starvation.

As she gradually comes to her senses, Clara notes her surroundings: beyond the cell, there are long waxed corridors and the atmosphere of a dusty museum, with those wax flowers under glass cases and engravings of Queen Victoria so praised by O'Donoghue for their civilising influence. To emphasise Clara's confusion and isolation, she can even see a garden through her cell window, and buses trundling up and down the street in the real world which is so tantalisingly close but so far away.

Eventually, Clara is considered well enough to be allowed outside, not to the beautiful garden, alas, but to an asphalt-covered exercise yard with a broken bench, one plane tree, and a daunting inscription on one of the high brick walls:

Baby

Blood

Murder

It is at this point that Clara is sufficiently recovered to take an interest in her fellow patients. These include a beautiful girl who looks like one of Renoir's models, whom she nicknames 'Sunny Breezes' on account of the fact that she can only talk about the weather, and two terrifying older women, one of whom possesses 'a face that could hardly be called a face for the features were partly obliterated and the skin was red-glazed and puckered as if the flesh had been burnt away' and another who is almost classically beautiful, with a broad forehead, greying curls and eyes 'that seemed to be carved out of green stone', but whose mouth is 'hideously deformed', with 'two long yellow eye-teeth [grown] down over the lower lip, like the fangs of an old tiger'.[33] It is this patient who tries to attack Clara and has to be restrained, but not before she has hit one nurse and knocked the other's cap off.

At this point, Clara begins to come to her senses and understand that she inhabits a strange 'Alice in Wonderland' world, in which her fellow patients twitter senselessly as they play croquet with no observance of the rules and there is even a 'duchess' in the form of a mad old lady who demands that Clara curtsy to her, since she is really a queen in hiding from potential assassins. 'The next moment it came to her. These women were mad. She was imprisoned in a place full of mad people.'

This marks the beginning of Clara's recovery, but explaining this insight to the sympathetic Dr Bennett proves challenging. Clara is frightened that she will never leave. When asked if she feels she is being kept at 'Nazareth' against her will, Clara bursts into tears: 'What's the good,' she sobs, 'if I say yes, [Dr Bennett]'ll think I'm mad. And if I say no, he'll think I don't want to go home'.[34] A further aspect of Clara's treatment which emerges is the intense loneliness she experiences as she realises she is no longer mad but that she is utterly without friends here. She explains that she felt so isolated having to be with the same people and not being able to talk to them that she had deliberately started to copy the way the other patients behaved, and even imitate their words and gestures as they seemed to understand each other in a strange sort of way. 'It was beginning to work,' she confides, 'and in time . . .' Fortunately, Clara is released on parole for a fortnight and subsequently discharged, but not without this disturbing insight into the nature of institutionalisation.

Clara's breakdown and subsequent treatment conform to preconceived theories of female hysteria: she is deemed to have lost her mind following an unhappy marriage, a divorce and an affair with a new lover. Clara receives the standard treatment at Bethlem, including the mechanical restraint advocated by Savage, the traditional hot and cold baths and the drugs. But her doctor is ultimately presented as a reassuring and sympathetic figure with a genuine desire to see her restored to sanity. When Clara goes home, she is appalled to discover that her parents had been preparing themselves for the fact that she might never recover. In this, Clara was a typical product of her class and gender. But while Clara was fighting for her sanity in 'Nazareth', the medical establishment was recovering from an extraordinary development which transformed the attitude towards hysteria in particular and mental illness in general, and affected the fate of Bethlem itself during the following century.

MODERN BEDLAM

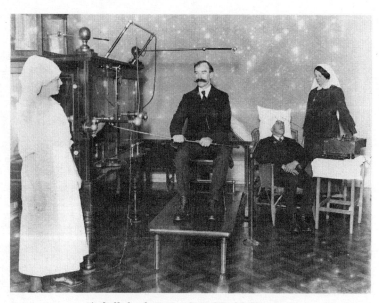

A shell shock victim from World War One.

There is an exhibit at the Imperial War Museum which at first glance appears to be some forgotten gem of the silent movie genre, crudely comic in effect, featuring soldiers twitching and shuddering spasmodically as though in anticipation of the 'Silly Walks' sketch from *Monty Python's Flying Circus*. But on close examination you realise that this is no comedy. Recorded for training purposes by World War One army doctors, these pathetic creatures are the victims of shell shock, the mysterious phenomenon that had a massive impact on the attitude to madness and its treatment by virtue of its sheer scale. British doctors were suddenly faced with around 80,000 cases of apparent mental breakdown among ostensibly fit and active men. Men, not frail young women, were succumbing to a fit of the vapours. It was unprecedented. The 'monolithic theory of hereditary degradation upon which Victorian psychiatry had been based was significantly dented as young men of respectable and proven character were reduced to mental wrecks after a few months in the trenches'.[1]

By December 1914, a report reached the director general of the Army Medical Services in London, stating that 7–10 per cent of officers and 3–4 per cent of other ranks in hospitals in Boulogne had suffered nervous or mental breakdowns. The army sent William Aldren Turner, a top neurologist, out to France to investigate. It was soon apparent that the problem was getting worse. By 1916, shell shock cases constituted up to 40 per cent of casualties from heavy fighting zones, and one doctor later commented that he had most of the officers and men from an entire regiment under his care at the 4th and 5th Army Advanced Neurological Centre.[2]

The Cambridge psychologist C. S. Myers invented the term shell shock in 1915 and it soon became popular with soldiers and civilians as an informal description of the phenomenon. However, medical and legal commentators distrusted the term for this very reason. Shell shock was far too vivid and populist a name for the dusty medico-legal lexicon. The term was officially banned by the Army Medical Service in 1917, but by then it was too late: shell shock, as a label for a broad spectrum of mental and physical symptoms, had entered the language.

According to official statistics, around 80,000 cases of shell shock passed through army hospitals, of which approximately 30,000 ended up in institutions in Britain. There were around 200,000 discharges from active service, leading to a drain in resources. At first, shell shock was assumed to have a physiological origin and the hysterical symptoms that characterised the condition were described as 'Disordered Action of the Heart'. There was also a reluctance to give psychiatric diagnoses because of the implied stigma, so patients were simply described as sick or debilitated, with a covert recognition that life in the trenches, experiencing extreme terror and anxiety on a daily basis, was scarcely normal, and enough to induce trauma in the most robust personality. This led to another, extraordinary development: while popular prejudice might have predicted that it would be the ordinary men of the regiment who sustained shell shock, the 'other ranks' who had not endured years of public school discipline, it was actually the officers, trained for command, who proved most susceptible. Young and isolated, they were out of their depth, facing a war for which no amount of drill or immersion in the military tactics of the Classics could have prepared them. Lacking essential leadership skills, they succumbed at twice the rate of the ranks. This had severe strategic implications, given the loss of officers in the earlier stages of the war. Shell shock also had terrible implications for morale: it undermined the army code of conduct, and, on occasion, seemed to trigger outbreaks of mass hysteria. The army's *esprit de corps*, which had been bolstered by the 'Pals' system of recruitment, in which entire villages and factories had volunteered together, had been destroyed, leaving a culture of cynicism and despair in the trenches.

Army doctors initially believed that shell shock represented a breach of discipline and constituted a form of malingering. It was suggested that patients suffering from the disorder should be sent to army prisons, asylums, or even court-martialled and shot. But by 1917 shell shock had reached such epidemic proportions that it would have been impossible to court-martial all the victims.

The War Office, GHQ on the Western Front and, most of all,

the Royal Army Medical Corps could formulate no explanation for shell shock when it first appeared, with its extraordinary range of symptoms. These included strange jerking movements of the limbs, indicating muscular contractions; blindness, tics, mental confusion, catatonia, obsessive-compulsive disorders, amnesia, insomnia, nightmares and panic attacks. Totally at a loss, army doctors referred to the condition as 'delusional insanity' and packed the patients back off to Blighty, to the Royal Victoria Hospital at Netley and the neurological hospitals in London. In spring 1915, Moss Side Asylum in Manchester was commandeered and renamed Maghull War Hospital, and by 1918 over twenty army hospitals in Britain took shell shock cases, along with smaller convalescent homes for officers. Even shell shock, it seems, had a class divide. While regular soldiers were more likely to suffer symptoms of hysteria – paralysis, blindness, deafness, contractions, mutism and limping – officers reported neurasthenic or chronic anxiety states with symptoms such as nightmares, insomnia, palpitations, dizziness and depression.[3]

The majority of the medical staff was perplexed: how had it come to this? Why were officers and men, particularly officers, giving way to hysteria? These were not pauper lunatics; their symptoms could not be dismissed as the hereditary consequence of generations of venereal disease, poverty, deprivation and alcohol abuse: these were England's finest, public schoolboys, Oxford and Cambridge Blues, devotees of the Horatian maxim *dulce et decorum est, pro patria mori* – 'it is sweet and fitting to die for one's country', a tag used to devastating effect in Wilfred Owen's horrific account of a gas attack. So how could these men, of all people, be going mad? There could only be one possible explanation: shell shock must be a result of actual physical damage to the central nervous system caused by the sound of exploding shells. Physical causes included concussion, carbon monoxide poisoning, changes in atmospheric pressure and even 'an invisibly fine molecular commotion in the brain'.[4]

But it soon became obvious that this was not a rational explanation: although soldiers who had been shelled were presenting with shell shock, so too were men who had never been near a blast. And far from being a sudden breakdown, many others were succumbing to the insidious onset of mental illness over a period of weeks or months.

Bafflement at the symptoms was followed by confusion as to suitable treatment for shell shock. At first, conventional 'rest cures', such as those used on delicate Victorian maidens, were attempted: milk diets, massage and bed rest. But patients were haunted by memories of their horrific experiences. One treatment for this was to distract the patients and encourage them to focus on happier, more positive memories, but with such a high level of trauma this method was doomed to fail. And there was another, more pressing need: the officers and men invalided out by shell shock were desperately needed back in action at the Front. Under pressure to restore their troops and make them operational once more, army doctors turned their attention to another treatment option: 'Faradisation' – otherwise known as Electric Shock Treatment.

The Canadian neurologist Dr Lewis Yealland treated an unnamed private at his private clinic at Queen's Square in 1917. This 24-year-old man was a veteran of Mons, the battle of the Marne, Ypres, Neuve Chapelle, Loos and Armentières. Sent to Salonica he had collapsed, ostensibly with heat exhaustion, and had been mute for nine months despite all attempts to cure him, including hypnotism, electric shocks to his neck and throat and cigarette burns on his tongue. Yealland was determined to get this young man to speak so that he could be sent back into action:

'You are a young man with a wife and child at home,' he told him. 'You owe it to them if not to yourself to make every effort to restore yourself. You appear to me to be very indifferent, but that will not do in such times as these . . . you must recover your speech at once.'[5]

Instead of replying, the young soldier only became more

depressed. Later that evening, he was taken down to the basement, strapped into a chair, and his mouth was propped open with a tongue depressor. Then electric currents were applied to his pharynx, causing him to startle backwards so strongly that leads were pulled out of the electrical battery. All the time, Yealland reminded the young man of the obligations of his masculinity and told him to behave like 'a hero', reminding him that someone who had survived so many battles really ought to be in control of himself. This went on for four hours. After the first hour, the patient could whisper 'Ah!' but this was not considered to be enough. The patient tried to get up and leave, but was forced back in the chair with the assurance that Yealland, not the patient, would decide when the treatment was over. The patient pointed at the electrical apparatus, as if to indicate that he was ready for more, but Yealland's response was: 'Suggestions are not wanted from you; they are not needed. When the time comes for more electricity you will be given it, whether you wish it or not.' Yealland later wrote that 'I had intended at that time to resort to electricity, but, owing to his attitude, I postponed its use and instead made him walk up and down the room repeating "ah, ah, ah," merely to keep him awake and to show him that his suggestion regarding the electricity would not be accepted.'[6]

Yealland returned to the battery and administered shocks until the patient began to stammer and cry. Even then, this was not enough: he continued applying strong shocks until the young man spoke, without stammering. He was obliged to say 'thank you' when it was over.[7] On another occasion, Yealland recalls that he told a patient that his feelings during the procedure were irrelevant. 'It makes very little difference to me what you think of your condition,' he told a young man who choked and twitched continuously, and dreamed of blood and exploding mines after six months in the Somme. 'I do not want to hear your views on the subject.' Yealland records that after ten minutes of strong electric shocks, the young man had stopped twitching. The patient later said that he no longer dreamed of blood and mines – instead he dreamed he was having electrical treatment in the trenches. Yealland regarded this as an indication that he had been successful. If it seems extraordinary to us that the young soldier put up with such appalling treatment, we should bear in mind the alternative: a court martial and the prospect of being shot. Despite attempts to treat what appeared to be a neurological disorder, shell shock was still regarded in some circles as a disciplinary rather than a medical condition, suffered by shamming malingerers.[8] One army lawyer claimed that by 1918, 'shell shock' had become a 'parrot-cry' at courts martial.

*

Yealland's barbaric treatment of shell shock patients gave way to a more enlightened approach, courtesy of C. S. Myers, who maintained that the way to treat shell shock was to regard it as a form of hysteria. Myers collaborated with William Aldren Turner, who had originally been sent out to France to investigate the causes of shell shock, and they put considerable energy into psychotherapy as a cure.[9]

Back in England, at the shell shock hospitals of Netley and Maghull, doctors began using psychotherapy as a treatment option, their methods concentrating on 'abreactive' or 'cathartic' techniques, designed to enable participants to relive painful experiences which had been suppressed. This brought condemnation from established British psychiatrists who regarded the theories of Freud and his peers as 'Teutonic Science'. (Psychiatry, as a discipline, had always been taken more seriously in Northern Europe. A tradition of psychiatric medicine had already been established in Germany and Austria before World War One.)

One psychiatrist, Sir Robert Armstrong Jones, dismissed psychoanalysis as a treatment option (for shell shock) by stating that it was 'probably applicable to people on the Austrian and German frontiers, but not to virile, sport-loving, open-air people like the British!'[10] One popular and enduring misinterpretation of Freud was that he was obsessed with sexuality, neglecting the fact that he had become increasingly preoccupied with death and 'thanatos' – not, as some have translated it, 'the death wish' but the complete and utter terror of death. It was W. H. R. Rivers, treating shell shock cases at Craiglockhart Military Hospital in Edinburgh, who realised that Freudian theory had a place in the battlefield. Rivers maintained that Freudian principles were appropriate when it came to dealing with the fundamental human experiences of death, which could cause psychiatric disease. Between them, Rivers and Myers devised a 'psychiatric fix' for shell shock which resulted in squads of fifty RAMC officers undergoing crash-courses in psychotherapy and dream analysis by the end of the war, GPs being encouraged to hand over their shell shocked patients to specialist psychotherapists and civilian doctors being trained as psychotherapists to work in specialist clinics set up by the Ministry of Pensions to deal with the floods of shell shocked ex-servicemen desperate for treatment.[11]

Myers in particular was responsible for a number of reforms, including pressing for a ban on the diagnosis shell shock, or any other informal diagnosis. Shell shock cases were described as 'NYDN – Not Yet Diagnosed (Nervous?)' and they were segregated from soldiers with psychotic conditions or who were awaiting court martial. He persuaded the authorities to open four Advanced Neurological Centres a few miles from the Front to deal with shell shock cases coming straight off the battlefields and out of the trenches. These centres were a combination of field hospitals and military camps, with NCOs in charge. This helped the army detect fraudulent cases where the symptoms were being faked, and detect cases of genuine mental breakdown. All of which makes Myers sound heroic, and so he was, in a psychiatric context, but it is worth bearing in mind that, like Rivers, his intention was that of his military controllers: to return soldiers to the line on behalf of the war effort, and that the acceptance of psychological therapies by the RAMC was a consequence of an industrial approach to warfare.

One positive outcome was that psychology and psychotherapy

were at least being taken seriously by mainstream British psychiatrists, even it was only in the context of an authoritarian tool. As for shell shock, despite military and medical resistance, the general public showed themselves only too willing to accept the condition. Victims of shell shock were treated sympathetically in the press and in Parliament, with the Under-Secretary of State for War delegating a committee of the Royal College of Physicians to investigate how the 'regiments of broken men' could best be looked after.[12] Athelstan Rendell MP asked how shell shock victims fared in asylums, and whether asylum doctors were qualified to treat them, while his colleague, Cecil Harmsworth, put a mental health Bill before Parliament designed to exempt shell-shocked servicemen from certification under the 1890 lunacy laws.[13] Shell shock had caught the sympathy and the imagination of the public, and been raised to 'the dignity of a new war disease before which doctors seemed well nigh helpless'.[14] It also brought about the recognition that psychotherapeutic techniques, based on the theories of Freud, might have a practical application and constitute an acceptable form of treatment. As one historian has observed:

> It was perhaps the First World War that most effectively brought home the artificiality of the distinction between the normal mind on the one hand and its abnormal conditions on the other. In the military hospitals the study of so-called shell shock revealed that symptoms quite as serious as the well-defined psychoses might arise through simple stress and strain and yet prove quickly curable by psychotherapeutic means. And thus it gradually became apparent that much of what had been considered abnormal might be discovered in the mind of the average man.

Shell shock did not disappear after the Armistice: around 114,600 ex-servicemen applied for pensions for shell shock between 1919 and 1929. These were not the same men who had gone off to war. They looked the same, when they came back, but 'something had altered in them. They were subject to queer moods and queer tempers, fits of profound depression alternating with a restless desire for pleasure. Many were easily moved to passion when they lost control of themselves, many were bitter in their speech, violent in opinion, frightening.'[15]

*

As we have seen, shell shock was no respecter of persons. The disorder claimed two of our most respected and celebrated war poets, Siegfried Sassoon and Wilfred Owen.

Sassoon (1886–1967) was a cricket-loving, fox-hunting country gentleman from a wealthy Anglo-Jewish family. Despite his name, Sassoon had no German connections: 'Siegfried' reflected his mother's passion for Wagner. After an undistinguished period at Clare College, Cambridge, Sassoon embarked on a writing career and was friendly with Robert Graves and Rupert Brooke. When war broke out in 1914, he joined up with typical machismo, enlisting in the ranks of the Sussex Yeomanry, before being commissioned the following year into the Royal Welch Fusiliers. The death of his brother at Gallipoli and of a good friend, David Thomas, drove him to acts of outrageous courage and revenge. His exploits were heroic and he earned the nickname 'Mad Jack' and the Military Cross, in 1916. On one occasion, Sassoon was so overwhelmed by the death of a comrade that he rode his horse into an enemy trench, lobbing grenades as he went, with all the passion of a fox hunter and the devastating aim of a spin-bowler.

However, by 1917, Sassoon had become disillusioned. Wounded in the shoulder, he was evacuated back to Britain. During his convalescence his discontent with the course of the war became more pronounced, a change which was reflected in his poetry:

'Good-morning; good-morning!' the General said
When we met him last week on our way to the line.
Now the soldiers he smiled at are most of 'em dead,
And we're cursing his staff for incompetent swine.

'He's a cheery old card,' grunted Harry to Jack
As they slogged up to Arras with rifle and pack.
But he did for them both by his plan of attack.[16]

Patriotism was replaced by intense criticism for the manner in which his military superiors conducted the war, and in July 1917, Sassoon published an open letter claiming that the war was being deliberately prolonged by those who had the power to end it. Sassoon narrowly avoided a court martial, thanks to the intervention of Robert Graves. Instead, he was diagnosed with shell shock and dispatched to Craiglockhart War Hospital in Edinburgh, where he was placed under the psychiatric treatment of Dr W. H. R. Rivers.

It was here, in 'Dottyville' as Sassoon called the hospital, that Sassoon met Wilfred Owen (1893–1918). Apart from their diagnosis, the two men could not have been more different. While vigorous, extrovert Sassoon had enjoyed army life, Owen, a shy, retiring young man who had already suffered one breakdown, had been horrified by the robust, crude company of the troops. Having enlisted in the Artists' Rifles, Owen had endured the horrific experience of being trapped in a shell hole for three days with his comrades, and developed shell shock. Sassoon, at ease with his homosexuality, boasted an extensive and sympathetic circle of gay friends, including Osbert Sitwell and K. Scott Moncrieff, translator of Proust. Religious and tormented, Owen was conflicted about his sexuality. But he hero-worshipped Sassoon, and the encounter was to change both men's lives. Bored to distraction by the convalescent regime, the pair contributed poetry to the hospital magazine. Sassoon encouraged Owen to write more honestly, more bitterly, about his experiences of war, while Owen became convinced that his ultimate duty was to return to the Front, even though Sassoon threatened to stab his friend in the leg if he tried. Sassoon subsequently returned to the Front, where his exploits were as reckless as ever. He was invalided out in 1918. Owen, meanwhile, faced no

pressure to return to active service and was offered work as a
teacher, but he felt it his duty to return. He was killed, in 1918, in
the last week of the war: his mother received the news of his death
as the church bells rang out to celebrate peace.

Owen produced a brief but enduring legacy reflecting his observation that 'the poetry is in the pity' and his work brought home to
civilians the bitter reality of war, such as this account of shell shock
patients:

> Who are these? Why sit they here in twilight?
> Wherefore rock they, purgatorial shadows,
> Drooping tongues from jaws that slob their relish,
> Baring teeth that leer like skulls' teeth wicked?
> Stroke on stroke of pain, – but what slow panic
> Gouged these chasms round their fretted sockets?
> Ever from their hair and through their hands' palms
> Misery swelters. Surely we have perished
> Sleeping, and walk hell: but who these hellish?
>
> These are men whose minds the Dead have ravished.
> Memory fingers in their hair of murders,
> Multitudinous murders they once witnessed.
> Wading sloughs of flesh these helpless wander,
> Treading blood from lungs that had loved laughter.
> Always they must see these things and hear them,
> Batter of guns and shatter of flying muscles,
> Carnage incomparable, and human squander
> Rucked too thick for these men's extraction.
>
> Therefore still their eyeballs shrink tormented
> Back into their brains, because on their sense
> Sunlight seems a blood-smear; night comes blood-black;
> Dawn breaks open like a wound that bleeds afresh.
> Thus their heads wear this hilarious, hideous,

Awful falseness of set-smiling corpses.
Thus their hands are plucking at each other;
Snatching after us who smote them, brother,
Pawing us who dealt them war and madness.[17]

*

In the treatment of shell shock, we can see the beginnings of the two major approaches to treating psychiatric disorders during the twentieth century: on the one hand, the psychoanalytic approach of Myers and Rivers, based on Freudian theory, and on the other, traditional medical psychiatry, enhanced by new developments, particularly electric shock treatment. These developments were to have particular significance for the future of Bethlem. By the 1920s – when Antonia White was undergoing her ordeal in the waxed corridors – it was clear that once again, the hospital needed to be rebuilt. The final scene in the transformation of Bethlem took place with the move from St George's Fields to Eden Park, in the sunlit uplands of suburban Kent. The hospital was built on a 240-acre site, previously the country estate of a banker, Lewis Loyd. There had been a mansion here, with trees and gardens, three lakes with cascades and a farm. The hospital built four separate houses in the villa style (reminiscent of a red brick university campus) and the rural atmosphere was maintained with pigs and cows, which the patients used to help muck out. The wards were carpeted and tastefully furnished, and the ground-floor bedrooms opened on to verandas so that bed-bound patients could be wheeled out to take the air. By this time, the majority of Bethlem's inmates were private patients who could pay their way[18] and who, significantly, were there by choice.

Choice, or being a voluntary patient, also played a part in the opening of a new hospital in London, with the help of funds donated by Dr Henry Maudsley to the LCC. Maudsley's wish was to establish a psychiatric hospital in a central position which would take patients on a voluntary basis, specialise in early and acute cases, and provide research facilities. According to its first medical superintendent, Dr Edward Mapother, it combined the character-istics of the European neurological and psychiatric clinics along with those of British hospitals. The Maudsley opened in Camberwell, across the road from King's College Hospital, in 1923, and consisted of several Georgian buildings in the 'Wrenaissance' style. Eventually, the medical school was taken over by the University of London and renamed the Institute of Psychiatry.[19] Meanwhile, the Tavistock Clinic, established in the Bloomsbury square of the same name, provided a centre for the development of the psychoanalytic theories and psychotherapeutic treatments which had been developed during World War One, inspired by the theories of Sigmund Freud, who died in Hampstead in 1939, having fled to England from Nazi Germany. The Viennese psy-chiatrist had a profound influence on our attitudes to mental illness. Still celebrated in some quarters, derided in others, Freud's theories lie at the heart of many modern treatment options. Who among us has not attempted, or at least heard of, the talking cure? Or accused a partner of being 'anal' when they insist on keeping a tidy house? Or hinted at their manager's 'repression' when the latter refuses to get up and dance at the company party? Or imposed ennui on their colleagues whilst recounting last night's dream?

To his critics, Freud will for ever be a caricature, an elderly cocaine fiend obsessed with sex (conveniently forgetting that cocaine was not a banned substance at the time, but prescribed as a euphoric, and Freud self-medicated with cocaine to treat his depression). Feminists have condemned Freud's attitude towards childhood sexual abuse, which he first recognised, and then denied. During his early investigations into the causes of mental distress, Freud recognised the prevalence of child abuse as a cause of hys-teria. But in later life, Freud changed his mind, claiming that such abuse constituted a fantasy on the victim's part, as they negotiated a difficult relationship with a parent or other authority figure.

Another criticism is that Freud's expertise derived from a very narrow sample of individuals from the Viennese bourgeoisie, privileged but neurotic: how could accounts of their struggles with personal demons possibly be relevant to other groups?

In his defence, Freud was one of the first psychiatrists to encourage his patients to talk intimately about their sexual desires and experiences and the influence of these on their lives and their sanity. The actual talking cure itself is a form of secular confession, and Freud's approach was deeply humane, inviting us to recognise the sometimes overwhelming nature of human experience, in the form of love, pain and loss. Freud's strength was to permit us to discuss our mental processes and reflect upon them, giving value and credence to our emotions, rather than attempting to blot them out with manacles, surgery or mind-altering substances. Freud's approach also provided an alternative treatment path for some patients: instead of incarceration, there was the possibility of consulting with their therapists in a private house, or attending hospital on an outpatient basis. In this respect, Freud was a successor to Robert Burton: if they were ever to meet in the Hereafter, the brilliant but depressive Oxford don would find much common ground with the Viennese doctor.

*

Sadly, Freud's progressive, enlightened attitude towards the mad was not universal during the aftermath of World War One. While the father of psychoanalysis presided over his Hampstead consulting rooms and listened sagely as his patients spoke to him from the celebrated couch, other branches of the medical profession demonstrated a more disturbing approach, arguing that those deemed feeble in mind and body should be eliminated for the sake of society. At first glance, we associate this attitude with Nazi Germany, where a National Socialist government was intent on producing a super race of 'Aryans' by the means of eugenics or selective breeding. Under the Nazis, thousands of physically and mentally ill men, women and children, Aryan and non-Aryan, were systematically murdered, in hospitals and death camps, and the slaughter would have continued in Britain had the German invasion of these shores been successful. What is even more alarming is that there were many members of the British medical establishment who supported the principles of eugenics and argued for the voluntary sterilisation of 'mental defectives'. Some even went so far as to advocate euthanasia. A. F. Tredgold, consulting physician to University College Hospital, London, argued that the 80,000 or more 'idiots and imbeciles' in Britain who were unemployable, a drain on the nation's resources and 'utterly helpless, repulsive in appearance, and revolting in manners' should have their existence painlessly terminated in an economical and humane procedure. 'It is doubtful if public opinion is yet ripe for this to be done compulsorily; but I am of the opinion that the time has come when euthanasia should be permitted at the request of a parent or guardian.'[20]

Although, mercifully, Tredgold's recommendations for a programme of mass euthanasia were not put into practice, many thousands of patients endured a form of living death in the overcrowded, underfunded Victorian asylums which, by the 1930s, had become monuments to therapeutic pessimism, filled with hopeless cases, the institutionalised, long-term sick and the mentally handicapped. In 1946, the newly formed National Health Service inherited around 100 asylums, with an average population of 1,000 patients each: something clearly had to be done about these 'mansions of misery'. Deliverance came from two main sources: the NHS itself, which had to take responsibility for the asylums; and the National Association for Mental Health (now MIND) founded in the same year and formed from a number of existing organisations. MIND continues to do sterling work on behalf of all people with mental health problems.

*

While NHS doctors and administrators set about reforming conditions and mental health campaigners pushed for better legislation, attitudes towards madness were undergoing another paradigm shift. Psychiatrists such as R. D. Laing (1927–89) were beginning to question the classic medical model of mental illness, in which the causes were organic, and, influenced by existentialist philosophers such as Søren Kierkegaard, Friedrich Nietzsche and Jean-Paul Sartre, suggested that madness (and sanity) were social constructs and that the mad might actually be the more perceptive individuals, desperately trying to adjust to societal norms while seeing through the pretence. Madness was an understandable response to trying to live an 'authentic' (honest) life in a shallow, dishonest world, and one aspect in particular caught Laing's imagination – dysfunctional family relationships. Given this diagnosis, appropriate treatment consisted of psychotherapy and allowing patients the opportunity to explore their inner turmoil, rather than administering large quantities of pharmaceuticals. In this sense, Laing only appears to have been developing Freud's approach, but his techniques were far more alarming. Laing turned against his clinical background in favour of alternative therapies such as 're-birthing' and founded a therapeutic community at Kingsley Hall, in east London. Unlike a conventional hospital, doctors were encouraged to drop their professional persona and engage with their patients as friends.

Laing's most famous patient was Mary Barnes (1923–2001), a former nurse who developed schizophrenia in her mid-thirties. Under Laing's influence, Mary attributed this condition to her 'abnormally nice' parents (one can only sympathise with Mr and Mrs Barnes at this display of monstrous ingratitude). When Mary was admitted to Kingsley Hall in 1965, Laing's solution was to encourage her to revert to an infantile state. Under his regime of 'Regression', Mary no longer spoke, but squealed; she was fed from a bottle and slept naked in a wooden box. Mary's days were spent screaming, crying, and covering herself in excrement. Mary became obsessed with her psychotherapist, Joseph Berke, who, on one occasion, claimed that she had provoked him so much that he hit her, bloodying her nose. When Berke apologised, Mary protested only that she loved him the more for it. It is clear at this point that the therapeutic relationship had been overstepped between doctor and patient. However, one day, Berke provided Mary with a box of crayons and some paper: the outcome was astonishing. From a state of infantilism, Mary emerged as a gifted artist, covering the walls with flaming suns, brilliant clouds and religious iconography. Within months, Mary was writing short stories to accompany her paintings and appearing barefoot at her book launch, speaking in a little-girl voice. She appeared to have made an astonishing transformation from the repressed, obsessive Catholic she had been prior to treatment. The rest of Mary's life was spent lecturing and painting, a testimonial to Laing's methods.

Kingsley Hall, however, was far from being an unqualified success, and closed in 1970. The following decade saw a plethora of alternative therapies such as Primal Scream and Transactional Analysis, many of which appear to have been a playground for dubious and narcissistic practitioners, unregulated by any professional code.

At the beginning of the 1980s, faced with the failure of the asylums, the NHS ushered in a system of closures. The massive Victorian hospitals such as Friern Barnet (formerly Colney Hatch) were shut down and the land sold off for private development. In their place came a scheme known as 'Care in the Community', an initiative which suggested that the mad would receive better treatment living at home or in hostels and visiting mainstream hospitals for their treatment. The concept of 'Care in the Community' originated with the right-wing libertarian Enoch Powell back in 1961, when he compared the great Victorian asylums with prisons and declared that they should be swept away.

Care in the Community proved disastrous. This is scarcely surprising as it was imposed by a government which believed that 'there is no such thing as society'. A fact which helpless, long-term, institutionalised mental patients discovered for themselves when they emerged blinking into the sunlight and found nothing there to support them. Instead, they faced a twilight world of shabby hotels and a bewildering benefits system. Lacking medical supervision, many failed to take their medication and relapsed, wandering the streets, sleeping rough, as riddled with lice and despair as any mediaeval Bedlam beggar. Those with families became the despair of their relatives, unable to meet their needs or have them readmitted to the hospital care they so desperately required. Friern Barnet, meanwhile, and the other mansions of the mad were sold off to property developers, the twilight wards and clammy cells transformed into bijou apartments for City folk.

Another tragic aspect of Care in the Community was a series of killings by mental patients who should never have been allowed out of hospital. In 1992, Jonathan Zito, a 27-year-old musician, was stabbed to death in Finsbury Park underground station in an unprovoked attack by Christopher Clunis, a schizophrenic. Mr Zito's wife subsequently set up the Zito Trust to campaign on the issue of the release of mentally ill patients. According to the Zito Trust, more than 100 people were killed by Care in the Community patients during the period 1993–8. The Trust claimed that approximately two people a month are murdered because of the failure to provide adequate care. One consequence of these tragic deaths is the perception that the mentally ill are more dangerous than the sane. In fact, an article in the *British Journal of Psychiatry* demonstrated conclusively, using Home Office statistics, that the proportion of homicides committed by people with a mental disorder (at most, ten per cent of all homicides in any case) has declined year on year, not only since the advent of community care, but ever since the late fifties when asylum populations were at their peak. 'Far from being the modern bogeyman, the majority of those with a mental illness are a greater danger to themselves than to others.'[21]

By 1990, even the Health Secretary Frank Dobson was admitting that 'care in the community has failed' and recommended secure units for seriously disturbed psychiatric patients. A new Mental Health Bill in 2002 brought controversy in its wake when it recommended that individuals with severe personality disorders should be detained indefinitely, even if they had not offended, although how any government could achieve this, given the shortage of hospital beds and prison cells, is debatable.

*

As we have seen over the centuries, the history of Bethlem has included many vivid, larger-than-life characters, from playwright Nathaniel Lee, drinking his talent away, to obsessional subeditor Alexander Cruden, from *soi-disant* spy James Tilley Matthews to would-be regicide Margaret Nicholson. The last personality to figure in these pages, the outspoken, humorous mental health activist Pete Shaughnessy proved himself a worthy successor. When in 1997 plans were announced to celebrate the 750th anniversary of Bethlem by the Bethlehem and Maudsley NHS Trust, Shaughnessy – a formidably articulate activist and founder member of Mad Pride – greeted them with disbelief. Shaughnessy, ever the master of the pithy soundbite, saw nothing to celebrate either in the original Bedlam, or in the current state of mental health care.[22] A patient at the Maudsley at the time, Shaughnessy was incensed when patients were offered a 'users' day' as part of the celebrations. 'I thought that was really token; that we were tacked on at the end of this really naff event,' he said. 'And then they said we're having a Thanksgiving Service at St Paul's, and I think that's probably when I snapped. We called that a Commemoration, for the people who have died and the sadness they've lived in.' Reclaim Bedlam's counter-demonstrations included a rally and march from the Imperial War Museum to the Maudsley in Camberwell; and a picket of the service at St Paul's, which involved a minute's silence on the steps outside.

Shaughnessy grew up in a working-class Irish family and attended drama school before working in a children's home and eventually fulfilling his childhood dream of becoming a bus driver, at the wheel of the number 36 to Peckham. But in 1992 he was viciously attacked by two passengers with an iron bar after going to the aid of his conductor. This incident was aggravated by the privatisation of the bus service, which saw Shaughnessy going on silent hunger strike outside the bus garage, and the breakdown of his relationship with his partner. He developed mental health problems which were later diagnosed as manic depression. Shaughnessy became an outspoken advocate for the mentally ill, forming Mad Pride. Like Gay Pride or Black Pride, Mad Pride saw a stigmatised group reappropriate language and force society to face its prejudices. 'Telling people I am mad is taking control of my madness and accepting it,' he said. 'By reclaiming language I'm turning my prison into a fortress.'

In 1995, Shaughnessy's younger sister, Theresa, was murdered by her boyfriend, who was later diagnosed as suffering from paranoid psychosis. Rather than distance himself from his sister's killer, Shaughnessy's response was to throw himself into the most contentious area of mental health care and examine how society responds to the criminally insane, becoming an advocate for patients at Broadmoor. Tragically, Shaughnessy lost his own battle with mental illness in 2002: on Sunday, 15 December, at about 6 p.m., at

Another inmate of Bethlem, Louis Wain was famous for his idiosyncratic cats.

Battersea Park railway station, he stepped off the platform into the path of a fast-moving train. The campaigner died from multiple injuries, having killed himself, according to the coroner, whilst the balance of his mind was disturbed. He was just forty years old.

*

Seven hundred and fifty years from its foundation, what can the modern visitor to Bethlem expect? Let me be your guide as we tour two 'Bethlems': the Imperial War Museum building in Lambeth, and the suburban hospital in Kent.

Hoping to recreate O'Donoghue's view of the institution, I arrive at the vestiges of Victorian Bethlem one cold and rainy afternoon in October, where I am received with sympathy by the staff, as if I too might be a potential inmate. At first, it is obvious that this building is now a museum – not a museum of madness but a museum of war, stuffed with an arsenal of military craft, including tanks and motorcycles and Spitfires dangling from the ceiling. But once I get behind the scenes, it is obvious that this was once an old Victorian hospital. Of course, lunatics no longer prowl the corridors; the cells are no longer havens for the weird, the mad and the misunderstood. Instead, the cells are offices, humming with modems and the gentle buzz of water-cooler chat. But those windows are still too small to squeeze through. Gazing through the thick glass panes across the lawn, I reflect that these are the same views Antonia White looked on, as she wondered if she would ever rejoin the vivid, noisy real world out on the Lambeth Road.

The distinctive ribbed iron ceilings have been painted over, and the wards have become storage bays for the museum's endless records. But the ghosts of Bethlem remain: staff speak with a humorous collective shudder of a reluctance to visit the stationery store in the basement: there is something of a chill in the air, down there, something not quite right. The museum of war is also a museum of death. There is no more fitting display of collective insanity than the Holocaust exhibition, with its scale models of con-centration camps and disturbingly rational account of the Nazi death machine, which would defy the imagination of Bethlem's most insane residents. Even James Tilley Matthews, persecuted by the Air Loom Gang, could not have envisaged such a deadly spectacle.

Arriving at the Bethlem Royal Hospital in Eden Park could not be more different from the day trippers arriving at Moorfields on a holiday, between a visit to the puppets and the Tower Menagerie. The railway station has helpful directions, and others are making the same journey, to visit the patients, but to console rather than to ridicule. There are no sideshows, or pickpockets, or dancing bears. There is an endless walk up a quiet street, lined with respectable suburban houses; and here is the hospital itself, with its smooth lawns and shady trees, the ideal therapeutic community, one of the most restful places I have ever seen.

As hospitals go, it is a paradise. But, lest we forget, the museum – which is open to the public – recalls 'Bedlam' in all its infamy. Here, you may inspect the restraints, the instruments for force-feeding, and meet the 'brainless brothers' face-to-face, larger than life and somewhat intimidating, crouched in the confines of a little room. In the casebooks you will find the sad histories of those who have already featured in this book. But you are not left without hope of redemption. The museum has regular exhibitions of patients' work and is a testament to art therapy. Among the items on display are works by Richard Dadd, Jonathan Martin (admitted in 1829 after attempting to burn down York Minster) and Louis Wain (1860–1939), famous for his cartoon cats, anthropomorphic creatures who were portrayed in an increasingly bizarre manner as Wain's psychosis progressed, their radiant colours glowing against psychedelic backdrops (Wain's parents were wallpaper designers and he seems to have been obsessed with brilliant colours and swirling designs). Unlike Dadd, who murdered his father, Wain was harmless, but too fragile to survive in the outside world. For Wain, Bethlem genuinely seems to have been a sanctuary, or, in the true sense of the word, an asylum.

And then, after looking round the museum, you are free to walk out and leave, thankful that you can do so, and reflecting that there but for grace go most of us. Walking in the grounds, one wonders what Simon FitzMary would have made of his legacy. Eden Park is a long way, literally and metaphorically, from the ramshackle hovel in Bishopsgate. Simon would have recognised some modern approaches: fringe treatments and complementary therapies such as herbal remedies and horoscopes were as familiar in the Middle Ages as they are today. Robert Burton would recognise the groaning shelves of self-help books as the natural successors to his *Anatomy of Melancholy*, although he would probably deplore the frenetic upbeat prose style. Beating and exorcism have mercifully been superseded by more enlightened approaches. It seems unlikely now that a man would rot in chains for twelve years, like poor William Norris. James Tilley Matthews would have blogged his conspiracy theories on the internet and Margaret Nicholson would have campaigners lobbying for her release and a stream of sympathetic visitors, while Antonia White's successors mine the rich seam of misery memoirs, battling Prozac or vodka or eating disorders.

This brings us to the end of this tour through 'Bedlam'. Like the jostling crowds who stared and jeered, and the concerned but curious commentators who came to watch and learn, we all possess a slightly voyeuristic interest in madness. This seems eternal: just as the crowds arrived at Moorfields on a holiday, so, a year or two ago, I participated in the eager throng traipsing around an exhibition dedicated to Hogarth at Tate Britain. The most popular exhibit was, inevitably, *The Rake's Progress*. Scores perused the fate of poor Tom Rakewell, and gawped at his eventual breakdown and incarceration, surrounded by mad stereotypes. A more cynical commentator might add that reality television programmes serve the same purpose, as millions examine and comment on the public spectacle of helpless, and often it seems senseless, individuals, losing their dignity on screen.

'Bedlam' itself may have disappeared, but madness is still a reality for many, requiring a life-long regime of medication and support. According to MIND, one in four of us will experience a mental health problem at some point of our lives. Each year more than 250,000 people are admitted to psychiatric hospitals and over 4,000 take their own lives. Among the population of 'the worried well', most of whom seem to be experiencing mild depression, perhaps following bereavement or redundancy, the popular option is a regular prescription for antidepressants, available with the super-market shopping and occasioning no more comment than a box of organic muesli or a bottle of vodka. Some of us prefer to endure 'melancholy' in its various manifestations and accept that this variety of madness is part of our identity. As a stoic of the old school, I am suspicious of the twenty-first-century notion of perpetual happiness, or the concept that I should be in a constant state of beatific calm. Over the years, I have learned to embrace melancholy, and welcome this dark side as my teacher, just as John Keats did when he celebrated 'the wakeful anguish of the soul'.

The poet experienced more than his fair share of misery during his short life: his father was killed by a fall from a horse when he was nine, and he nursed his mother during her terminal tuberculosis, succumbing to the same disease at twenty-six. Despite this, and the knowledge that he would soon cease to be, Keats recognised that to live is to suffer, and that there is no love without pain. For Keats, as for Robert Burton, to experience melancholy is to understand the nature of mortality:

'Ode on Melancholy'

No, no, go not to Lethe, neither twist
    Wolf's-bane, tight-rooted, for its poisonous wine;
Nor suffer thy pale forehead to be kiss'd
    By nightshade, ruby grape of Proserpine;
Make not your rosary of yew-berries,

Nor let the beetle, nor the death-moth be
    Your mournful Psyche, nor the downy owl
A partner in your sorrow's mysteries;
    For shade to shade will come too drowsily,
        And drown the wakeful anguish of the soul.

But when the melancholy fit shall fall
    Sudden from heaven like a weeping cloud,
That fosters the droop-headed flowers all,
    And hides the green hill in an April shroud;
Then glut thy sorrow on a morning rose,
    Or on the rainbow of the salt sand-wave,
        Or on the wealth of globèd peonies;
Or if thy mistress some rich anger shows,
    Emprison her soft hand, and let her rave,
        And feed deep, deep upon her peerless eyes.

She dwells with Beauty – Beauty that must die;
    And Joy, whose hand is ever at his lips
Bidding adieu; and aching Pleasure nigh,
    Turning to Poison while the bee-mouth sips:
Ay, in the very temple of delight
    Veil'd Melancholy has her sovran shrine,
        Though seen of none save him whose strenuous tongue
Can burst joy's grape against his palate fine;
    His soul shall taste the sadness of her might,
        And be among her cloudy trophies hung.

Notes

1: FOUNDATION

1. See O'Donoghue, *The Story of Bethlehem Hospital from its Foundation in 1247*, p. 2
2. Ibid. p. 3
3. Ibid. p. 5
4. Ibid.
5. See Andrews, *The History of Bethlem*, p. 28
6. See O'Donoghue, *The Story of Bethlehem Hospital*, pp. 19–20
7. Ibid. p. 28
8. Ibid. p. 30
9. Ibid.
10. Ibid. p. 72
11. Ibid. p. 86
12. http://www.bethlemheritage.org.uk
13. See O'Donoghue, *The Story of Bethlehem Hospital*, p. 36
14. Ibid. p. 37
15. Ibid. p. 43
16. Ibid. p. 39
17. Ibid. p. 45

2: MEDIAEVAL MADNESS AND MEDICINE

1. See O'Donoghue, *The Story of Bethlehem Hospital*, p. 28
2. Ibid.
3. Ibid. p. 69
4. Ibid. p. 66
5. See Scull, *Museums of Madness*, pp. 18–19
6. See Andrews, *The History of Bethlem*, p. 107
7. See O'Donoghue, *The Story of Bethlehem Hospital*, p. 88
8. See Hunter and Macalpine, *Three Hundred Years of Psychiatry*

(1535–1860), p. 2

9. See Andrews, *The History of Bethlem*, p. 99
10. See Simon, *Mind and Madness in Ancient Greece*, p. 32
11. See Garland, *The Eye of the Beholder*, p. 138
12. Ibid. p. 126
13. Deuteronomy 28: 28–9
14. Mark 5: 2–15
15. See O'Donoghue, *The Story of Bethlehem Hospital*, p. 72
16. Ibid. p. 133
17. Ibid. p. 86
18. See Scull, *Madhouses, Mad-Doctors, and Madmen*, p. 30
19. See O'Donoghue, *The Story of Bethlehem Hospital*, p. 86
20. Ibid. p. 72
21. See Hunter and Macalpine, *Three Hundred Years of Psychiatry (1535–1860)*, p. 12
22. See Andrews, *The History of Bethlem*, p. 52
23. See O'Donoghue, *The Story of Bethlehem Hospital*, p. 75
24. Ibid. p. 79
25. Ibid. p. 82
26. Ibid.
27. Ibid. p. 89
28. Ibid. p. 91
29. Ibid. p. 92
30. Ibid. p. 94

3: A MAD WORLD, MY MASTERS

1. See Andrews, *The History of Bethlem*, p. 18
2. See O'Donoghue, *The History of Bethlehem Hospital*, pp. 110–11
3. Ibid. p. 111
4. Ibid. p. 128
5. See Andrews, *The History of Bethlem*, p. 49
6. Ibid.
7. Ibid. p. 88
8. Ibid. p. 89
9. Ibid. p. 51
10. Ibid. p. 133
11. See Hunter and Macalpine, *Three Hundred Years of Psychiatry (1535–1860)*, p. 90
12. See O'Donoghue, *The Story of Bethlehem Hospital*, p. 148
13. Ibid. p. 150
14. Ibid.
15. See Porter, *Madness*, p. 66
16. See Shakespeare, *A Midsummer Night's Dream*, V. i. 7

17. See Shakespeare, *Hamlet*, V. i. 150–5
18. See Shakespeare, *King Lear*, I. v. 46–7
19. Ibid. III. ii. 1–9
20. See *The Penguin Dictionary of Quotations*, p. 5
21. See O'Donoghue, *The Story of Bethlehem Hospital*, p. 139
22. See Shakespeare, *King Lear*, II. iii. 9–20
23. Ibid. III. vi. 29–32
24. Shakespeare, *Hamlet*, IV. v. 60–1
25. See O'Donoghue, *The Story of Bethlehem Hospital*, p. 146
26. Ibid. p. 147
27. Ibid. pp. 135–7
28. Ibid. p. 139
29. See Andrews, *The History of Bethlem*, p. 102
30. See Mueller, *The Anatomy of Robert Burton's England*, p. 94
31. Ibid. pp. 95–6
32. See Ussher, *Women's Madness*, p. 51
33. Ibid. p. 52
34. See Hunter and Macalpine, *Three Hundred Years of Psychiatry (1535–1860)*, p. 32
35. Ibid.
36. See Mueller, *The Anatomy of Robert Burton's England*, p. 91
37. See Hunter and Macalpine, *Three Hundred Years of Psychiatry (1535–1860)*, pp. 68–75
38. See O'Donoghue, *The Story of Bethlehem Hospital*, p. 156

4: MYSTICAL BEDLAM

1. See Masters, *Bedlam*, p. 41
2. Ibid.
3. See Burton, *The Anatomy of Melancholy*, vol. I, p. 87
4. See O'Donoghue, *The Story of Bethlehem Hospital*, p. 158
5. Ibid. p. 168
6. See Hunter and Macalpine, *Three Hundred Years of Psychiatry (1535–1860)*, p. 107
7. Ibid. pp. 103–5
8. Ibid. p. 91
9. See O'Donoghue, *The Story of Bethlehem Hospital*, p. 178
10. See Russell, *Scenes from Bedlam*, p. 72
11. Ibid.
12. Ibid.
13. Ibid.
14. See Andrews, *The History of Bethlem*, p. 300
15. Ibid. p. 303
16. See Mueller, *The Anatomy of Robert Burton's England*, pp. 13–14

17. Ibid. p. 14
18. Ibid. pp. 14–15
19. Ibid. pp. 16–17
20. Ibid. p. 17
21. See Hunter and Macalpine, *Three Hundred Years of Psychiatry (1535–1860)*, p. 90
22. Ibid. p. 2
23. See Burton, *The Anatomy of Melancholy*, vol. III, pp. 359–60
24. Ibid. p. 390
25. Ibid. p. 381
26. Ibid. p. 385
27. See Mueller, *The Anatomy of Robert Burton's England*, p. 71
28. Ibid. p. 74
29. See Burton, *The Anatomy of Melancholy*, vol. I, p. 14
30. Ibid. p. 24
31. See Mueller, *The Anatomy of Robert Burton's England*, p. 26
32. See Burton, *The Anatomy of Melancholy*, vol. I, p. 461
33. Ibid. p. 166
34. Ibid. p. 164
35. Ibid. p. 166
36. See Burton, *The Anatomy of Melancholy* (1859 edition), p. x
37. See Burton, *The Anatomy of Melancholy*, vol. I, pp. 15–16
38. See Burton, *The Anatomy of Melancholy* (1859 edition), p. x
39. Ibid.
40. See Mueller, *The Anatomy of Robert Burton's England*, p. 6
41. Ibid. p. 7
42. See O'Donoghue, *The Story of Bethlehem Hospital*, p. 179
43. Ibid.
44. Ibid. p. 398
45. Ibid.
46. See O'Donoghue, *The Story of Bethlehem Hospital*, p. 181
47. Ibid. pp. 182–3
48. See Hunter and Macalpine, *Three Hundred Years of Psychiatry (1535–1860)*, p. 143
49. Ibid.
50. http://www.pendle.net/Attactions/quakers.htm
51. http://acaciapair.com/Acacia.John.Bunyan/Sermons.Allegories/Grace.Abounding/index.html
52. See Masters, *Bedlam*, p. 52
53. See O'Donoghue, *The Story of Bethlehem Hospital*, p. 169
54. Ibid. p. 170
55. Ibid. p. 397
56. Ibid. p. 142
57. Daniel V: 5–28

58. See O'Donoghue, *The Story of Bethlehem Hospital*, p. 172
59. See Russell, *Scenes from Bedlam*, p. 101
60. Ibid.
61. See O'Donoghue, *The Story of Bethlehem Hospital*, p. 176
62. See Russell, *Scenes from Bedlam*, pp. 102–3
63. Ibid. p. 102
64. See O'Donoghue, *The Story of Bethlehem Hospital*, p. 189
65. Ibid. p. 142
66. Ibid. p. 193

5: THE 'PALACE BEAUTIFUL'

1. See O'Donoghue, *The Story of Bethlehem Hospital*, pp. 216–17
2. See Stow, *Survey of London*, vol. I, book I, p. 192
3. See Batten, *The Architecture of Dr Robert Hooke FRS*, pp. 91–3
4. See Andrews, *The History of Bethlem*, p. 234
5. Ibid.
6. Ibid. p. 240
7. Ibid. p. 242
8. Ibid.
9. See Batten, *The Architecture of Dr Robert Hooke FRS*, pp. 91–3
10. See O'Donoghue, *The Story of Bethlehem Hospital*, p. 212
11. Ibid. pp. 212–13
12. See Stevenson, *Medicine and Magnificence*, p. 83
13. See O'Donoghue, *The Story of Bethlehem Hospital*, p. 231
14. See Batten, *The Architecture of Dr Robert Hooke FRS*, pp. 91–3
15. See Andrews, *The History of Bethlem*, p. 232
16. See O'Donoghue, *The Story of Bethlehem Hospital*, pp. 218–19
17. See Andrews, *The History of Bethlem*, p. 233
18. Ibid. p. 178
19. See Masters, *Bedlam*, p. 49
20. See O'Donoghue, *The Story of Bethlehem Hospital*, p. 238
21. See Ainsworth, *Jack Sheppard*, p. 213
22. See O'Donoghue, *The Story of Bethlehem Hospital*, p. 211
23. Ibid.
24. Ibid. p. 251
25. Ibid. p. 249
26. Ibid. p. 250
27. Ibid.
28. Ibid.
29. Ibid. p. 244
30. Ibid. p. 209
31. See Hunter and Macalpine, *Three Hundred Years of Psychiatry (1535–1860)*, p. 233

32. Ibid. pp. 234–5
33. See Andrews, *The History of Bethlem*, p. 203
34. Ibid. p. 269
35. See Hunter and Macalpine, *Three Hundred Years of Psychiatry (1535–1860)*, p. 185
36. Ibid. pp. 228–9
37. Ibid.
38. Ibid. p. 216
39. Ibid. pp. 218–20
40. See Andrews, *The History of Bethlem*, p. 272
41. Ibid. pp. 350–1
42. See O'Donoghue, *The Story of Bethlehem Hospital*, pp. 229–30
43. See Russell, *Scenes from Bedlam*, pp. 104–5
44. Ibid. p. 104
45. Ibid.
46. See O'Donoghue, *The Story of Bethlehem Hospital*, pp. 226–7

6: THE MIRROR OF MADNESS

1. See O'Donoghue, *The Story of Bethlehem Hospital*, p. 258
2. Ibid. p. 259
3. See Parry-Jones, *The Trade in Lunacy*, p. 13
4. See Scull, *Museums of Madness*, p. 24
5. Ibid.
6. See Hunter and Macalpine, *Three Hundred Years of Psychiatry (1535–1860)*, pp. 265–7
7. See Porter, *The English Malady*, p. xvi
8. Ibid. p. xvii
9. Ibid. p. xi
10. Ibid. p. xxvi
11. See Macalpine and Hunter, *George III and the Mad-Business*, pp. 287–8
12. Ibid. p. 291
13. See O'Donoghue, *The Story of Bethlehem Hospital*, pp. 281–2
14. See Hunter and Macalpine, *Three Hundred Years of Psychiatry (1535–1860)*, pp. 538–542
15. Ibid. pp. 348–50
16. See Masters, *Bedlam*, pp. 49–50
17. See Parry-Jones, *The Trade in Lunacy*, p. 10
18. See Hunter and Macalpine, *Three Hundred Years of Psychiatry (1535–1860)*, p. 199
19. Ibid. pp. 198–9
20. Ibid. p. 358
21. See Scull, *Undertaker of the Mind*, p. 97
22. See Hunter and Macalpine, *Three Hundred Years of Psychiatry*

(1535–1860), p. 359

23. Ibid. p. 360
24. Ibid. p. 361
25. Ibid. pp. 362–3
26. See Scull, *Museums of Madness*, p. 128
27. Ibid. p. 126
28. See Hunter and Macalpine, *Three Hundred Years of Psychiatry (1535–1860)*, p. 267
29. See Scull, *Undertaker of the Mind*, pp. 174–5
30. See Scull, *Museums of Madness*, pp. 125–6
31. Ibid.
32. See Andrews, *The History of Bethlem*, p. 269
33. See Hunter and Macalpine, *Three Hundred Years of Psychiatry (1535–1860)*, pp. 411–18
34. Ibid. p. 408
35. Ibid. p. 405
36. Ibid. p. 412
37. Ibid.
38. Ibid. pp. 415–16
39. Ibid. pp. 402
40. See Andrews, *The History of Bethlem*, pp. 276–7
41. See O'Donoghue, *The Story of Bethlehem Hospital*, pp. 239–40
42. See Masters, *Bedlam*, p. 47
43. See O'Donoghue, *The Story of Bethlehem Hospital*, p. 411
44. See Masters, *Bedlam*, pp. 59–60
45. See O'Donoghue, *The Story of Bethlehem Hospital*, p. 281
46. See Hunter and Macalpine, *Three Hundred Years of Psychiatry (1535–1860)*, p. 424
47. See O'Donoghue, *The Story of Bethlehem Hospital*, p. 408
48. Ibid. pp. 265–6
49. Ibid. p. 266
50. Ibid. p. 282
51. Ibid. p. 283
51. Ibid. p. 272
52. Ibid. p. 271
53. Ibid. pp. 273–4
54. Ibid.
55. Ibid.
56. See Hunter and Macalpine, *Three Hundred Years of Psychiatry (1535–1860)*, p. 417
57. See Kermode and Hollander (eds.), *The Oxford Anthology of English Literature*, vol. II, pp. 26–7
58. See Dickens, *Barnaby Rudge*, vol. I, p. 372
59. http://www.nottingham.ac.uk/hrc/projects/burney/letters/gordon.phtml

60. See Dickens, *Barnaby Rudge*, vol. II, p. 135
61. Ibid. p. 133
62. *Catholic Encyclopaedia*: http://www.newadvent.org/cathen/06649.c.htm

7: 'OUR KING IS MAD'

1. See O'Donoghue, *The Story of Bethlehem Hospital*, p. 316
2. See Macalpine and Hunter, *George III and the Mad-Business*, p. xiii
3. Ibid. p. 100
4. See Porter, *The Faber Book of Madness*, p. 50
5. See Macalpine and Hunter, *George III and the Mad-Business*, p. 18
6. Ibid. p. 19
7. Ibid. p. 25
8. Ibid. p. 31
9. Ibid. p. 36
10. Ibid. p. 38
11. See Parry-Jones, *The Trade in Lunacy*, p. 75
12. Ibid. p. 75
13. See O'Donoghue, *The Story of Bethlehem Hospital*, p. 317
14. See Macalpine and Hunter, *George III and the Mad-Business*, pp. 52–3
15. Ibid. p. 60
16. Ibid. p. 65
17. Ibid. p. 78
18. Ibid. p. 90
19. Ibid. p. 91
20. Ibid.
21. See Masters, *Bedlam*, p. 86
22. See Parry-Jones, *The Trade in Lunacy*, p. 76
23. See Macalpine and Hunter, *George III and the Mad-Business*, p. 97
24. Ibid. p. 101
25. Ibid.
26. Ibid. p. 102
27. Ibid. pp. 102–3
28. Ibid. p. 107
29. Ibid.
30. Ibid. p. 122
31. See O'Donoghue, *The Story of Bethlehem Hospital*, p. 318
32. See Hunter and Macalpine, *Three Hundred Years of Psychiatry (1535–1860)*, pp. 534–7
33. Ibid.
34. Ibid. p. 254
35. Ibid. p. 256
36. See Russell, *Scenes from Bedlam*, p. 105
37. Ibid.

38. Ibid. p. 106
39. Ibid. p. 109
40. Ibid.
41. See Masters, *Bedlam*, p. 92
42. See Russell, *Scenes from Bedlam*, p. 109
43. Ibid. p.110
44. Ibid.
45. See Andrews, *The History of Bethlem*, p. 421
46. See Hunter and Macalpine, *Three Hundred Years of Psychiatry (1535–1860)*, pp. 699–700
47. See Masters, *Bedlam*, p. 104
48. Ibid. p. 98
49. Ibid. pp. 151–2
50. See Andrews, *The History of Bethlem*, p. 420
51. See Masters, *Bedlam*, p. 101
52. See Smyth, *Sketches in Bedlam*, p. 165
53. See O'Donoghue, *The Story of Bethlehem Hospital*, pp. 328–9
54. See Masters, *Bedlam*, p. 144
55. See Metcalf, *The Interior of Bethlehem Hospital*, p. 13
56. Ibid. p. 16
57. Ibid. p. 11

8: SCANDAL!

1. See O'Donoghue, *The Story of Bethlehem Hospital*, p. 287
2. Ibid. pp. 296–301
3. Ibid. p. 312
4. Ibid. p. 303
5. See Andrews, *The History of Bethlem*, p. 409
6. Ibid. p. 409
7. See Hunter and Macalpine, *Psychiatry for the Poor*, p. 11
8. Ibid. p. 28
9. Ibid. p. 24
10. Ibid. pp. 29–30
11. Ibid. p. 31
12. Ibid. p. 32
13. Ibid. p. 17
14. Ibid. p. 18
15. See Andrews, *The History of Bethlem*, p. 436
16. Ibid.
17. See O'Donoghue, *The Story of Bethlehem Hospital*, p. 330
18. See Andrews, *The History of Bethlem*, p. 442
19. Ibid. p. 443
20. See Masters, *Bedlam*, pp. 145–6

21. Ibid. p. 147
22. See Report of the Commissioners of Lunacy, 1852, p. 29
23. See Andrews, *The History of Bethlem*, pp. 468–9
24. See Report of the Commissioners of Lunacy, 1852, p. 52
25. See Andrews, *The History of Bethlem*, p. 472
26. Ibid.
27. See O'Donoghue, *The Story of Bethlehem Hospital*, p. 333
28. See Andrews, *The History of Bethlem*, p. 477
29. See Report of the Commissioners of Lunacy, 1852, p. liv
30. See Andrews, *The History of Bethlem*, p. 47

9: UNDER THE DOME

1. See Hunter and Macalpine, *Three Hundred Years of Psychiatry (1535–1860)*, p. 919
2. Ibid. p. 920
3. See Andrews, *The History of Bethlem*, p. 506
4. See Busby, Alison, *The Guardian*, 28 August 2007
5. See O'Donoghue, *The Story of Bethlehem Hospital*, p. 339
6. See Masters, *Bedlam*, p. 156
7. See Hunter and Macalpine, *Three Hundred Years of Psychiatry (1535–1860)*, p. 1020
8. See *The Quarterly Review*, vol. 101 (1857), pp. 361–2
9. See Andrews, *The History of Bethlem*, p. 502
10. See Russell, *Scenes from Bedlam*, p. 154
11. See Smyth, *Sketches in Bedlam*, p. 1
12. Ibid. p. 64
13. Ibid. p. 68
14. Ibid. p. 266
15. See Bethlehem Records, 1850, no. 55
16. Ibid. no. 51
17. Ibid. no. 44
18. Ibid. no. 33
19. Ibid. no. 16
20. Ibid. no. 15
21. Ibid. no. 12
22. Ibid. no. 63
23. See Russell, *Scenes from Bedlam*, p. 111
24. See Bethlehem Records, no. 83
25. See Russell, *Scenes from Bedlam*, p. 151
26. See Masters, *Bedlam*, p. 160
27. Ibid. p. 161
28. See Andrews, *The History of Bethlem*, p. 496
29. See Masters, *Bedlam*, p. 162

30. Ibid. p. 160
31. Ibid. pp. 163–6
32. See Dickens, *Household Words*, pp. 381–91
33. Ibid. pp. 382–3
34. Ibid. p. 384

10: MAD WOMEN

1. See Showalter, *The Female Malady*, p. 90
2. See Russell, *Scenes from Bedlam*, p. 155
3. See Masters, *Bedlam*, p. 163
4. See Small, *Love's Madness*, p. 15
5. See Bethlehem Records, no. 33
6. See Small, *Love's Madness*, p. 33
7. See Showalter, *The Female Malady*, p. 90
8. Ibid. p. 10
9. Ibid. p. 129
10. See Collins (ed. Sweet), *The Woman in White*, p. xxvii
11. See Smyth, *Sketches in Bedlam*, p. 262
12. Ibid. p. 291
13. http//www.mdx.ac.uk/www/study/ylamb.htm#Revealed
14. See Sutherland, *Victorian Fiction: Writers, Publishers, Readers*, p. 67
15. Ibid. p. 69
16. Ibid. p. 71
17. See Collins (ed. Sweet), *The Woman in White*, p. xxix
18. See Sutherland, *Victorian Fiction: Writers, Publishers, Readers*, p. 64
19. Ibid. p. 66
20. See Dickens, *Great Expectations*, pp. 54–5
21. Ibid. pp. 366–7
22. See Brontë, *Jane Eyre*, p. 379
23. Ibid. p. 380
24. Ibid. p. 381
25. Ibid. pp. 528–9

11: TRANSFORMATION

1. See Russell, *Scenes from Bedlam*, p. 152
2. Ibid. p. 153
3. Ibid. p. 156
4. Ibid. p. 157
5. See Trombley, *All That Summer She Was Mad*, p. 116
6. Ibid. p. 108
7. Ibid. p. 144
8. Ibid. p. 145

9. Ibid. p. 148
10. Ibid. p. 153
11. Ibid. p. 152
12. See Showalter, *The Female Malady*, p. 104
13. Ibid. p. 106
14. Ibid. p. 107
15. Ibid.
16. Ibid. p. 110
17. See Dickens, *Household Words*, p. 490
18. Ibid. pp. 496–7
19. See Porter, *The Faber Book of Madness*, pp. 38–9
20. Ibid. p. 44
21. http://www.mdx.ac.uk/www/study/4_09.htm
22. See Hunter and Macalpine, *Psychiatry for the Poor*, p. 207
23. See Hunter and Macalpine, *Three Hundred Years of Psychiatry (1535–1860)*, pp. 638–9
24. See http://www.mdx.ac.uk/www/study/mhtim.htm#1902
25. Ibid.
26. See http://wisdomtools.com/poynter/manual.pdf
27. See Hunter and Macalpine, *Three Hundred Years of Psychiatry (1535–1860)*, pp. 215–16
28. Ibid. p. 216
29. See Andrews, *The History of Bethlem*, p. 527
30. See White, *Beyond the Glass*, p. 211
31. Ibid. p. 213
32. Ibid.
33. Ibid. p. 236
34. Ibid. p. 260

12: MODERN BEDLAM

1. See Stone, Martin, 'Shellshock and the Psychologists', in *The Anatomy of Madness*, vol. III, p. 245
2. Ibid. p. 249
3. See Showalter, *The Female Malady*, p. 174
4. Ibid. p. 168
5. Ibid. p. 176
6. Ibid. pp. 176–7
7. Ibid.
8. See Stone, 'Shellshock and the Psychologists', p. 253
9. Ibid. p. 254
10. Ibid. p. 247
11. Ibid. p. 243
12. Ibid. p. 254

13. Ibid.
14. Ibid.
15. See Showalter, *The Female Malady*, p. 190
16. See Sassoon, 'The General', in Parsons (ed.), *Men Who March Away*, p. 75
17. See Owen, 'Mental Cases', in Parsons, *Men Who March Away*, p. 140
18. See Russell, *Scenes from Bedlam*, pp. 13–14
19. Ibid.
20. See Tredgold, *A Text-Book of Mental Deficiency*, in Andrew Roberts, Mental Health Timeline
(http://www.mdx.ac.uk/www/study/mhhtim.htm)
21. See Olden, Mark, *The Guardian*, 23 January 2003, p. 22; Seaton, Matt, *Evening Standard Magazine*, 17 March 2000
22. See Wilson, *The Chronicle Review*, vol. 54, no. 19, p. B11

Bibliography

Ainsworth, W. H., *Jack Sheppard*, London: George Routledge, 1898

Alexander, Franz, *The History of Psychiatry: An Evaluation of Psychiatric Thought and Practice from Prehistoric Times*, London: Allen & Unwin, 1967

Andrews, Jonathan (ed.), *The History of Bethlem*, London: Routledge, 1997

Barham, Peter, *Closing the Asylum: The Mental Patient in Modern Society*, Harmondsworth: Penguin Books, 1997

Brontë, Charlotte, *Jane Eyre*, Peterborough, Ont.: Broadview Literary Texts, 1999

Burton, Robert, *The Anatomy of Melancholy* (3 vols.), London: G. Bell & Sons, 1924

Burton, Robert, *The Anatomy of Melancholy* (ed. 'Democritus Minor'), n.p.: William Tregg & Co., 1859

Bynum, W. F. and Porter, Roy, *The Anatomy of Madness: Essays in the History of Psychiatry*, London: Routledge, 1985

Cohen, J. M. and M. J., *The Penguin Dictionary of Quotations*, Harmondsworth: Penguin, 1960

Collins, Wilkie, *The Woman in White* (edited with an introduction by Matthew Sweet), Harmondsworth: Penguin Books, 1999

Dickens, Charles, *Barnaby Rudge: A Tale of the Riots of 'Eighty*, London: Chapman & Hall, 1897

Dickens, Charles, *Great Expectations*, Harmondsworth: Penguin Popular Classics, 1994

Dickens, Charles, *The Uncollected Writings of Charles Dickens: Household Words, 1850–1859*, London: Allen Lane, 1969

Garland, Robert, *The Eye of the Beholder: Deformity and Disability in the Graeco-Roman World*, Ithaca, NY: Cornell University Press, 1995

Hollingshead, Greg, *Bedlam*, Toronto: HarperCollins, 2004

Hunter, Richard and Macalpine, Ida, *Psychiatry for the Poor: 1851 Colney Hatch Asylum–Friern Hospital 1973: A Medical and Social History*, Folkestone: Dawsons, 1974

Hunter, Richard and Macalpine, Ida, *Three Hundred Years of Psychiatry (1535–1860)*, Oxford University Press, 1963

Jones, Colin and Porter, Roy (eds.), *Reassessing Foucault: Power, Medicine, and the Body*, London: Routledge, 1994

Jones, Kathleen, *Asylums and After: A Revised History of the Mental Health Services from the Early 18th Century to the 1990s*, London: Athlone, 1993

Kermode, Frank and Hollander, John (eds.), *The Oxford Anthology of English Literature*, vol. II, Oxford: Oxford University Press, 1979

Macalpine, Ida and Hunter, Richard, *George III and the Mad-Business*, London: Allen Lane, 1969

MacDonald, Michael, *Mystical Bedlam: Madness, Anxiety and Healing in Seventeenth-Century England*, Cambridge: Cambridge University Press, 1981

Masters, Anthony, *Bedlam*, London: Michael Joseph, 1977

Metcalf, Urbane, *The Interior of Bethlehem Hospital*, n.p.: Metcalf, 1818

Mueller, William Randolph, *The Anatomy of Robert Burton's England*, Berkeley and Los Angeles: University of California Press, 1952

O'Donoghue, Rev. E. G., *The Story of Bethlehem Hospital from its Foundation in 1247*, London: T Fisher Unwin, 1914

Oppenheim, Janet, *Shattered Nerves: Doctors, Patients, and Depression in Victorian England*, Oxford: Oxford University Press, 1991

Parry-Jones, William, *The Trade in Lunacy: A Study of Private Madhouses in England in the Eighteenth and Nineteenth Centuries*, London: Routledge & Kegan Paul, 1972

Parsons, I. M. (ed.), *Men Who March Away: Poems of the First World War*, London: Chatto & Windus, 1965

Porter, Roy, *The Faber Book of Madness*, London: Faber & Faber, 2003

Porter, Roy, *George Cheyne: The English Malady (1733)*, London: Routledge, 1991

Porter, Roy, *Madness: A Brief History*, Oxford: Oxford University Press, 2002

Porter, Roy, *Mind-forg'd Manacles: A History of Madness in England from the Restoration to the Regency*, London: Athlone, 1987

Quiller-Couch, Arthur (ed.), *The Oxford Book of English Verse 1250–1900*, Oxford: Oxford University Press, 1912

Report of the Commissioners of Lunacy, 1852

Russell, David, *Scenes from Bedlam: A History of Caring for the Mentally Disordered at Bethlem Royal Hospital*, London: Baillière Tindall/RCN, 1996

Scull, Andrew T., *Madhouses, Mad-Doctors, and Madmen: The Social History of Psychiatry in the Victorian Era*, London: Athlone Press, 1981

Scull, Andrew T., *The Most Solitary of Afflictions: Madness and Society in Britain, 1700–1900*, New Haven, CT and London: Yale University Press, 1993

Scull, Andrew T., *Museums of Madness: The Social Organization of Insanity in Nineteenth-century England*, London: Allen Lane, 1979

Scull, Andrew T., *Undertaker of the Mind*, Berkeley and Los Angeles: University of California Press, 2001

Shakespeare, William, *The Complete Works*, Oxford: Blackwell, 1949

Shorter, Edward, *A History of Psychiatry: From the Era of the Asylum to the Age of Prozac*, New York and Chichester: John Wiley & Sons, 1997

Showalter, Elaine, *The Female Malady: Women, Madness and English Culture, 1830–1980*, London: Virago, 1987

Simon, Bennett, *Mind and Madness in Ancient Greece: The Classical Roots of Modern Psychiatry*, Ithaca, NY: Cornell University Press, 1978

Small, Helen, *Love's Madness*, Oxford: Clarendon Press, 1996

Smyth, James, *Sketches in Bedlam*, London: Sherwood, Jones & Co., 1823

Stevenson, Christine, *Medicine and Magnificence*, New Haven, CT and London: Yale University Press for the Paul Mellon Centre for Studies in British Art, 2000

Sutherland, John, *Victorian Fiction: Writers, Publishers, Readers*, Basingstoke: Macmillan, 1995

Trombley, Stephen, *All That Summer She Was Mad: Virginia Woolf and Her Doctors*, London: Junction Books, 1981

Troyer, Howard William, *Ned Ward of Grubstreet: A Study of Sub-literary London in the Eighteenth Century*, Cambridge, MA: Harvard University Press, 1946

Ussher, Jane M., *Women's Madness: Misogyny or Mental Illness?*, London: Harvester Wheatsheaf, 1991

White, Antonia, *Beyond the Glass*, London: Virago Modern Classics, 1979

Index